Kimberley History

People, Exploration and Development

Proceedings of the Kimberley Society
Kimberley History Seminar
held at The University of Western Australia
27 March 2010

Edited and compiled by
Cathie Clement, Jeffrey Gresham and Hamish McGlashan

First published in 2012 by
Kimberley Society Inc., PO Box 8471, Perth Business Centre, Perth, Western Australia, 6849
www.kimberleysociety.org

Reprinted 2016

Disclaimer

The views expressed in the papers published in these Proceedings are those of the authors and do not necessarily reflect the opinions of the Kimberley Society. The Society takes no responsibility for the accuracy of the information presented in the papers, nor does it take any responsibility for ensuring that permission has been obtained for the use of the photographs and maps. The Society has published those items in good faith after requesting all authors to meet relevant legal obligations prior to submitting images for publication.

Caution

Indigenous readers are advised that this volume contains references to, and images of, people who have passed away. The volume also contains quotations in which some of the language and views are outdated. No offence is intended by the reproduction of that material in its historical context.

National Library of Australia
Cataloguing-in-Publication entry:
Clement, Cathie.
Kimberley history: People, exploration and development
ISBN: 978-0-9587130-2-3 (paperback)
Includes bibliographical references.
1. Kimberley (W.A.) – Discovery and exploration. 2. Kimberley Region (W.A.) – History.
I. Gresham, Jeffrey John. II. McGlashan, Hamish Edgar. III. Title.
994.14

Design and production Maria Duthie Design
Printed in Australia by Scott Print

This publication is printed using vegetable based inks and paper stock that is chlorine free and manufactured from pulp that is sourced from sustainable plantation grown timber. Both printer and paper manufacturer are certified to the highest internationally recognized standard for environmental management.

Cover images from top Bradshaw (Gwion Gwion) rock paintings include detailed depictions of weapons, accoutrements and ceremonies. Photo – Michael Morwood; 'The Mermaid Beached in Careening Bay'. Hand coloured engraving by W. Hatherell, c. 1887, based on a sketch by Phillip P. King. Courtesy of Antique Print Room, Sydney (www.antiqueprintroom.com); Evening muster, Carlton Hill Station. Photo – © Roger Garwood 2012.

Opposite Pindan cliffs north of James Price Point, west coast of the Dampier Peninsula, north of Broome. Photo – Kevin Kenneally

Left The Bungle Bungle Range, Purnululu National Park, Ea[illegible] Kimberley.
Photo – Mike D[illegible]naldson

Contents

Contributors

Mark Bin Bakar is an Indigenous Australian, a musician, comedian and radio announcer based in Broome. He is well known for his television character Mary Geddarrdyu or Mary G. Mark has been actively involved in seeking justice for members of the Stolen Generations with part of this involvement being through his Chairmanship of the Kimberley Stolen Generations Corporation. Mark was announced "Western Australian of the Year" in December 2007, and in May 2009 was appointed Chair of the Aboriginal and Torres Strait Islander Arts Board. He recently was a recipient of an Honorary Doctorate from Edith Cowan University for his work in the Aboriginal community and his commitment to reconciliation.

Geoffrey Bolton AO, one of Western Australia's best known historians, was educated at the University of Western Australia and Oxford University. He held various academic posts before retiring in 1996. His early research involved the exploratory expeditions of Alexander Forrest and he has authored 13 books, most recently *Land of Vision and Mirage: Western Australia since 1826*. Geoff is a Trustee of the Western Australian Museum and Chairperson of its Maritime Archaeology Advisory Committee.

Bill Bunbury is a broadcaster/documentary maker of 40 years experience and has received five international and national awards, including the United Nations Peace Prize in 1986 for his documentary on the Vietnam War "The War Rages On". He is the author of 11 books based on his work in Australian social history. Bill is currently Adjunct Professor, History and Communications at Murdoch University and is still doing part time production for the ABC.

Cathie Clement OAM has a doctorate from Murdoch University and practises as a historian and heritage consultant. Her research and writing, which focuses on Australia's North-West, encompasses events that range from early maritime exploration to recent entrepreneurial activity. Her main research interests are the contact between Indigenous people and others, the colonisation of the region, and the gold rush of 1886. Cathie was the founding president of the Kimberley Society. A *Studies in Western Australian History* volume titled *Ethics and the practice of history*, which she edited, was launched at the Kimberley History seminar.

Opposite
Purnululu National Park
in the east Kimberley
Photo – Mike Donaldson

Christine Choo, historian, social worker and social researcher, is an Honorary Research Fellow at the University of Western Australia. She has been involved in a number of community based social welfare and history projects and has published on race and gender issues. Her publications include *Aboriginal Child Poverty* (1990), *Mission Girls* (2001) and *History and Native Title*, a co-edited volume of *Studies in Western Australian History* (2003).

Michael Cusack is a retired farmer with ancestral links to the former Lillimilura Station in the Kimberley. He has led and participated in many 4WD and walking expeditions to the region and has carried out extensive research on the 1891 Kimberley expedition led by Joseph Bradshaw. This research led to the rediscovery of Bradshaw's cave where he had documented the so called Bradshaw (Gwion Gwion) rock art paintings. This finding had eluded other explorers for a hundred years.

Mike Donaldson is a geologist and has been bush walking in the Kimberley for more than 20 years. He has a keen interest in Aboriginal rock art and was co-editor of the Society's book, *Rock Art of the Kimberley* and has recently published major books on the rock art of the Burrup Peninsula and the Mitchell Plateau. Mike was involved with Ian Elliot in compiling and editing Frank Hann's diaries and their subsequent publication in the book *Do Not Yield to Despair*. He is a past president of the Kimberley Society.

Ian Elliot is a professional historian who spent many years with the Department of Land Administration researching exploration diaries for cartographic purposes in the Mapping Branch. He commenced the transcription of Frank Hann's diaries that eventually led to the publication of *Do Not Yield to Despair.* Ian is still involved in modern desert exploration and is the author of several historical books.

Jeffrey Gresham is a geologist with over 40 years of industry experience both in Australia and internationally. He has been visiting and walking extensively in the Kimberley for the past 16 years and has a keen interest in the history of the region. He has published a number of scientific papers and is the author of the book *Kambalda: History of a Mining Town*. He is currently President of the Kimberley Society.

Kevin Kenneally AM is a botanist and has conducted research on the vegetation, flora and natural history of the Kimberley for more than 35 years. He was involved in the first biological survey of the Prince Regent Reserve in 1974. Kevin has authored and co-authored numerous scientific papers and was co-recipient with Tim Willing of the 1994 CSIRO Medal for Research Achievement for the book *Broome and Beyond – Plants and People of the Dampier Peninsula*. Kevin was awarded a Churchill Fellowship in 1979, the Australian Natural History medallion in 1984 and the Pride of Australia Medal in 2009.

Kevin is a past president of the Kimberley Society and is currently an Adjunct Professor in the Faculty of Natural and Agricultural Sciences at the University of Western Australia and an Honorary Research Associate with the Western Australian Herbarium and the WA Museum.

Hamish McGlashan is a retired gynaecologist who worked for five years in the Kimberley. For more than 25 years he has carried out expeditions on foot throughout the region, concentrating on retracing the tracks and findings of early European explorers. He is the immediate past President of the Kimberley Society.

Michael Morwood, one of Australia's leading archaeologists, is Professor of Archaeology at the University of Wollongong. He has carried out extensive research in the Kimberley region and on the Indonesian archipelago. Known popularly as a discoverer of the "Flores Hobbit", Michael has published numerous papers and is the author of the book *Visions of the Past: The Archaeology of Australian Aboriginal Art.*

Phillip Playford AM, with degrees from the University of Western Australia and Stanford University in the US, has an international reputation as one of Australia's leading geologists with much of his work being in the Kimberley region. He has been the author and co-author of many significant scientific publications. He is also well known for his historical research, particularly his work on the early Dutch ship wrecks and is the author of *Carpet of Silver,* the story of the wreck of the *Zuytdorp*. Phil was awarded the prestigious Royal Society of Western Australia Science Medal in 2001.

Alison Spencer was born in Melbourne, but moved to Western Australia as a child. She graduated with a history degree from Murdoch University in 1979, before relocating to Broome in 1980. From then until retiring in 2007, Alison worked mainly in the field of Aboriginal education. Despite poor health, she continues to live in Broome.

Tony Quinlan is a retired civil engineer and his great grandfather perished at Camden Harbour.

Tim Willing was born in East Africa (Kenya), graduated from the School of Oriental and African Studies at the University of London, and has lived in Broome since 1980. In 1985 he was awarded a Churchill Fellowship and undertook tropical horticultural studies in Africa and Madagascar, and in 1994 he was a co-recipient of the CSIRO Medal for Research Achievement for the book *Broome and Beyond – Plants and People of the Dampier Peninsula.* Until 1996 Tim was a horticulturalist with the Shire of Broome and he subsequently worked as a Conservation Officer with the Department of Conservation and Land Management in Broome. He has made numerous journeys along the Kimberley coast as a scientific guide aboard charter vessels for Pearl Sea Coastal Cruises based in Broome.

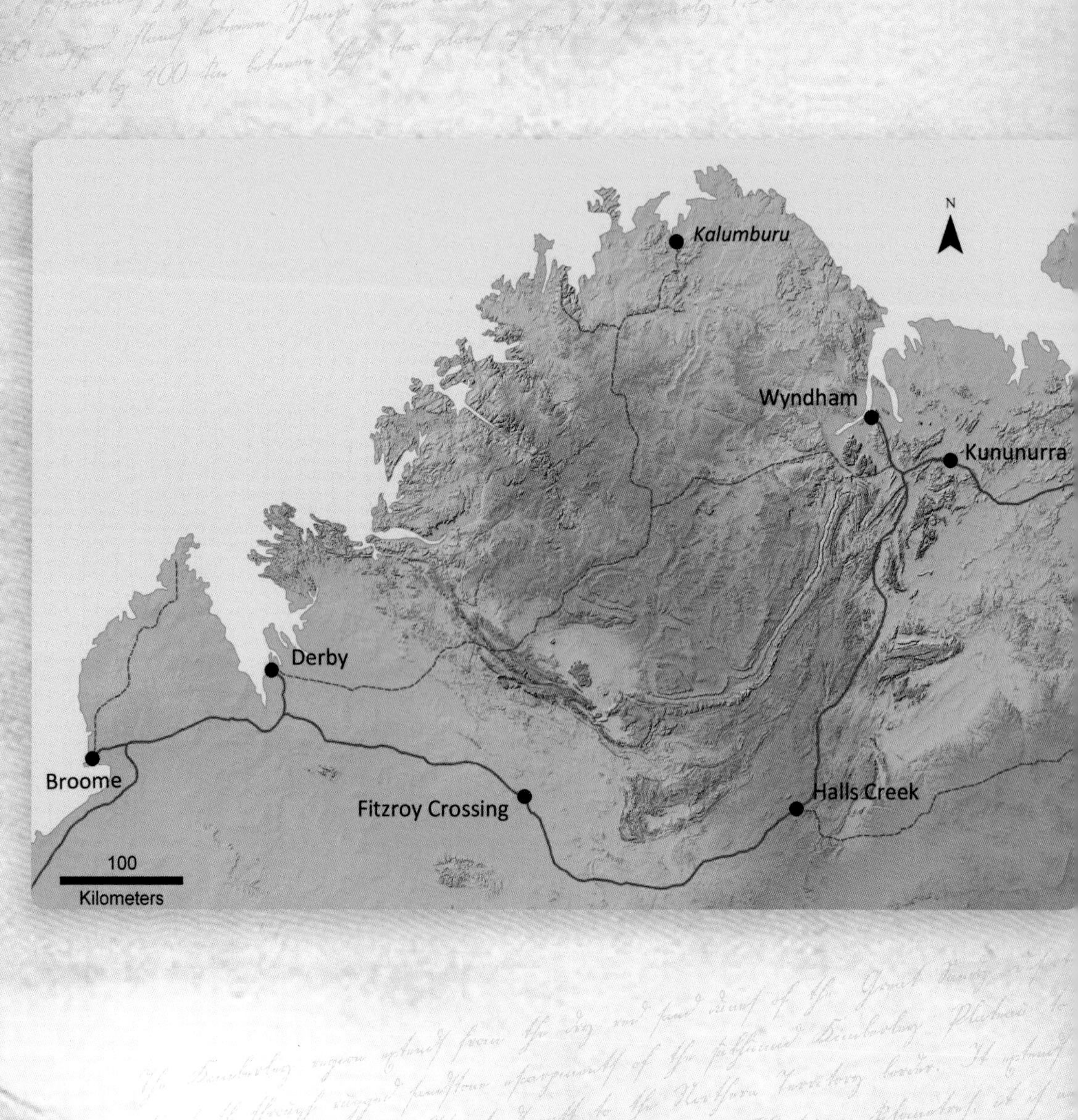
N
Kalumburu
Wyndham
Kununurra
Derby
Broome
Fitzroy Crossing
Halls Creek
100
Kilometers

Introduction

Jeffrey Gresham

The region

The Kimberley region extends from the dry red sand dunes of the Great Sandy Desert in the south through rugged sandstone escarpments of the subhumid Kimberley Plateau to the Timor Sea in the north. It extends east to the Northern Territory border. Covering some 423,500 square kilometres, it is nearly twice the size of the state of Victoria and three times the size of England. Numerous islands off the northern coast, and the many gulfs, headlands and the irregularity of the coastline attest to the current historically high sea levels and the so-called 'drowned' topography of the region. There are more than 2,500 mapped islands between Yampi Sound and the mouth of the King Edward River. In a straight line it is approximately 400 kilometres between those two places whereas it is nearly 1,300 kilometres around the actual coastline.

The region has a tropical monsoonal climate. The wet season extends from November to March and the dry season from April to October. Annual rainfall peaks at 1,500 mm per annum in the north-west part of the plateau and drops off to 350 mm per annum in the semi-arid south. Temperature ranges can be extreme with summer daytime temperatures frequently exceeding 40°C and winter night-time temperatures sometimes going below zero on the higher parts of the plateau and in the desert regions to the south.

Most of the northern portion of the Kimberley is characterised by savannah style vegetation with mature trees and grasslands. Rivers to the north are commonly lined with paperbarks and pandanus. The river patterns are commonly defined by joints or faults in the underlying bedrock and most flow north or west. In places they incise deep gorges within the sandstone. Where the rivers meet the ocean, mangrove colonies are often developed. Throughout much of the northern Kimberley small patches of rain forest are preserved.

Opposite
Topographic image of the Kimberley Region showing major roads and towns.
Derived from SRTM digital elevation model (courtesy of NASA).

The rocks of the region contain a geological record that spans the last 1,900 million years of the Earth's history. The oldest rocks in the Kimberley form the Lennard Hills in the west Kimberley and the Bow River Hills and the Halls Creek ridges in the east Kimberley. These comprise metamorphosed sediments, volcanics and granites.

The main part of the Kimberley, known as the Kimberley Plateau, comprises generally flat lying sedimentary rocks and basaltic lavas. Sandstones were deposited about 1,800 million years ago by major river systems that flowed from north to south across the whole region. Large volumes of concordant basalt lava flows that are a characteristic of the Mitchell Plateau are sandwiched between different sandstone sequences across the Kimberley. Subsequent to around 1,790 million years ago the region has seen several periods of geological activity that has resulted in deposition of further sedimentary sequences, largely around the margins of the Kimberley Plateau, and there is evidence for periods of major glaciations.

The current landscape of the Kimberley has been evolving over a period of at least 250 million years. Periods of uplift resulted in peneplanation of the land surface and deeply incised rivers. A lengthy period of tropical conditions 70 to 50 million years ago resulted in the development of a lateritic cap, particularly over the volcanic rocks, which are more susceptible to weathering. This is another characteristic feature of the Mitchell Plateau.

As sea levels rose from approximately 120 metres below current levels following the end of the last glacial maximum around 20,000 years ago, the Kimberley coastline became drowned with the sea filling what were once river valleys. This phenomenon gives the coastline its distinctive irregular outline.

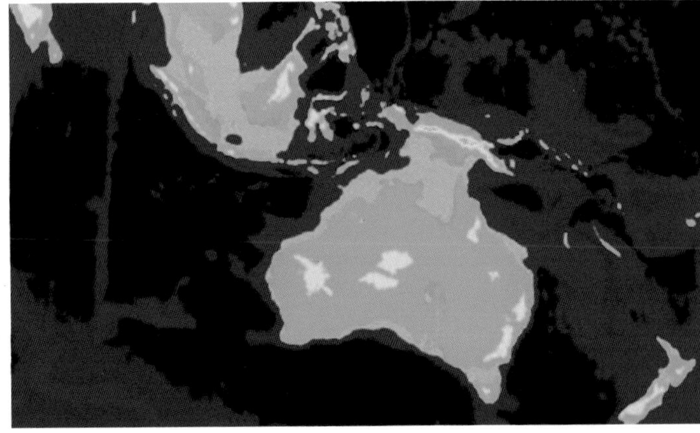

Right Outline (light blue) of the Sahul (Australia-New Guinea) and Sundaland (Asia) landmasses at the last glacial maximum around 20,000 years ago. Courtesy of Karl-Heinz Wyrwoll.

Aboriginal occupation of the Kimberley

A growing body of archaeological work indicates that Aboriginal people arrived in Australia at least 55,000 years ago and it is possible that one of the first places occupied, given its proximity to Timor and New Guinea, was the Kimberley area. Sea levels were probably about 80 metres below current levels however it is obvious from paleo-bathymetric maps that the early arrivals traversed between 100 and 200 kilometres of open water. Also obvious, from the extensive and prolific rock art (both Gwion Gwion and Wandjina styles) that occurs throughout much of the Kimberley, is that significant numbers of Aborigines lived and travelled throughout the region for thousands of years. In this volume Mark Bin Bakar, an Indigenous Australian, presents a powerful paper that articulates the strong connectedness of the Kimberley Aboriginal people to the land and the importance of maintaining that connection. Mike Morwood, one of Australia's leading archaeologists, summarises both previous and present archaeological work in the Kimberley and discusses the migration of modern man to Australia.

Above and left
Examples of Bradshaw (Gwion Gwion) and Wandjina rock art from the Kimberley.
Photos – Michael Cusack (above) and Mike Donaldson (left)

European exploration of the Kimberley

There is some uncertainty as to exactly when the first European contact was made in the Kimberley but that contact was obviously made from the coast as European exploration of the globe and the search for new resources extended south. The thousands of years of uninterrupted Aboriginal occupation was quickly brought to a conclusion once the first explorers and settlers arrived.

Although the first officially recorded European visit to the Kimberley coast was by Abel Tasman in 1644, other undocumented visitors who included Macassans in search of the sea slug trepang may have preceded Tasman. Cathie Clement presents a comprehensive summary of the maritime exploration of the Kimberley coast. Phillip Parker King made four northern Australian voyages between 1818 and 1822 mapping the coast in detail and naming many features along it. During his 1820 voyage on the ship *Mermaid* he was forced to careen and repair the vessel for 16 days at a place now called Careening Bay. Members of the crew recorded the visit by inscribing the ship's name on a large boab tree close to the beach.

Following the exploration and mapping of the Kimberley coast a series of important exploratory expeditions opened up this vast and isolated region. Hamish McGlashan discusses in detail the first European penetration of the Kimberley interior by George Grey and his party in 1837–38. Grey commenced his expedition at the height of the wet season and his ambitious plan to travel south to the developing Swan River Colony was not achieved. He did record in some detail the occurrence of Wandjina rock paintings in the Glenelg River area. Comparatively little other exploration then occurred before Alexander Forrest's 1879 expedition, which is described by Geoffrey Bolton. Forrest's attempt to penetrate into the interior of the Kimberley was thwarted by the rugged King Leopold Ranges

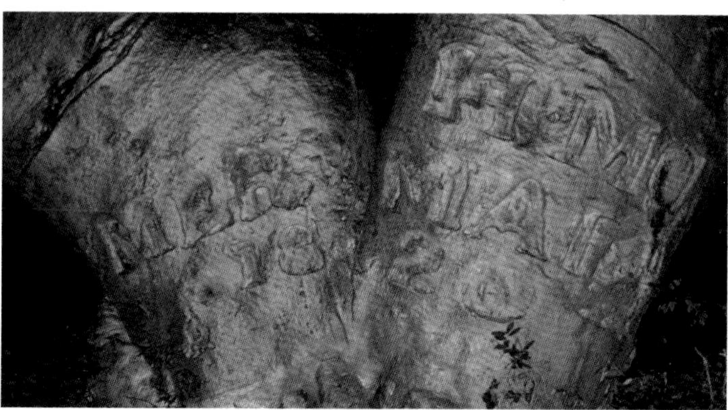

Right Boab tree at Careening Bay. Photo – Jeffrey Gresham

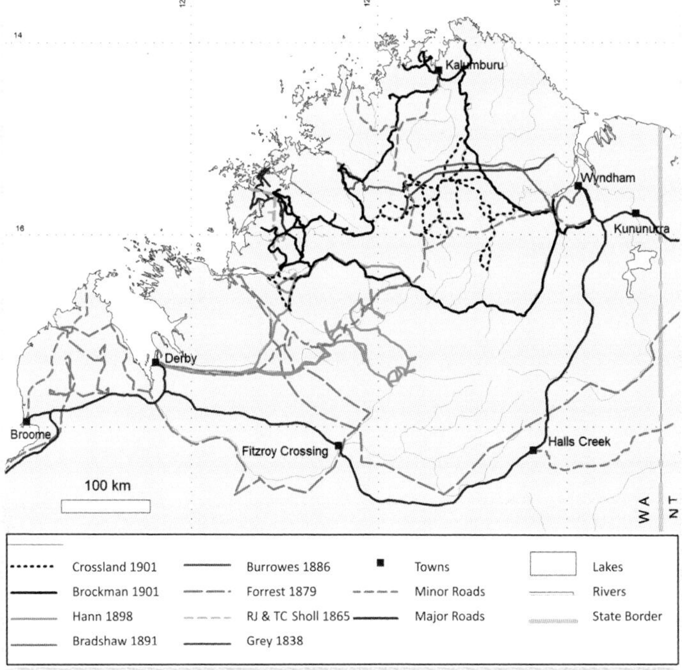

that proved impossible to cross with his horses. He therefore made his way back from the Walcott Inlet and proceeded east along the Fitzroy River, discovering the Ord before crossing into the northern territory of South Australia. He observed how favourable some of the country was for development of a pastoral industry and that development duly occurred. Mike Cusack details Joseph Bradshaw's expedition west from Wyndham in 1891 in search of further pastoral land. Bradshaw's objective was to get to the Prince Regent River where he had, sight unseen, applied for an extensive lease holding. Bradshaw's navigational skills were lacking and he ended up in the Roe and Moran Rivers nearly 80 kilometres north of his leases. It was in this area that he found and documented the so-called Bradshaw or Gwion Gwion rock paintings. Mike Donaldson and Ian Elliot document Frank Hann's 1898 expeditions and Frederick Brockman's 1901 epic exploration. Hann, who was also looking for pastoral country, was successful in penetrating the King Leopold Ranges. He did find extensive tracts of country favourable for pastoral development but never took up any leases in the area. Brockman and his party spent more than six months and travelled more than 2,300 miles (3,680 kilometres) exploring the northern interior of the Kimberley. Starting and completing their journey at Wyndham they penetrated west to the area between the Charnley and Prince Regent rivers and as far north as the mouths of the King Edward and Drysdale rivers. Brockman's expedition essentially completed the exploration of the Kimberley region.

Above Exploration routes in the Kimberley. Courtesy of Mike Donaldson

Early settlements in the Kimberley

The early European explorers gave varying views of the country they had seen but some enthused about the pastoral potential of the land. This was done largely in ignorance of the seasonal nature of the climate in the region and also the barren, rocky terrain of much of the country. However, with much of the more accessible southern land already taken, speculation was often rife in the pastoral industry. Tony Quinlan discusses the failed settlement at Camden Harbour in 1865. Tony's paper has a special poignancy given that his great grandfather, Michael Quinlan, drowned during an encounter with Aborigines close to the settlement. Sadly this was not the only loss of life during this abortive exercise and the place was abandoned less than a year after it was established.

Following his 1891 exploratory expedition, Joseph Bradshaw together with Aeneas Gunn and others established a settlement at Marigui in the shadow of Mt Trafalgar at the mouth of the Prince Regent River in 1892. Kevin Kenneally describes the development and short-lived nature of this venture. The harshness of the environment made any economic pastoral venture in this area an impossibility.

Above Ruins at Camden Harbour.
Photo – Jeffrey Gresham

Early industrial development in the Kimberley

The worldwide demand for phosphate in the middle of the 19th century led to the development of the first extractive industry in the Kimberley. Tim Willing and Alison Spencer document the extraction of guano from various islands around the Kimberley coast from the early 1870s. Although not large by world standards the mining activities resulted in the payment of limited royalties to the Western Australian Government.

Following Forrest's 1879 expedition and his recognition of the pastoral potential of the Fitzroy and Ord areas, the Kimberley was opened up for leasing in 1881. Geoffrey Bolton describes the early development of the sheep and cattle industry in the region.

By the early 1880s gold discoveries and mining had transformed the economies of the eastern colonies. Phillip Playford presents the story of the Kimberley gold rush centred on Halls Creek of 1885–1886. Although only limited gold was produced from the Halls Creek field it was an important event in the history of Western Australia and the development of the Kimberley region.

Above Ruins of Lillimilura Station. Photo – Mike Donaldson

Opposite
Garimbu Creek in Garimbu Gorge.
Photo – Jeffrey Gresham

Other aspects of early Kimberley history

Following the early European occupation and development in the Kimberley, and the displacement and change that these events brought to the Aboriginal people of the region, the churches moved to establish missions in the area. Christine Choo discusses the establishment of both Catholic and Protestant missions in the region and the impacts, both positive and negative, that these institutions brought to the people.

Bill Bunbury looks at the impact of settlement and development in the Kimberley, focussing on changes in the pastoral industry since the 1960s. His paper reinforces the connection of the Aboriginal people to the land and the dislocation to their lives and traditions that these changes wrought.

Given the limited time available to the presenters at the seminar this volume contains important additional and relevant information that was not included in the presentations.

The future

This volume documents some of the early history of the Kimberley region. It can be clearly seen that certain exploratory events triggered other events that progressively opened up the region. Not all of these events were either successful or of benefit to the region and its original inhabitants. Despite these developments the area still remains one of the great wilderness areas of the world, sparsely populated and with limited infrastructure. A major challenge exists in preserving and protecting the special character of the Kimberley. However there are pressures for additional tourist and industrial developments that will continue to change the character of the area. Hopefully, by appreciating the early history of the region and the impacts these events have had on the landscape and people, future developments can be progressed with minimal impact on this special part of Australia.

Acknowledgments

All papers in the volume have been edited and I wish to acknowledge the work done by my fellow members of the seminar subcommittee – Cathie Clement, Hamish McGlashan, Mike Donaldson, and Kevin Kenneally – in preparing the volume for publication. Acknowledgment is also due to Maria Duthie, for her design work, and to the members of the Kimberley Society Council and others who contributed to the success of the seminar, which was enjoyed by 150 people.

References

Department of Environment and Conservation (DEC). *A Synthesis of Scientific Knowledge to Support Conservation Management in the Kimberley Region of Western Australia.* The Department, 2009 (2009224_kimberleysciencerpt_finalweb.pdf at www.dec.wa.gov.au).

Donaldson, M. and Kenneally, K. (eds). *Rock Art of the Kimberley: Proceedings of the Kimberley Society Rock Art Seminar.* Kimberley Society, Perth, 2007.

Tyler, I. *Geology & Landforms of the Kimberley.* Department of Conservation and Land Management, Como (WA), 1996, revised edition, 2000.

My Home the Kimberley: An Aboriginal perspective of Kimberley history

Mark Bin Bakar

I firstly acknowledge that we gather here today on Nyoongar country and that I feel that we need to continue the acknowledgments despite what Mr Abbott or Mr Tuckey may say. This is the greatest thing that our country can do in empowering Aboriginal people to keep their place, and entice mainstream to celebrate and be part of this unique protocol and to respect the diverse Aboriginal people that make up our nation.

This is the Australia that we should aspire to, we should not, as a nation, disregard the secret, sacred, unique, ancient civilization of the oldest living culture in the world, in having its place, protocols and culture respected, as true Australians, inclusively. The diversity and uniqueness of the landscape of our country gives us pride and the joy of knowing that we share this great country, together.[1]

I am honoured to have been invited to speak in this forum, focusing on one of the last frontiers of our country, of our state, the rough and rugged escarpment and plateaus, the ancient and prehistoric formations that created the amazing colours, shapes and mystery. In all its roughness, dangers and isolation, it also brings and provides the sanctuary for the human body, soul and spiritual wellbeing of man to be embraced and submerged in a part of our country that, from the moment you step into it, you know you are being swallowed into a vortex of spiritual presence.

Some may say God touches you, others feel the presence of a Great Spirit or life form that welcomes you into a land that is old as time itself and, despite where you travel and where you may decide to live after leaving this place, a calling captures you to carry in your heart and mind, this very powerful and unique place. It commands you to respect the place.

The terrain formed hundreds of millions of years ago and, before a great drop in sea levels, a barrier reef system similar to the Great Barrier Reef encircled much of what we know as the Kimberley.

Opposite
(Top) Horizontal Falls, Talbot Bay.
Photo – Jeffrey Gresham
(Bottom) Aboriginal men with spears.

It can be seen today in the Napier, Oscar and Ningbing Ranges. Geikie Gorge, Windjana Gorge, Tunnel Creek and Mimbi Caves are some of its more notable remnants.[2]

The Aboriginal people always used this terrain to their advantage for confrontations and for hunting food. Their ability to become part of the elements and live amongst the rough terrain was a natural partnership.

For tens of thousands of years prior to a foreign foe, an ancient race of inhabitants walked this land and was in perfect balance with the environment. The beauty of this is the relationship between the Aboriginal people, the environment, the elements and the animals which shared this ancient land. This perfect partnership had allowed the place to weave itself into an exceptional mix of many different languages, cultures, dance and art. The differences practised between saltwater people, river people, desert people and hill people provided a setting that allowed diversity of human relationships to prosper.

Aboriginal people had their dreaming, an understanding of where they sat in terms of the environment, animals and universe. The skill to wander the land with no or limited water and hunt and gather food, this shaped Aboriginal people as a great Nomadic race, moving from place to place, following the seasons, foods and wildlife. Ceremony was also very important and so a system was in place that allowed people to carry out all cultural responsibilities and also self sustainability.

Right Karajarri muscians and cultural performers John Bennet and Mervyn Mulardy.
Photo – Guy Ghouse 2000

If one carried out all the cultural responsibilities and the tribes abided by the laws then the elements and the lands always provided food and nourishment. Aboriginal people understood nature. They could look at plants and know that fish and sea creatures were now ready for catching and eating. Know that animals were now safe to kill for food and that certain fruits and berries were also ready for consumption. Know that to eat things at the wrong time can poison you.

This ancient place covers an area of approximately 423,000 square kilometres in the far north of Western Australia and makes up one sixth of the State. Three times the size of England, it is fringed by the Timor Sea to the north, the Indian Ocean to the west, the Great Sandy Desert to the south, and the Northern Territory border to the east.

This place is called the Kimberley.

The diverse landscapes within the region range from savannah woodlands to river gorges with lush, tropical vegetation. The land has prospered despite human intervention.

The Kimberley is much steeped in Aboriginal culture as it has been home to the Aboriginal people for tens of thousands of years; it has even been credited as possibly their first base on the Australian mainland.

Above Kimberley coast, near Bigge Island.
Photo – Mike Donaldson

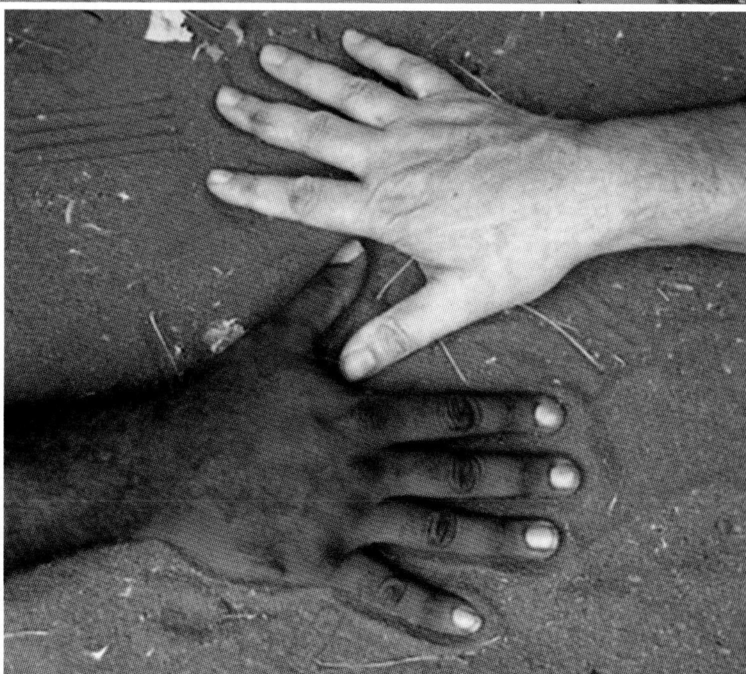

Above The coastline on Cape Leveque.

Right Hands: Black and white.
Photos – Mark Bin Baker

Aboriginal people practiced their culture, law, song, and dance and had laws that governed the people to live appropriately, to assist in a great capacity to survive. The values and beliefs that kept everyone safe and balanced with nature was as God had intended. An absolute engineered system that even prevented incest. An example of explaining skin grouping that I use is "Who I am to marry in a traditional society is already determined before my grandmother is born".

Many languages, cultures and differences made a unique small part of our continent to be dispersed in its own way, yet still one mob. And that mob shares spiritual philosophies that have been recorded as being the oldest continuous religious traditions on the planet.

Kimberley Aboriginal people's exposure to outsiders occurred quite slowly. The first known sighting of Europeans was in 1644 when a Dutch ship captained by Abel Tasman visited the coast. In 1688 William Dampier and others arrived in the *Cygnet* and had contact with the Bardi people at the northern end of Cape Leveque. He described the Aboriginal people he met as 'the miserablest People in the world'. Yet his time with them clearly fitted the sort of first contact that is said to have been characterized by open trust and curiosity.[3]

Papers by my fellow contributors tell of exploration on the coast, by Phillip Parker King and others, and then on land, led by George Grey in 1838.[4] There is also coverage of Alexander Forrest crossing from the west coast to the Northern Territory in 1879, setting himself up as a land agent specialising in Kimberley pastoral leases, and contributing to the activity that saw sheep go to the West Kimberley and cattle to the East Kimberley.[5]

They also tell of Philip Saunders and Adam Johns finding gold in 1882, Hall and Slattery finding some more in 1885, and the rush to Halls Creek then taking place.[6] Those events led to the Kimberley having resource-based industries as well as a strong pastoral industry that employed many Aboriginal people. Their stories are part of the region's history, especially their mustering, branding and droving of the cattle.

Droving continued until the early '60s when road improvements gave trucks better access. The Gibb River Road was constructed to help move cattle from the isolated stations that operated in the inland area behind the ranges.

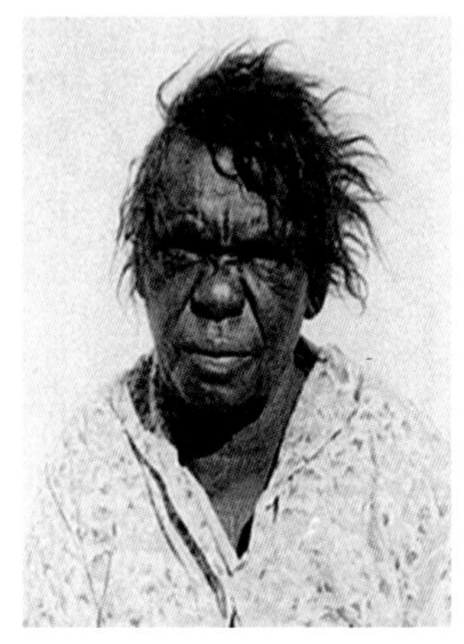

Above The author's great grandmother, Jenni.

So let's jump forward now as all of you here today are strong connoisseurs who are or have been heavily intoxicated with the smell, taste, and spirit of this place called The Kimberley. This place that brings us all together in oneness for the love of what we have called at least once, 'God's Country'.

My mother is a stolen generation woman snatched from her mother because of the colour of her skin. Her mother had no say in where her child went and the very essence of what was broken was the abuse. This was the right to have a mother. She never really reconnected to her mother again. She like many suffered under a corrupted calculating system that was intended to eradicate the Aboriginal and assimilate the little coloured children of European men who felt they had the right to exploit Aboriginal people. This was the way it was. Aboriginal people were Flora and Fauna. But how can a nation hold its head high with this dark history?

But it can, by simply owning this history. This history belongs to all Australians. It does not matter if it was right or wrong, good or bad, the fact is we cannot undo the past but we can own it for all. Lest we forget. The Kimberley was not immune to the massacres, destruction, abuse and manipulation of the Aboriginal people. The power of this land and capacity to own a people is what can never be broken.

The Kimberley is the home and the burial ground of thousands of years of language, culture and generations that connects all Aboriginal people back to the Kimberley, back to country. Identity is the most important element of the human spirit. When one has lost one's identity then one becomes a lost soul. Like a feeling of not being loved by a mother.

This is what connects you and me. This is what brings us together as the Kimberley is a special place that needs to be protected as once the spirit is gone then we have a waste land.

Just recently I travelled to Halls Creek to film a piece with ABCTV on myself for Message Stick and we met at my mother's brother's camp. He is a man who has struggled to have a relationship with his sister, my mother. They grew up apart from each other and in fact did not have any brother, sister relationship. This only started to happen because I came back home to the Kimberley and started the journey of finding my blood line and country.

We also made a special point of having my grandfathers there as well. Matt Dawson, Munro Dawson and Bruce Wallaby. These men spent most of their lives on Margaret River Station. Why did they stay there

and not move around? Because that's where their father came from.

Their connection to the country was what determined them to remain there. This was their country, their home. They did not grow up anywhere else but the country of their father. He was a Kitja, Djaru and Goonian man, his wife was a pure Kitja woman from Bedford Downs.

She was a sister to the late Salleh Malay. So I am a Kitja, Djaru, Goonian Kimberley Aboriginal man with a bit of other races also making up my heritage. But I identify as an Aboriginal. My skin name is Jawandi.

I looked into the eyes of these great old Aboriginal men, and saw the loss. The chaos of their children's lives totally shattered by alcohol and the ostracism by society. The failure of our country to look after these fellow Australians.

They never drank alcohol; they are now in their 70s and 80s. They worked all their lives since they were 13 years of age.

Master horsemen, who worked and played a significant part in the building of the cattle industry. They got very little pay and yet still today remain humble and forgiving. They are now at the end of their lives and wait to join their ancestors. It broke my heart to see the injustice and the chaos.

History has dealt out a raw deal for Aboriginal people. They have been behind the eight ball since the start. The tokenism and the patronising attitude towards them are, to a degree, still installed in other people's attitudes towards these great people.

Above Evening muster, Carlton Hill Station. Photo – © Roger Garwood 2012

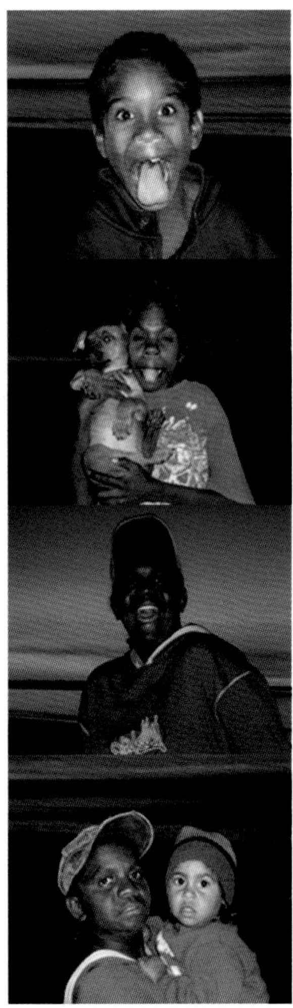

Above Young Aboriginal people from Djarindjin Community, north of Broome.
Photo – Mark Bin Bakar

Aboriginal people are Aboriginal people. They belong in a particular place and try so hard to balance their lives within the western system. But at the same time, these old grandfathers of mine obtained one amazing skill besides being great cattlemen and horsemen. They learnt the art of speaking and having a conversation with white men.

They became mates on the land. But the system had failed and so the eradication of Aboriginal cattlemen, due to having to be paid wages, changed their lives forever.[7] I cry in my heart for these great noble men. They are the black ringers.

Now my grandfather says to me, grandson you have to come bush with me and walk the country. You have to learn and understand our country because this is where you belong. You can be a star, you can travel the world but you belong here. Your mother is my daughter, through my sister, so our blood very strong. The rivers call us. Your mother born in river bed, black fellow hospital. A great sense of pride strikes out at me and my mother.

What a great honour to be bestowed onto you, to be born in an ancient traditional birth tree. A women's tree. I am so moved by their humbleness. This is what I had lost, my birthright to be a Kimberley Aboriginal man who is very clear, in where I sit with my people. To know my traditional language, to know my culture and cultural responsibilities to country, people and ancestors. This is for all Aboriginal people.

He says to me "Jaja, you not a Guddia, you got the same blood running in your veins, you belong to we". I learnt the value of what identity means and where you belong which is so important to Aboriginal people.

This is the greatest enemy to the youth, because those who have lost a lot through government policy etc. cannot pass on to the young and so the young people are also lost and are trying to find their place back in their cultural place. Inside of their body and mind, they are lost and struggle with this anxiety, which easily gets confused between depression and anger.

Not understanding why they feel like they feel, which causes more mental suffering which disguises itself as ego and machismo.

We now also have mining and industry breathing down our necks because it's all about the economy and making money. This is fine as long as Aboriginal people along with people of the Kimberley

are happy with the way we use the land and not destroy an ancient landscape and people for greed. We all have a responsibility to protect the Kimberley and find ways to uniquely allow industry to operate where possible and culturally appropriate, but also to include the people of the lands.

Now we have a new threat that has the capacity to destroy the native species of animals that can cripple the Kimberley and turn it into a wasteland where life has the potential to not exist.This is the migration of the cane toad, a serious threat and a terrible experiment that has found its way from Queensland into the Kimberley via the great floods.

The rivers are suffering along with the native animals and we as people who are passionate about the Kimberley have a responsibility to get behind preventative measures of eradicating the cane toad.

The animals, birds and all creatures that help pollinate and fertilise not only the growth of the Kimberley but also the spirit in the land. When all the native animals are gone, and all we have left is cattle then we have a dying region. The balance that I talked about earlier between Aboriginal people, the land and the environment has been slowly destroyed and we need to take action now.

The greatest environmentalists are the Aboriginal people, and by introducing the pests and weeds to manage an eco system, we will only destroy the fragile and very well balanced existing system.

Above King George Falls.
Photo – Jeffrey Gresham

Mining and development is now fast becoming an additional burden on the Kimberley and we must carefully consider the ancient cultures that have existed there, the Aboriginal people, first and foremost, and find a way forward to balance the way we use and tamper with this ancient land.

The Kimberley is the last frontier; we cannot afford to destroy the existing ancient culture, the landscape, the wildlife and the eco system that has sustained itself and us for thousands of years. Are we going to destroy it in a matter of a few generations?

Equity and respect must be dually dispersed in the way we manage mining and development whilst protecting and catering for the Aboriginal people of the Kimberley.

This prompts me to say that we as a collective must be vigilant and protect the Kimberley that we love so much. The very ancient rock art and visual art including traditional dance, language and culture must be recognised as also being an integral part in the economic sustainability of the identity and the uniqueness of the Aboriginal people who make up the Kimberley.

We have in the palms of our hands, the capacity to absolutely eradicate and destroy the ancient art, culture, dance and language, not to mention the country, due to our ignorance. If we look towards a denser populated area of western influence that has failed to take these considerations into account, we find exactly this, in terms of the Aboriginal people.

The Kimberley needs one voice that speaks for all the Aboriginal people of the Kimberley in partnership with all levels of Government. This will allow clarity and capacity to protect, consolidate and negotiate with all relevant parties and groups in protecting the Kimberley. We are talking about an ancient sacred ground.

I would like to grab this opportunity to acknowledge past and present great champions within the Aboriginal people of the Kimberley who have shown leadership and have built the foundations to allow us to see the fragility and the capacity to destroy God's own country – the Kimberley. A person who comes to mind is Uncle Sam Lovell who has been able to balance tourism and protection of Aboriginal artwork in country whilst embracing the Great Spirit that lies in the Kimberley.

The discovery of the Gwion Gwion (Bradshaw) paintings dated to be at least 17,000 years old and the recent bat paintings, and not to mention the amazing ancient Wandjinas, is a clear indication of the tenacity and the ability of Aboriginal people to sustain their own

culture way beyond the writings of the Bible and the building of the Pyramids or even Stonehenge.

Aboriginal people and their culture have become an invaluable resource for the future of tourism in Australia and the Kimberley region. Their knowledge of the country and the sacred places that are scattered through it are priceless gems in a fast changing world. This history and heritage is something that all Australians should be proud of. People like Uncle Sam Lovell break down the division that does occur between Aboriginal people and non-Aboriginal people.

However the massacres and murders that had been imposed on Aboriginal people will never ever be forgotten. Aboriginal people never forget and, through the nature of their culture, have an oral tradition that passes stories down through generations. These stories are considered and accepted as fact and will continue to be passed on and accepted as fact.

Aboriginal people have been victims of cruelty and racism since the explorations to the Kimberley and warriors like Jandamarra stood up against the powers of that era. Today the Kimberley is going through a new phase with all the pressures as well as the inadequacies of government services and so the historical confrontations and hostilities have not really changed, hence, the social dysfunction, youth suicide and limited education.

Above Aboriginal elder from Wugubun Community, south of Kununurra.
Photo – Mark Bin Bakar

We must allow greater access to education and to continue to support the communities in their struggle in managing alcohol and drug use and domestic violence.

The Kimberley is not only home to the native species, the ancient artwork, the ancient culture, the Aboriginal people, it is also home to non-Aboriginal people of diverse background and cultures who make up the new Kimberley.

Potentially, the greatest threat however, is that we all fail to take responsibility and protect this part of Australia, as it always was protected prior to colonisation. We must value what history has given us, learn from it, embrace it, share it and own it. We must protect the oldest uniqueness in the world, the Aboriginal people, their law, culture, languages, art and custodial responsibilities to the land. We all love the Kimberley; we all must look after it, in partnership.

Australian Aboriginal history is the only history that grows both ways – forward into the present and backwards into the past as new scientific methods indicate that archaeological sites are much older than originally thought.

I wrap by finally saying that the Kimberley also has her own royalty. I also work with this lady who is of royalty from the Kimberley. She is a direct descendant of Mary Queen of England. Mary G is the queen of the Kimberley and so she makes claim to all the minerals and wealth that lies embedded in the ground and sea as inherited.

She is ok to share a little bit, however she also trying to find the perfect husband, to no avail to date. She is now starting to believe that the perfect man does not exist.

Notes

1 The photographs in this paper, unless otherwise acknowledged, have been provided by Mark Bin Bakar and are sourced from his personal collection.

2 See 'Kimberley (Western Australia)', http://en.wikipedia.org/wiki, for more information about the geology, history and other aspects of the region.

3 See http://en.wikipedia.org/wiki/Timeline_of_Aboriginal_history_of_Western_Australia for more detail about the arrival of outsiders.

4 See Cathie Clement, 'Maritime exploration on the Kimberley coast', and Hamish McGlashan, 'George Grey's expedition 1837-1838: first European penetration of the Kimberley interior', this volume.

5 See Geoffrey Bolton, 'Alexander Forrest's expedition 1879 and early development of the cattle industry', this volume.

6 See Phillip Playford, 'The Kimberley gold rush of 1885-1886', this volume.

7 See Bill Bunbury, 'Impacts of settlement and development in the Kimberley 1965–2010', this volume, for coverage of this period.

Above Mary G.

Opposite
King Edward Falls on the King Edward River.
Photo – Jeffrey Gresham

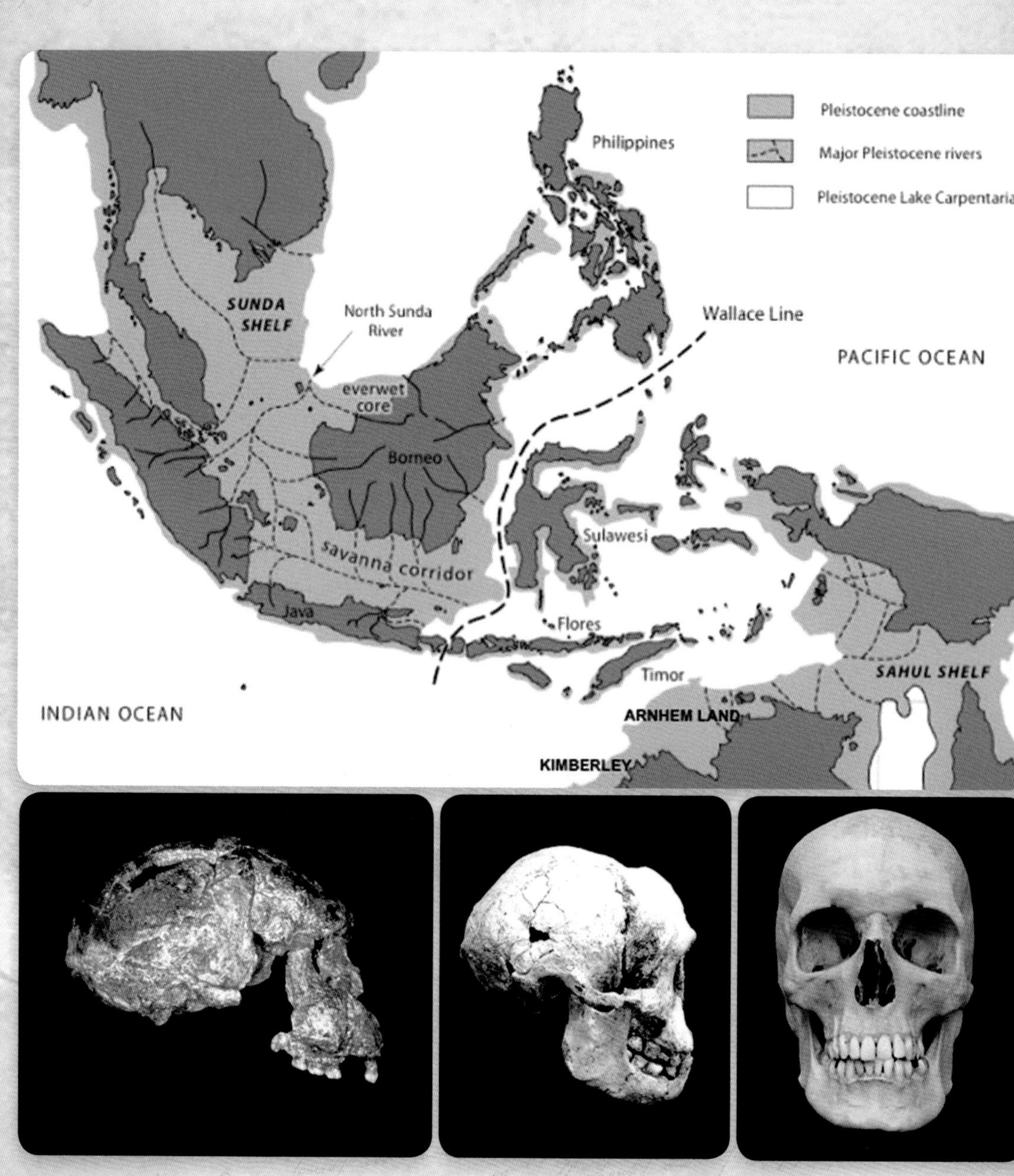
Pleistocene coastline
Major Pleistocene rivers
Pleistocene Lake Carpentaria
Philippines
SUNDA SHELF
North Sunda River
Wallace Line
PACIFIC OCEAN
everwet core
Borneo
Sulawesi
savanna corridor
Java
Flores
Timor
SAHUL SHELF
INDIAN OCEAN
ARNHEM LAND
KIMBERLEY

Archaeology of the Kimberley, Northwest Australia

Michael J. Morwood

The Kimberley has unique potential for tackling major issues in world and Australian archaeology. This results mainly from its geographical location and especially its proximity to island Southeast Asia, and its geology. In this paper, I outline some of the general implications, what we know about the archaeological and rock art sequences in the region, and priorities for future research.

The wider context: island Southeast Asia

On the basis of the length of required water-crossings at times of lowered sea level, Northwest Australia, including the Kimberley and Arnhem Land, was a likely beachhead for human colonists crossing from continental Asia (Sunda) to Greater Australia (Sahul).

Three human species are known to have occupied adjacent island Southeast Asia during the Pleistocene – *Homo erectus, Homo floresiensis* and *Homo sapiens* (modern humans), but only the latter appears to have managed the crossing to Sahul.

In fact, evidence from Australia comprises the best-dated and earliest evidence for the worldwide dispersal of modern humans out of Africa, where our species first appeared around 195,000 years ago, on the basis of both genetic and archaeological evidence (Hudjashov et al. 2007; McDougall *et al.* 2005; Oppenheimer 2004). In Sunda and Sahul the earliest skeletal and/or behavioural evidence for modern humans is found about 45,000 years before present (BP) at sites such as Niah Cave in Sarawak, Leang Burung 2 in Sulawesi, Jeremalai Cave in East Timor, and Nauwalabila, Malakununja, Widgingarri 1, Devils Lair and the Willandra Lakes in Australia (e.g. Barker et al. 2007; Bowler et al. 2003; O'Connor 2007; Gillespie 2002; Glover 1981; Roberts et al. 1994). Modern human colonisation from Sunda to Sahul is therefore generally thought to have been rapid, complete and unidirectional (e.g. Birdsell 1977). However, the discovery of evidence for *Homo floresiensis*, an endemic species that survived on Flores until at least 18,000 years ago, shows that earlier hominin

Opposite
(Top) Location of Kimberley and Arnhem Land in relation to Southeast Asia.
(Bottom from far left) Three hominin species are known from Southeast Asia – *H. erectus, H. floresiensis* and *H. sapiens* (modern humans).
Photos – Peter Brown

populations in mainland and island Southeast Asia could co-exist with modern human occupation of the region for at least 30,000 years (Brown et al. 2004; Morwood et al. 2005).

Even at low sea levels, at least four sea crossings were needed to reach Sahul from Sunda – with one of these crossings being at least 100 kilometres (Birdsell 1977; Figure 2). In addition, the strength of the prevalent, north-south currents, the Indonesian Throughflow, made the required west-east crossings difficult, as shown by the natural faunal impoverishment of the islands-in-between (i.e. before humans began to translocate animals). In fact, the only land mammals that managed the entire crossing themselves from Sunda to Sahul were rodents and modern humans. One clear implication is that Sahul was not colonised accidentally by 'a pregnant woman adrift on a mangrove log', but required deliberate crossings by groups of people with a sophisticated marine technology – including means for harvesting marine resources, as well as making ocean crossings. Evidence for tuna fishing in the earliest levels of Jeremalai in East Timor around 42,000 years ago amply testifies to this, as does over-the-horizon peopling of Manus Island in West Melanesia by 21,000 BP (Fredericksen et al. 1993).

Colonisation of island Southeast Asia then Sahul was, therefore, probably rapid but not necessarily unidirectional (Macaulay et al. 2005). Initial occupation of Sahul would have been along the now submerged coastal plain, given that since the last interglacial, 125,000 years ago, sea levels have been consistently lower than today's (Bowdler 1997). However, river systems, such as the Fitzroy, Mitchell, King Edward and Drysdale, would have served as access routes for penetration of inland regions.

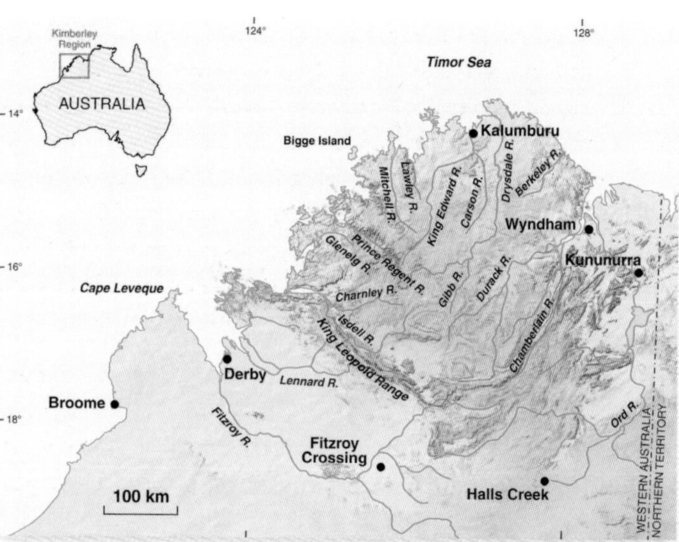

Right Location of Kimberley in Northwest Australia, with major river systems.

Cultural contact, exchange and movement of people between Northwest Australia and Asia probably occurred for the whole duration of human presence in this part of the world. That such input did occur is demonstrated by the introduction of the dingo to Australia about 4,000 years ago (Gollan 1984). In addition, there is a range of more ambivalent technological evidence for Asian cultural contact, such as the mid-Holocene appearance of stone points and backed blades around 4,000 BP.

As well as a possible beachhead for initial colonisation of Sahul, Northwest Australia served as a point of contact for continued Asian influences, including technological, linguistic and genetic inputs. For instance, there is abundant historical, as well as archaeological evidence for systematic contact between Indonesian seafarers and Aboriginal people in the Kimberley and Arnhem Land (Macknight 1976; Morwood & Hobbs 1997). In this context, it is significant that Aboriginal cultures in Northwest Australia share a number of long term cultural traits that set them apart from those in the rest of the continent; for instance, edge-ground, hafted axes occur in the earliest sites in the Kimberley, Arnhem Land and Cape York Peninsula, but do not appear in the rest of Australia until 4,000 BP at most (Geneste et al. 2010; Morwood & Trezise 1989); while bifacial, pressure flaked points were only made in Northwest Australia.

The linguistic and artistic complexity of the Kimberley, Arnhem Land and adjacent areas in historic times has similar implications (Blake 1988). At the time of European contact there were about 300 Aboriginal languages in Australia, which could be grouped into 17 language phyla. However, 16 of these phyla are found

Above In Australia, Pleistocene hafted ground axes and bifacially pressure flaked points are only known from the northwest of the continent.
Photo – Michael Morwood

only in Northwest Australia; the remainder of the continent only has languages of the Pama-Nyungan language phyla. In addition, these same two regions have rock art sequences which share many characteristics, but which are very different from those in other parts of Australia. Some of this complexity relates to climatic fluctuations and in situ cultural developments, but some relates to Asian input.

Evidence from archaeological excavations

Although little archaeological research has yet been undertaken in the Kimberley, it clearly has a long and complex prehistoric sequence including changes in land use, projectile technology and rock art. At this stage, the oldest, published dates for human presence in the Kimberley specifically and Australia generally comes from Carpenter's Gap 1 and Riwi in the southern Kimberley limestones (O'Connor 1996). Non-basal radiocarbon ages of about 45,000 BP, suggest that dates for initial occupation of the Kimberley may be the same as those claimed for Arnhem Land on the basis of Optically Stimulated Luminescence (OSL) – i.e. 53,000 to 60,000 BP (Roberts et al. 1994).

All OSL dates of this age range come from Arnhem Land and the Kimberley, even though the technique has been used to date 'early' occupation sites elsewhere in Australia. There is therefore a possibility that these two areas, which have environmental barriers to the south and east, and an extensive coastline flanking island Southeast Asia, could have been occupied by peoples well before the rest of the continent. As well as stone artefacts, bone and plant remains, Carpenter's Gap yielded a slab of the roof coated with red pigment in deposits about 42,000 years old (O'Connor & Fankhauser 2001). This is a minimum age for rock paintings at the site; although not enough survived to be able to tell what was being painted.

By 30,000 BP human use of the Kimberley had intensified, with sites such as Widgingarri, Widgingarri 2 and Koolan Shelter 2 along the southern Kimberley coast, and Drysdale 3 in the northern inland being occupied for the first time. Later, at the height of the Last Glacial Maximum (LGM) an occupation hiatus seems evident at most sites suggesting abandonment of much of the Kimberley in response to increasing aridity. Presumably, people moved to better-watered areas or refuges if this was an option. For instance, at Carpenter's Gap very limited use of the site continued throughout the LGM indicating that (semi)-permanent waters were retained in deep gorges of the Napier Range.

In this light, it is significant that Miriwun Shelter on the Ord River, east Kimberley, was first occupied in the LGM and continued in use up until the end of the Pleistocene, when conditions began to improve around 12,000 years ago. The Ord is the most likely catchment in the general region to have retained permanent water at this time. Over much of the Kimberley, there is little evidence of continuity of occupation between Pleistocene and Holocene times. See Table 1. Presumably, people moved to better-watered areas if this was an option, or to the coastline, which at the LGM was 200 kilometres farther west than at present. Coastal shelf sites were submerged by the post-glacial rise in sea level, making their archaeological records beyond reach of recovery.

Period	Epoch	Million Years
	Holocene	0 to 0.012
Quaternary	Pleistocene	0.012 to 2.6

Left Table 1. Pleistocene and Holocene Timelines.

Opposite
Carpenter's Gap archaelogical site, the location of the oldest evidence of human occupation in the Kimberley.
Photo – Mike Donaldson

Pleistocene stone artefact assemblages in the region largely comprised amorphous flaked assemblages of fine-grained quartzite, silcrete and chert, but also included fragments of edge-ground axes made on volcanics or metamorphics. Edge-ground axes of this age range are only found in the Kimberley, Arnhem Land and Southeast Cape York Peninsula, which have the earliest evidence for edge-ground technology anywhere (Morwood & Trezise 1989).

Widgingarri 1, Koolan, Carpenter's Gap and Riwi are unusual for north Australian sites in that they have well-preserved organic remains in all levels and these provide good evidence for environmental and economic change over time. At Koolan 2 on Koolan Island, for instance, bone recovered from the excavation shows a generalised exploitation of inland terrestrial fauna. With the exception of Tasmanian Tiger and Tasmanian Devil, all species represented in the Pleistocene levels are still available on the mainland, but some contact with the coast is also evident in fragments of baler shell and pearl shell dated to 28,000 and 19,000 BP respectively. The pearl shell was transported to the site at a time when the coastline was 200 kilometres away; indicating that people occupied the now-drowned coastal shelf, and that inland and coastal groups were linked by long-distance exchange. Shell beads found at Riwi similarly document long-distance exchange and the value of exotic, decorative items (Balme & Morse 2006).

Re-occupation of the Kimberley generally, as conditions improved and sea levels rose, then stabilised, is first evident at Koolan from 10,500 BP. In addition to terrestrial fauna, the diet of people at the site now included marine shellfish. From stabilisation of sea level around 6,500 years ago, there appears to have been an exponential increase in the number of occupied sites, which included shell middens along the newly established coast (Veitch 1996).

The mid-Holocene appearance of stone spear points at Kimberley sites is an important chronological marker, but there is uncertainty as to the exact timing as the small number of stone points and the loose sandy deposits at some sites make accurate dating difficult. However, evidence from a number of excavations indicates that stone points were introduced to the region between 5,000 and 3,000 years ago (Bowdler & O'Conner 1991; O'Connor 1996).

Later in the sequence, sporadic contact between European navigators and local Aboriginal people began in the 17th century (e.g. Tasman in 1644, Dampier in 1688), but the first large-scale and regular contacts between Kimberley Aborigines and 'outsiders' date to the mid-17th century, with Indonesian seafarers visiting north Australian waters to collect trepang.[1] The linguistic, genetic, ideological and material effects of this contact between Indonesian and Aboriginal groups included use of a 'Malay' *lingua franca* by Aboriginal groups along the coast; the introduction of new diseases, such as smallpox; and access to exotic raw materials, such as glass and steel.

Archaeological evidence for Indonesian trepangers is seen in the large number of trepang processing sites along the Kimberley and Arnhem Land coastlines (Crawford 1969; Howard 2009; Macknight 1976; Morwood & Hobbs 1997; Stone 1999). The only date yet available for an Indonesian site in the Kimberley comes from Tamarinda, near Kalumburu, where a Dutch East Indies coin recovered by Ian Crawford dates to AD 1823. However, a beeswax depiction of an Asian prau in West Arnhem Land has yielded a radiocarbon age of 1667 AD, which provides a minimum date for the beginnings of the Australian trepang industry.

In historical times, following European occupation of the Kimberley, massive changes occurred in Indigenous land use, technology, demography, social life, art, ceremony and interaction with other groups. And, if anything, the pace of change is now accelerating. Notable, but little researched aspects of the associated archaeological record include the impacts of early European settlement, pastoralism, European/Aboriginal trepanging, missions, World War II, designation of National Parks and recognition of Native Title (e.g. Beasy & Beasy 1995, Crawford 2001).

Kimberley rock art

The Kimberley rock art sequence is likely to prove one of the longest and most complex anywhere in the world; rivalled only by the rock art of western Arnhem Land, with which it shares early stylistic traits (Chaloupka 1993; Lewis 1984). Partly this longevity relates to the hardness and stability of the King Leopold and Warton Sandstones, which comprise the majority of rock art surfaces in the region.

As with West Arnhem Land, the numerous rock painting styles in the Kimberley sequence have emphasis on figurative motifs, with a degree of detail not evident in Aboriginal rock art in most other regions, and with clear visual cues for recognition of depicted subjects (see Walsh & Morwood 1999). The sequence of rock art styles, inferred from studies of superimpositions and differential

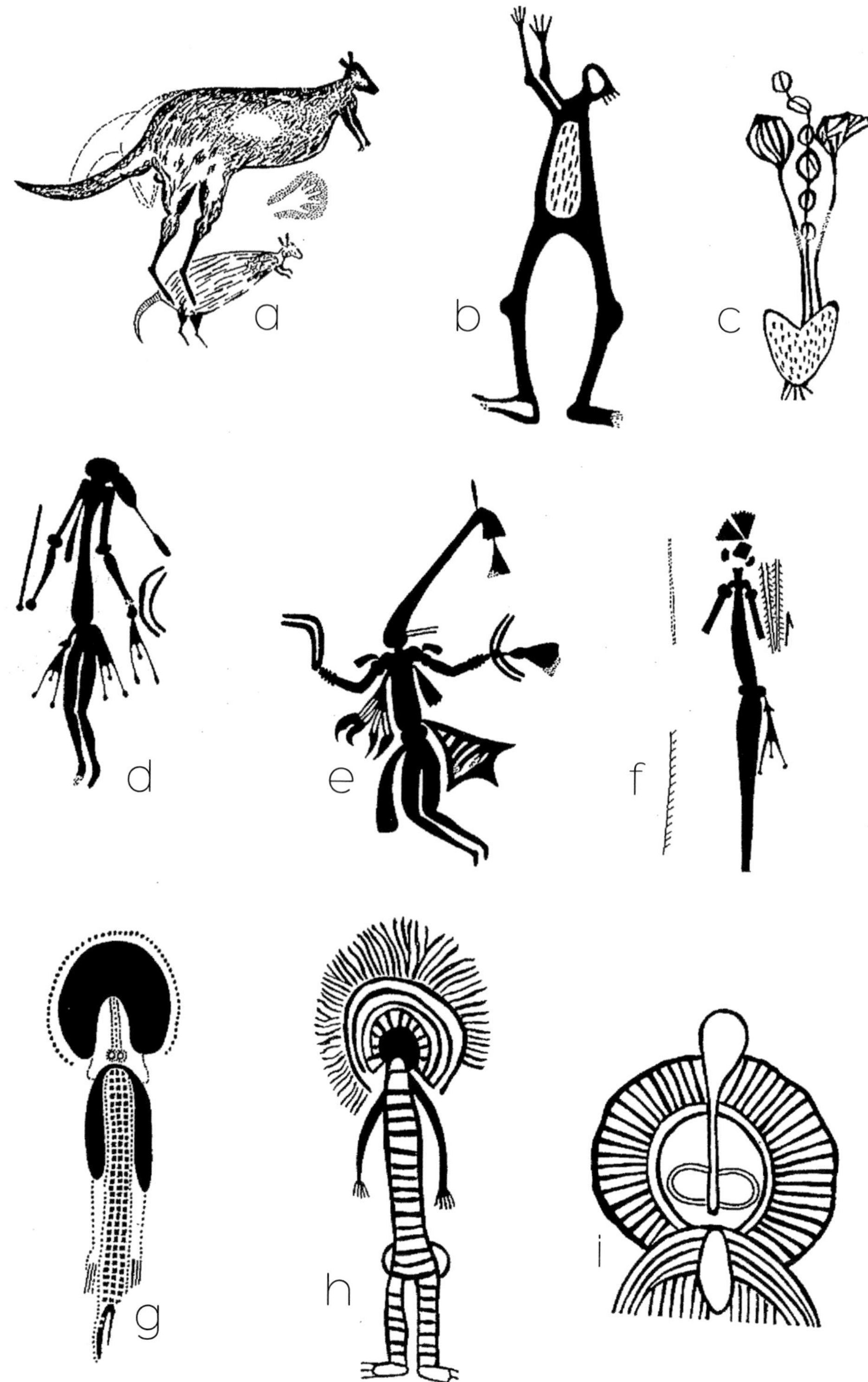
a
b
c
d
e
f
g
h
i

weathering, shows that there have been associated changes in artistic conventions, subject matter, context of production and function (e.g. Crawford 1970, 1977; Welch 1993; Walsh 1988, 2000). Some of this complexity may relate to the geographical proximity of the Kimberley to Southeast Asia and outside culture contact, including early European contact as evidenced by the well-known rock paintings of Europeans and their watercraft on the west coast of Bigge Island (Crawford 1970).

Once dates for rock art are available, changes in depicted subjects and cultural context can be compared with contemporaneous technological and economic changes represented in archaeological excavations. The few dates now available for the Kimberley rock art sequence mean that a little of this potential can be used.

We can assume that the first people to occupy the region included artists. Although there is no direct evidence of this yet in the Kimberley, archaeological excavations in Arnhem Land to the east have recovered lumps of high quality red ochres in levels dated by OSL to 53,000–60,000 BP (Roberts et al. 1994). Art was part of the cultural heritage of the first people to reach Australia.

The earliest direct evidence for rock art in the Kimberley comes from Carpenter's Gap, where rock paintings date to a minimum of 42,700 BP (O'Connor & Fankhauser 2001). This not only establishes the minimum time-depth of the Kimberley rock painting sequence, but is also now the earliest evidence for rock painting anywhere in the world. In comparison, the famed Palaeolithic art tradition of Western Europe began about 32,000 years ago (Bahn & Vertut 1992).

The oldest surviving rock painting motifs evident in the Kimberley sequence comprise large depictions of animals, humans and yams, as well as stencilled hands and implements – a phase of rock art production termed the Irregular Infill Animal Period (Walsh 1988, 2000). This phase is followed by the Bradshaw (Gwion Gwion) rock painting style, characterised by depictions of humans with great attention to anatomical detail, accoutrements and composition, only matched in Australia by the Dynamic Figure paintings of West Arnhem Land (Chaloupka 1993; Lewis 1984). Differential weathering of paintings within the following Bradshaw painting developmental sequence indicates that they may span a considerable time. For instance, the earliest Tassel and Sash Bradshaws are concentrated in the region where the exposed rock is extremely hard, although isolated examples occur as far south as the Napier

Opposite
The Kimberley rock art sequence is long and complex. Styles as nominated by Walsh (2000) include – a-c) Irregular Infill Animal; d) Tassel Bradshaw; e) Sash Bradshaw; f) Clothes Peg; g) Horseshoe Head; h) Clawed Hand; i) Wandjina (from Morwood et al. 1994).

Range and as far east as the Keep River in the Northern Territory (Morwood & Hobbs 2000). In contrast, later paintings of the Clothes Peg Figure style are more evenly distributed throughout the general Kimberley region, suggesting that they are considerably younger.

Based on the evidence of differential weathering and superimpositions, there may have been a discontinuity in the rock art sequence between the end of the Bradshaw rock painting style and the following Clawed Hand Period style (Walsh 2000), which may correspond to the abandonment of much of the Kimberley during the LGM. For instance, OSL dating of a mud wasp nest partially covering a painted anthropomorph yielded an age of 16,400 years (Roberts et al. 1997).[2] If the motif is a 'late Bradshaw' as claimed, then this provides a minimum age for this enigmatic rock art style.

In contrast, the Clawed Hand Period painting style seems of Holocene age, for late panels of the style include depictions of stone spear points that were introduced to the Kimberley after 5,000 BP (Walsh & Morwood 1999). An age range of 10,500 to 4,500 BP for Clawed Hand Period paintings is therefore a reasonable first estimate. On the basis of Accelerator Mass Spectrometer (AMS) radiocarbon ages for associated charcoal pigments and stylistic transitions, the Clawed Hand style seems to have ultimately given rise to the Wandjina rock painting style, featuring large anthropomorphic beings lacking mouths and usually depicted on a background of white pigment. Direct radiocarbon ages for Wandjina paintings and beeswax figures indicate that simple Wandjina motifs featured in the rock art from about 4,500 BP, but the major Wandjina sites with multiple repaintings are all less than 1,250 years old (Morwood et al. 2010). Wandjina paintings continued as a focus of Aboriginal religious beliefs in the Kimberley until recent times (e.g. Blundell 1975).

Establishing a wider archaeological context for different rock painting styles in the Kimberley allows rare insights into past Aboriginal ideologies, technologies and material culture. Certainly, the activities, accoutrements, weapons and animals vividly depicted in early rock paintings contrast markedly with the sparse evidence of bones, plant remains and stone artefacts recovered from archaeological excavations. As well as marked discontinuities in the sequence, there are notable continuities, as in the artistic (and probably associated ideological) developments during the Holocene that ultimately gave rise to the Wandjina rock painting style of recent times.

The major problem with use of the Kimberley rock art as a source of information about the past is dating. At present, there are very few numerical dates available to anchor the rock art sequence and, with one exception, all are of Holocene age (Morwood & Hobbs 2000) – and some have questioned the credentials of the exception (Max Aubert: pers. comm.). In fact, to all intents and purposes, the older Kimberley rock art styles remain of unknown age and duration. They may be of LGM age or older, as claimed (Roberts et al. 1997; Walsh 2000); but also could be of terminal Pleistocene/ early Holocene antiquity. Obtaining multiple, well provenanced age determinations for early rock art styles must be a priority for future archaeological research in the region.

Above Bradshaw (Gwion Gwion) rock paintings include detailed depictions of weapons, accoutrements and ceremonies.
Photo – Michael Morwood

Conclusions

The Kimberley cultural sequence was complex, underwent major changes, had at least one lengthy hiatus, and included foreign contacts. The evidence could hardly be otherwise given its time depth, the fact that it spans major climatic fluctuations, and the proximity of the region to Asia. However, it is not necessary to evoke the intrusion of different racial groups to explain aspects of the Kimberley cultural sequence – nor is it necessary to argue for a direct line of descent to counter such arguments.

At present only a handful of sites have been excavated in the vast Kimberley region, despite its potential for documenting the initial arrival of modern people in Australia and subsequent cultural contacts with Asia; and most of these excavations have been undertaken in the southern or coastal sections. In addition, the age and duration of early Kimberley rock art styles remains unknown, as do their specific environmental and cultural contexts.

Hopefully, two complementary projects now underway will help rectify some of these gaps in coverage: '*Change and continuity: archaeology and art in the North Kimberley, Northwest Australia*' specifically targets the Mitchell and Lawley River hinterland sections of the North Kimberley (Morwood et al. 2008), while '*Life ways of the First Australians*' continues work on sites in the limestone belt in the South Kimberley. Both projects will include systematic surveys to locate new sites; excavations at a range of open and shelter sites; application of new dating techniques; and training of students, people from local communities and other stakeholders in a range of archaeological techniques.

Opposite
Mark Moore with Joseph Karadada and Yinica Perston excavating at 'Reindeer Rock' on the Lower Mitchell River, June 2010.
Photo – June Ross

Acknowledgments

The Australian Research Council, Kimberley Foundation, WA Department of Environment and Conservation, Heliwork and Kandiwal Aboriginal Corporation all generously support the North Kimberley research project being undertaken by June Ross (University of New England), Kira Westaway (Macquarie University), Mark Moore (University of New England) and myself. Kandiwal Aboriginal Corporation has also given permission for use of the photos used in this paper.

Notes

1 See Cathie Clement, 'Maritime exploration on the Kimberley coast', this volume, for further discussion.

2 Note that a series of AMS radiocarbon dates for mineral accretions associated with Bradshaw paintings establish minimum ages for these ranging from 1490 to 3880 BP (Watchman et al. 1997). The range of minimum ages and uneven distribution of oxalate crusts even across the same painting indicate that the formation process is episodic, could be considerably delayed or even involve stripping of previous deposits. Ages determined for the samples described as 'Accr.paint' or 'Under-paint' almost certainly apply to crusts formed after the painting. Contrary to Watchman et al. (1997), all these AMS dates should therefore be taken as minimum ages. In fact, a range of other evidence indicates that the crusts are very much younger than the underlying Bradshaw paintings.

References

Balme, J. 2000. Excavations revealing 40,000 years of occupation at Mimbi Caves, south central Kimberley, Western Australia. *Australian Archaeology* 51: 1–5.

Balme, J. & Morse, K. 2006. Shell beads and social behaviour in Pleistocene Australia. *Antiquity* 80: 799–811.

Barker, G., et al. 2007. The 'human revolution' in lowland tropical Southeast Asia: the antiquity and behavior of anatomically modern humans at Niah Cave (Sarawak, Borneo). *Journal of Human Evolution* 52: 243–61.

Beasy, J. & Beasy, C. 1995. *Truscott: the diary of Australia's secret wartime Kimberley airbase*. Australian Military History Publications, Loftus (N.S.W).

Birdsell, J. B. 1977. The recalibration of a paradigm for the first peopling of Greater Australia. In: J. Allen, J. Golson & R. Jones (eds) *Sunda and Sahul: Prehistoric Studies in Southeast Asia, Melanesia and Australia*: 113–67. Academic Press, London.

Blake, B. J. 1988. Redefining Pama-Nyungan: towards a prehistory of Australian languages. *Aboriginal linguistics*: 1–90.

Blundell, V. 1975. *Aboriginal adaptation in north-west Australia*. Ph.D. thesis, University of Wisconsin-Madison.

Bowler, J. M., et al. 2003. New ages for human occupation and climatic change at Lake Mungo, Australia. *Nature* 421: 837–40.

Bowdler, S. & O'Connor, S. 1991. The dating of the Australian Small Tool Tradition, with new evidence from the Kimberley, W.A. *Australian Aboriginal Studies*, 1991 No. 1: 53–62.

Bowdler, S. 1997. The Pleistocene Pacific. In D. Denoon, 'Human settlement', in D. Denoon (ed.) *The Cambridge History of the Pacific Islanders*, pp. 41–50. Cambridge University Press, Cambridge.

Brown P., et al. 2004. A new small-bodied hominin from the Late Pleistocene of Flores, Indonesia. *Nature* 431: 1055–61.

Chaloupka, G. 1993. Journey in time: *The World's Longest Continuing Art Tradition*. Reed, Chatswood (N.S.W.).

Crawford, I. 1969. *Late Prehistoric Changes in Aboriginal Cultures in Kimberley, Western Australia*. PhD thesis, University of London.

Crawford, I. C. 1970. *The art of the Wandjina*. Oxford University Press.

Crawford, I. C. 1977. The relationship of Bradshaw and Wandjina art in north-west Kimberley. In: P. J. Ucko (ed.), *Form in indigenous art*, pp. 357–69. Australian Institute of Aboriginal Studies, Canberra.

Crawford, I. 2001. *we won the victory: Aborigines and Outsiders on the North-West coast of the Kimberley*. Fremantle Arts Centre Press, Fremantle.

Dortch, C. 1977. Early and late industrial phases in Western Australia. In: R.V.S. Wright (ed.) *Stone tools as cultural markers*, pp. 104–32. Australian Institute of Aboriginal Studies, Canberra.

Fredericksen, C., et al. 1993. Pamwak rockshelter: a Pleistocene site on Manus Island, PNG. In: M. Smith, et al. (eds), *Sahul in Review: Pleistocene Archaeology in*

Australia, New Guinea and Island Melanesia, pp. 144–52. Canberra: Department of Prehistory, Research School of Pacific and Asian Studies, Australian National University. *Occasional Papers in Prehistory* 24.

Geneste, J-M., et al. 2010. Earliest evidence for ground-edge axes: 35,400±410 cal BP from Jawoyn Country, Arnhem Land. *Australian Archaeology* 71: 66–9.

Gillespie, R. 2002. Dating the first Australians. *Radiocarbon* 44(2): 455–72.

Glover, I. C. 1981. Leang Burung 2: an Upper Palaeolithic rock shelter in south Sulawesi, Indonesia. *Modern Quaternary Research in Southeast Asia* 6: 1–38.

Gollan, K. 1984. The Australian dingo: in the shadow of Man. In: M. Archer, G. Clayton (eds), *Vertebrate zoogeography and evolution in Australasia*. Hesperian Press, Perth, pp. 921–8.

Howard, P. 2009. *Past and present: an ethno-historical and archaeological study of the North Australian trepang industry.* B.A. Hons thesis. University of Wollongong.

Hudjashov, G., et al. 2007. Revealing the prehistoric settlement of Australia by Y chromosome and mtDNA analysis. *Proceedings of the National Academy of Sciences* 104: 8726–30.

Lewis, D. 1984. Mimi on Bradshaw. *Australian Aboriginal Studies* 2: 58–61.

Macaulay, V., et al. 2005. Single, rapid coastal settlement of Asia revealed by analysis of complete mitochondrial genomes. *Science* 308: 1034–6.

Macknight, C. C. 1976. *The voyage to Marege.* University of Melbourne Press, Melbourne.

McDougall, I., et al. 2005. Stratigraphic placement and age of modern humans from Kibish, Ethiopia. *Nature* 433: 733–6.

Morwood, M. & Trezise, P. 1989. Edge-ground axes in Pleistocene Greater Australia: new evidence from S.E. Cape York Peninsula. *Queensland Archaeological Research* 6: 77–90.

Morwood, M. J., Walsh, G. L., Watchman, A. 1994. The dating potential of rock art in the Kimberley, N. W. Australia. *Rock Art Research* 11(2): 79-87.

Morwood, M. J. & Hobbs, D. R. 1997. The Asian connection: preliminary report on Indonesian trepang sites on the Kimberley coast, N.W. Australia. *Archaeology in Oceania* 32: 197–206.

Morwood, M. J. & Hobbs, D. R. 2000. The archaeology of Kimberley art. In G. L. Walsh, *Bradshaw art of the Kimberley*, pp. 34–7. Takarakka Nowan Kas Publications, Toowong (Qld).

Morwood, M. J., et al. 2005. Further evidence for small-bodied hominins from the Late Pleistocene of Flores, Indonesia. *Nature* 437: 1012–17.

Morwood, M. J., Ross, J. & Donaldson, M. 2008. *Northwest Kimberley Archaeological Survey 20th – 27th April 2008.*' Unpublished Report to Kimberley Foundation Australia.

Morwood, M. J., Walsh, G. L. & Watchman, A. L. 2010. AMS radiocarbon ages for beeswax and charcoal pigments in North Kimberley rock art. *Rock Art Research* 27(1): 3–8.

O'Connor, S. 1996. Thirty thousand years in the Kimberley: results of excavations of three rockshelters in the coastal west Kimberley, W.A. In: P. Veth & P. Hiscock (eds), *Archaeology of northern Australia*, pp. 26–49. *Tempus* 4, Anthropology Museum, University of Queensland, Brisbane.

O'Connor S. 2007. New evidence from East Timor contributes to our understanding of earliest modern human colonisation east of the Sunda Shelf. *Antiquity* 81: 523–35.

O'Connor, S. & Fankhauser, B. 2001. Art at 40,000 bp? One step closer: an ochre covered rock from Carpenter's Gap Shelter 1, Kimberley region, Western Australia. In: A. Anderson, I. Lilley, S. O'Connor (eds), *Histories of old ages. Essays in honour of Rhys Jones.* Pandanus Books, Australian National University, Canberra, pp. 287–300.

Oppenheimer, S. 2004. *Out of Eden: The peopling of the world.* Robinson, London.

Roberts, R. G., Jones, R., Spooner, N. A., Head, M. J., Murray, A. S., Smith, M. A. 1994. The human colonisation of Australia: optical dates of 53,000 and 60,000 years bracket human arrival at Deaf Adder Gorge, Northern Territory. *Quaternary Science Reviews* 13: 575–83.

Roberts, R., et al. 1997. Luminescence dating of rock art and past environments using mud-wasp nests in northern Australia. *Nature* 387 (12 June): 696–99.

Stone, G. 1999. *The archaeology of fishing: interpreting the evidence for the trepang industry in the North Kimberly.* B.A. Hons thesis, University of New England, Armidale.

Taçon, P. S. C., et al. 2010. A minimum age for early depictions of Southeast Asian praus in the rock art of Arnhem Land, Northern Territory. *Australian Archaeology* 71: 1–10.

Veitch, B. 1996. Evidence for mid-Holocene change in the Mitchell Plateau, northwest Kimberley, Western Australia. In: P. Veth & P. Hiscock (eds), *Archaeology of northern Australia*, pp. 66–89. *Tempus* 4, Anthropology Museum, University of Queensland, Brisbane.

Walsh, G. L. 1988. *Australia's greatest rock art.* E. J. Brill-Robert Brown & Associates, Bathurst.

Walsh, G. L. 2000. *Bradshaw art of the Kimberley.* Takarakka Nowan Kas Publications, Toowong (Qld).

Walsh, G. L. & Morwood, M. J. 1999. Spear and spearthrower evolution in the Kimberley region, N.W. Australia: evidence from rock art. *Archaeology in Oceania* 34(2): 45–58.

Watchman, A. L., et al. 1997. AMS radiocarbon age estimates for early rock paintings in the Kimberley, N.W. Australia: preliminary results. *Rock Art Research* 14(1): 18–26.

Welch, D. 1993. The early rock art of the Kimberley, Australia: developing a chronology. In: J. Steinbring & A. Watchman (eds), *Time and space*, pp. 13–21. Occasional AURA Publication No. 8, Australian Rock Art Research Association, Melbourne.

Maritime exploration on the Kimberley coast

Cathie Clement

Delving into the history of coastal exploration can provide a sense of how the natural environment once looked, how newcomers perceived it, and whether contact occurred.[1] The readily available sources of information include published editions of early mariners' journals.[2] Although never free of embellishment, the journals are invaluable in that they present their authors' observations as part of a continuum that takes in both the past and the future.

We can delve deeper by going to old manuscripts and charts but, as we go back in time, the information becomes fragmented and tenuous. For that reason, this paper only provides an overview of early exploratory voyages that are known to have been made to the Kimberley. It focuses on people and contact, and, because the next paper is about George Grey, it starts at the time of his 1837–1838 visit. From there, it drifts back to earlier visits.

J. Lort Stokes and HMS *Beagle*

One of the mariners whose work complemented Grey's land-based exploration was Lieutenant J. Lort Stokes, the assistant surveyor on HMS *Beagle*. Stokes and his fellow officers perused and augmented the work of other mariners who had preceded them. Those men included Phillip Parker King (1818–1822), Nicolas Baudin (1803 & 1801), William Dampier (1699 & 1688) and Abel Tasman (1644).

In starting with HMS *Beagle*, we are looking at a time when a single colonial settlement existed on Australia's northern coast. Situated at Port Essington, on land that is now part of the Northern Territory, it had been preceded by other British settlements, since abandoned. The presence of this tiny outpost not only protected Britain's claim to the northernmost portions of the colony of New South Wales but also offered scope for the establishment of trade with South East Asia.[3] The explorers who ventured into northern Australia considered those things but some of them were more interested in searching for the great rivers that were believed to empty into the sea along the northern coast.[4]

Opposite
'The Mermaid Beached in Careening Bay'. Hand coloured engraving by W. Hatherell, c. 1887, based on a sketch by Phillip P. King. Courtesy of Antique Print Room, Sydney (www.antiqueprintroom.com).

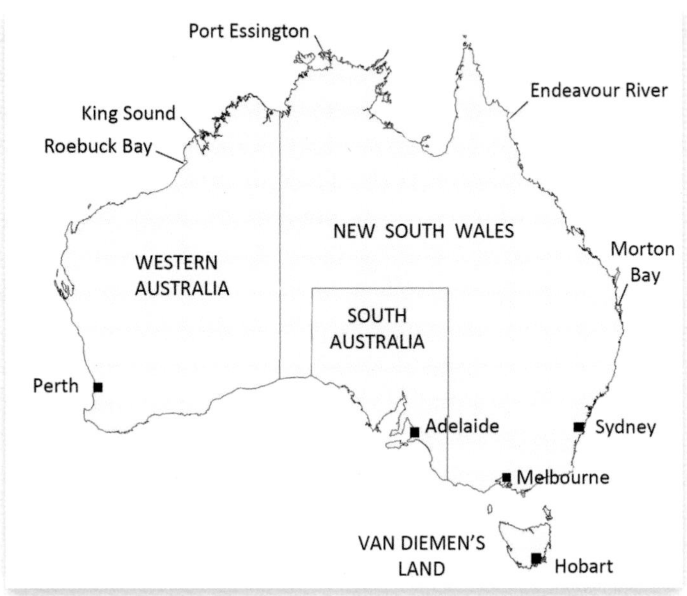

The mariners from the *Beagle* bestowed English names on numerous bays, islands and other coastal features. Those names included King's Sound, later shortened to King Sound, and the Fitzroy River, both of which honoured highly respected mariners.[5]

On 14 February 1838, on the western side of King Sound, Stokes and his companions found another reason to bestow a name:

> We named this Skeleton Point from our finding here the remains of a native, placed in a semi-recumbent position under a wide spreading gum tree, enveloped, or more properly, shrouded, in the bark of the papyrus. All the bones were closely packed together, the larger being placed outside, and the general mass surmounted by the head, resting on its base, the fleshless, eyeless skull 'grinning horribly' over the right side. Some of the natives arrived shortly after we had discovered this curious specimen of their mode of sepulture ; but although they entertain peculiar opinions upon the especial sanctity of 'the house appointed for all living,'—a sanctity we certainly were not altogether justified in disregarding—they made no offer of remonstrance at the removal of the mortal remains of their dead brother.[6]

It is impossible to imagine the feelings or thoughts of the Aboriginal people who watched the mariners remove the skeletal remains. Stokes obviously felt some qualms about his involvement but it was common for mariners and explorers to appropriate bones and skulls either for scientific study or as curiosities. In this instance, George Grey took the remains to England where they were deposited in the museum of the Royal College of Surgeons.[7] Some artefacts and skeletal remains have been, and are being, repatriated to the Kimberley and other parts of Australia but many will never be returned.[8]

Above The colonial situation when HMS *Beagle* visited the north Australian coast.

While such behaviour is condemned today, the mariners' interest in Aboriginal practices and customs did provide us with information about those things. Stokes, for instance, commented on the shelters he saw, stating that most were no more than 'a slight rudely thatched covering, placed on four upright poles, between three and four feet high'.[9]

On Bathurst Island, north-west of Cockatoo Island, he felt compelled to record a much different hut for posterity. His description, written on 25 March 1838, reads:

> Stout poles from 14 to 16 feet high formed the framework of these snug huts -- for so indeed they deserve to be termed -- these were brought together conically at the roof; a stout thatching of dried grass completely excluded both wind and rain, and seemed to bespeak the existence of a climate at times much more severe than a latitude of 16 degrees 6 minutes south, would lead one to anticipate. The remains of small fires, a well greased bark pillow, a head ornament of seabird's feathers, together with several other trifling articles, strewn upon the floors of these wigwams, proved that they had been very recently inhabited.[10]

The huts on Bathurst Island reminded Stokes and other men on the *Beagle* of some they had seen on the south-east coast of Tierra del Fuego (in the vicinity of Cape Horn). The huts were also quite different to those seen by earlier mariners.

Above The 'Substantial Native Hut' depicted by J. Lort Stokes in *Discoveries in Australia*, vol. 1, p. 172.

Phillip Parker King and the Aborigines

During his four voyages along the northern Australian coast, Captain King took notice of shelters built by Indigenous people.[11] Some were at Careening Bay, now known for the boab tree marked with the name of the *Mermaid* in 1820. King's journal carried sketches of his encampment there and some of the adjacent shelters.

King's description of one of the more complex shelters, which was on a hill, read:

> Two walls of stones, piled one upon the other to the height of three feet, formed the two ends ; and saplings were laid across to support a covering of bark or dried grass : the front, which faced the east, was not closed ; but the back, which slanted from the roof to the ground, appeared to have been covered with bark like the roof.[12]

In the 17 days spent ashore at Careening Bay, King and his crew were glad not to encounter any Aborigines, or, as he labelled them, Indians. They had experienced contact at other places along the coast; not all of it amicable.

During the previous year's voyage, while searching for fresh water at Vansittart Bay (approximately 170 kilometres to the north-east) in early October, they had come across 40 small fire-places in a straight line along a beach. Beside each one were stones on which people had been breaking seeds. The presence of husks indicated recent occupation. A wide search produced no fresh water but revealed materials indicative of earlier visits by outsiders.[13]

Above 'Huts of the Natives. Careening Bay. NW Coast of Australia, [1820]', from Phillip Parker King – album of drawings and engravings, 1802–1902. Courtesy of State Library of New South Wales (Call No. PXC 767, Digital: a3464054).

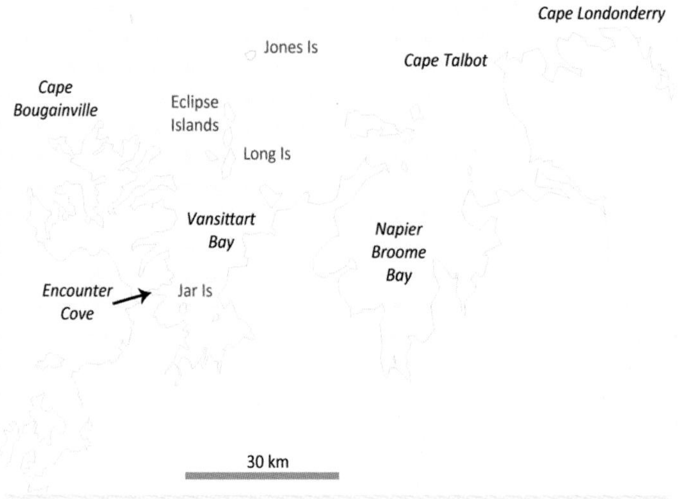

Asian fishermen had been visiting the northern Australia coast for many years, with more than a thousand making the voyage each year. The industry itself is believed to have begun in about 1700, with Muslim fishermen from South-East Asia meeting a Chinese demand for dried bodies of edible holothurians. The names of the holothurians include trepang, *bêche-de-mer*, sea slug and sea cucumber.[14]

King had come across some of these fishermen on the Arnhem Land coast and he was aware that French mariners had seen others west of Vansittart Bay. He was aware too, from discussions with fishermen at Timor in 1818, that the Indigenous people did not welcome these visits. Consequently, King worried that his visits would result in hostility solely because those people would not be able to discriminate between his party and Asian fishermen.[15]

Whether any discrimination occurred is unknown but, a day after King and his companions saw the 40 fireplaces, they provoked mild hostility. He wrote of a brief confrontation that ended when he fired his musket over the heads of 'natives' who were preparing to throw spears at his party. Everyone then withdrew. On the adjacent Jar Island, the mariners found a broken earthenware pot. King appears to have named the island in connection with that find, which led him to blame 'the mischievous disposition of the natives' on prior contact. Other names he bestowed at that time included Encounter Cove, recalling the confrontation, and Vansittart Bay. A week later, when rats were found to have holed two more of his ship's water casks, King headed for Timor to obtain fresh water.[16]

Above Vansittart Bay, Jar Island and Encounter Cove.

Nicolas Baudin and the Asian fishermen

A large fishing party encountered during a French scientific research voyage in April 1803 caused consternation. Sailing eastward in the *Geographe* and the *Casuarina*, Captain Nicolas Baudin and Sub-Lieutenant Louis de Freycinet remained some distance from the mainland as they charted the outer islands of the Bonaparte Archipelago. They saw plenty of smoke from freshly lit fires but no other signs of humans. They would not have been surprised to see Indigenous people among the islands but they were not expecting to meet Asians.

Baudin noted that the fishermen 'were all of Malay origin and were dressed and armed absolutely in the style of the inhabitants of Timor'. The size of their fleet, comprising some 24 or 26 boats, prompted him to organise protection for the men he sent to determine whether he was dealing with residents or visitors. The fishermen were visitors. They used the north-west monsoon to sail southward in December or January each year; fished for trepang west of Cape Londonderry; and then used the south-easterly winds to go home in about April or May.[17] Those winds were well known to seafarers and were shown on charts and maps that included a 'Map for the clarification of the History of the Possessions and the Trade of the Europeans in both Indies'.[18] See map opposite. It was published in Amsterdam in 1775.

Possessions and trade

The colours on Bonne's map belie the tensions of the time. The acquisition, transport and sale of exotic resources underpinned the economic growth of France, Spain, Portugal, Britain, the Dutch Netherlands, and various other countries. Periodical wars occurred; navies protected trade routes and harbours; and numerous armed, privately-owned vessels augmented naval strength. Manned by privateers or corsairs, those vessels carried permits that authorised them to raid the ships and harbours of their country's enemies. That volatile situation prevailed until 1856 when the signatories to the Declaration of Paris agreed to refrain from commissioning privateers.[19]

While the powerful European nations were busy exploiting the rich resources of the East and the West Indies during the 18th century, the Asian fishermen were possibly the only outsiders to visit the Kimberley coast. We have no way of knowing when they first fished on that coast, or when their contact with the Indigenous people began. Nor can we establish whether the Indigenous people adopted or adapted any outside technology in the hundred years prior to Baudin's arrival. Despite that, we do have tantalising fragments on which to muse.

Above The leader of the French expeditions in Kimberley waters. Engraving by William Macleod, c. 1886. Courtesy of Antique Print Room, Sydney (www.antiqueprintroom.com).

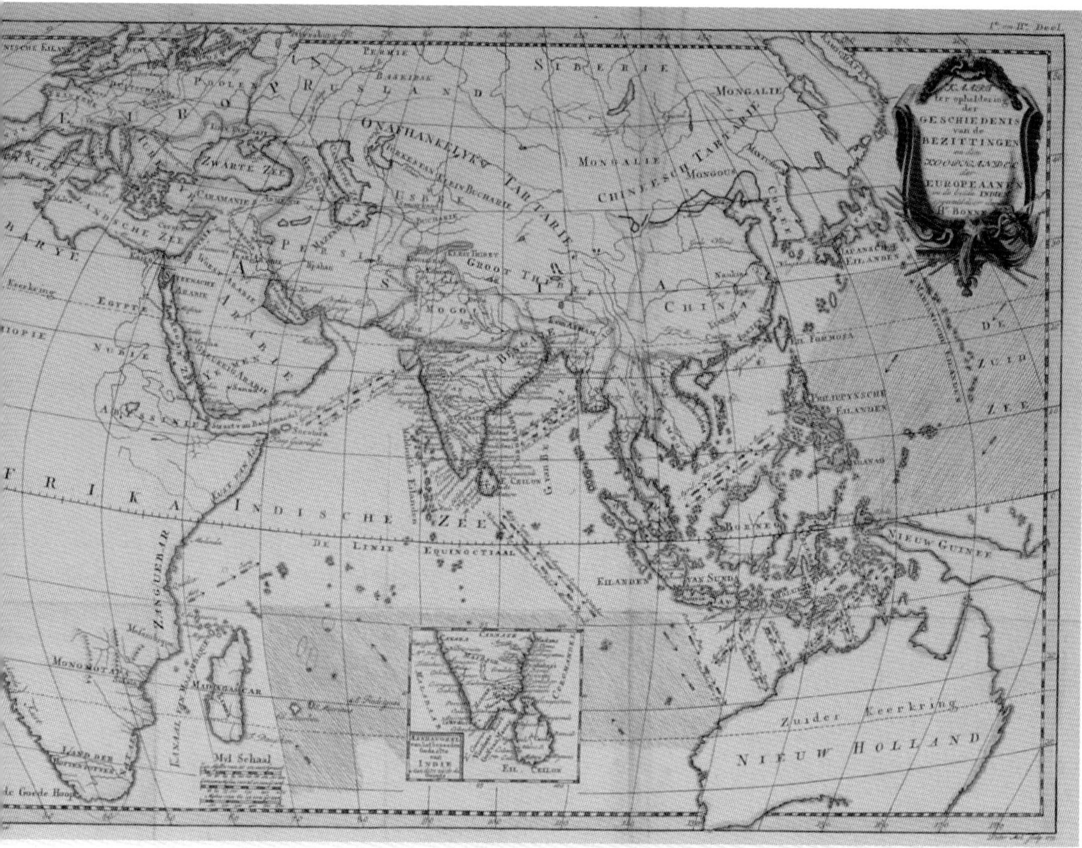

Much of the evidence relevant to 17th century visits to the coast comes from the pens of two men who not only had extensive experience of trading networks but also wanted to share their knowledge with the world. One was Alexander Dalrymple, an employee of the British East India Company. The other was William Dampier.

In the years 1759 to 1762, Dalrymple sailed among the islands of the East Indies where he documented trading activity and compared its low volume to the flourishing commerce identified by old Spanish histories. The obvious differences prompted him to propose that Britain penetrate the Dutch monopoly by creating an emporium near North Borneo. Such a site, equidistant from Korea, Japan, the east coast of India, and the north coast of New Holland, would, he thought, attract trade from within a radius of 1,000 miles (1,609 kilometres).[20] Dalrymple also collected information about voyages to Australia and, in 1767, he released that information in a book that he hoped would induce the British Government to engage him to complete the charting of the Australian coast.[21] That task went to Captain Cook but copies of Dalrymple's work continued to inform people interested in the earlier voyages.

Above Kaart ter opheldering der Geschiedenis van de Bezittingen en den Koophandel der Europeaanen inde beide Indien. Hand coloured copper engraving of a map drawn by R. Bonne in c. 1775.
Courtesy of Antique Print Room, Sydney (www.antiqueprintroom.com).

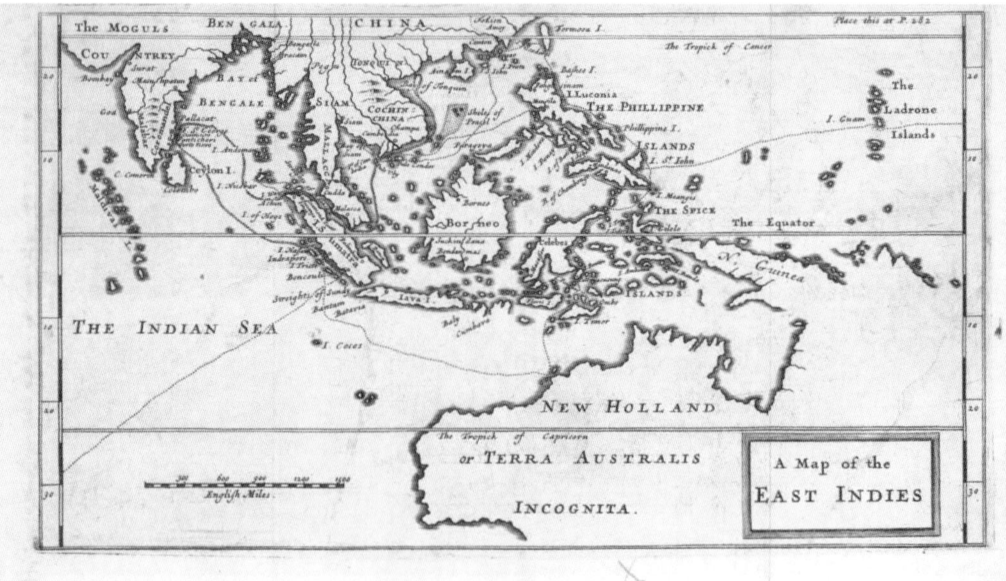

Above A map of the East Indies with track of Dampier's voyage showing his 1688 landing place. Published in *A Collection of Voyages*, James and John Knapton, London, 1729. Courtesy of National Library of Australia (NLA Map NK11186).

William Dampier

Dampier, who died before Dalrymple was born, worked as a privateer in the West Indies before sailing to the East Indies aboard the *Cygnet* with Captain Swan in 1686. After becoming familiar with that locality, the crew left Swan and several of his men in the Philippines, stole the *Cygnet*, and eventually used the monsoon winds to sail through the islands and visit the Kimberley coast in 1688. Dampier was in the company of privateers the whole of that time but he claimed that neither he nor the ship's surgeon 'had any Knowledge of the Plot that had been laid to leave Capt. Swan and run away with the Ship'.[22] In 1699 he returned to the Kimberley coast in command of HMS *Roebuck* but, after losing that badly deteriorating ship off Ascension Island in 1701, he was court martialled and again found work as a privateer.[23]

Other writers have focussed on Dampier's valuable contribution to botanical knowledge.[24] Here, his observations about Aboriginal people are more pertinent. His contact with those people occurred during an interval of at least five weeks from mid-January 1688, both on the mainland and on islands near One Arm Point.[25] Later, he wrote:

> We saw no sort of Animal, nor any Tracks of Beasts but once, and that seemed to be the Tread of a Beast as big as a great Mastiff Dog. There are a few small Land-birds, but none bigger than a Blackbird, and but few Sea-fowls. Nor is the Sea very plentifully stored with Fish unless you reckon the Manatee and Turtle as such. Of these Creatures there is plenty, but they are extraordinarily shy, though the Inhabitants cannot trouble them much, having neither Boats nor Iron...

They have no Houses but lie in the open Air without any covering, the Earth being their Bed and the Heaven their Canopy. Whether they cohabit, one Man to one Woman or promiscuously, I do not know, but they do live in Companies of 20 or 30 Men, Women and Children together. Their only Food is a small sort of Fish, which they get by making Wares of Stone across little Coves or Branches of the Sea. Every Tide brings in the small Fish and leaves them there for Prey to these People, who constantly attend to search for them at Low-water. This small Fry I take to be the top of their Fishery. They have no Instruments to catch great Fish, should they come and (rarely) be left behind at Low-water. Nor could we catch any Fish with our Hooks and Lines all the while we lay there. In other Places at Low-water they seek Cockles, Mussels and Periwinkles. There are fewer still of these Shellfish, so that their chiefest dependence is upon what the Sea leaves in their Wares.[26]

Dampier's emphasis on the local people's reliance on fish traps contrasts sharply with the marine prowess for which those people have since become famous. Written evidence regarding their use of rafts dates only from the time of the visits by King and Stokes. King was quite taken with the rafts and, as well as sketching one that he saw at Hanover Bay, he used a woodcut of that 'mode of conveyance' on the title page of Volume 2 of his published journals. The first 'native raft' that Stokes saw on the Kimberley coast was near where Dampier and his shipmates had careened their vessel in 1688. According to Stokes:

It was formed of nine small poles pegged together, and measured ten feet in length by four in breadth ; the greatest diameter of the largest pole was three inches. All the poles were of the palm tree, a wood so light, that one man could carry the whole affair with the greatest ease. By it there was a very rude double-bladed paddle.[27]

That raft was nothing like another one seen near the beach adjacent to the huts on Bathurst Island. Stokes noted that it was 'in such a position as must have required the exertions of several men to have placed it there; being heavier than either of our boats'. He also elaborated on its construction:

It was framed of the dead trunk of a mangrove tree, with three distinct stems growing from one root, about 18 feet long, and 4 1/2 broad. The roots at one end closely entwined, as is the habit of the tree, formed a sufficient bulwark at the stem, while an elbow in the centre of the trunk, served the same purpose at the stern: a platform of small poles, well covered with dried grass, gave a sufficient flooring to this rude specimen of a raft. I could not survey it without allowing my thoughts to carry me away in pleasing reflections upon the gradual progress of human ingenuity by the advance of which, the same intellect that first contents itself with the mere floating of the single tree, at length shapes a forest into timbers and launches the floating fortress in triumph on the deep![28]

One question that arises here is whether the Indigenous people of the Kimberley were using rafts in Dampier's time. He was adamant that those he saw were not:

> At another time our Canoe, seeking Game among these Islands, espied a drove of these Men swimming from one Island to another. For they have no Boats, Canoes or Bark-logs. They took up Four of them and brought them aboard. Two of them were middle-aged. The other two were young Men, about 18 or 20 Years old. To these we gave boiled Rice, and with it boiled Turtle and Manatee. They greedily devoured what we gave them, but took no notice of the Ship or anything in it, and when they were set on Land again, they ran away as fast as they could.[29]

Dampier and his shipmates had turtle and manatee (dugong) on hand because they were accompanied by two or three 'Moskito Men' whose sole job was to harpoon those creatures. Those men came from a section of coast between Cape Honduras and Nicaragua, and Dampier described them as follows:

> They have extraordinarily good Eyes, and will descry a Sail at Sea farther, and see anything better than we. Their chiefest Employment in their own Country is to strike Fish, Turtle or Manatee. For this they are esteemed and coveted by all Privateers. For one or two of them in a Ship will maintain 100 Men, so that when we careen our Ships, we choose commonly such Places where there is plenty of Turtle or Manatee for these Moskito Men to strike: and it is very rare to find Privateers destitute of one or more of them, when the Commander or most of the Men are English.[30]

Given that Dampier saw no rafts, canoes or fishing spears, there is room to wonder whether the Bardi people learnt about such things from the 'Moskito Men'. The available documentary evidence does not reveal whether Dampier's visit preceded those of the first Asian fishing parties. It is known, however, that Captain Cook saw Aboriginal people using canoes and elaborate fishing spears in 1770 when he sailed along Australia's north-eastern coast.[31]

With regard to 20th century accounts of changes in Kimberley water craft, Ian Crawford wrote:

> The main focus of the Aboriginal accounts is on canoes. Indonesians had them and Aborigines wanted them. The traditional craft of the area was the double layered raft, often referred to as a catamaran. It remained the dominant water craft among the Worora and Sunday Islanders on the west coast, but although it appeared in Aboriginal legends, it was displaced along the northern coast of the Kimberley. Canoes were regarded as superior to rafts in some circumstances. With its narrow form, the canoe was more manoeuvrable and less susceptible to the influences of tide and wind.[32]

Abel Tasman

Once we go beyond Dampier's visit, the documentary evidence for contact on the Kimberley coast is second hand at best. Much has been said about the Dutch putting Australia on the map but, when it comes to identifying where Abel Tasman landed in northern Australia in 1644, we have to rely on the conclusions drawn by later mariners.

Tasman's depiction of the Australian coast first appeared on a map revised by the Dutch cartographer Joan Blaeu in 1645. Three years later, Blaeu released a newly-drawn world map, which was widely circulated and showed the same coastline. The English apparently became privy to the information by 1650 or 1655.[33]

In 1688, Dampier and his shipmates had access to details of New Holland in what he referred to as their 'Drafts' and 'Plots'.[34] He displayed no knowledge of Tasman's landing places or voyages.[35] By 1699, he had a copy of Tasman's chart, complete with soundings.[36] In noting the availability of that chart, Matthew Flinders later lamented that 'none bearing his name can now be found'. Flinders took care to inform himself about early exploration on the Australian coast, studying not only the available charts but also the material collected by Dalrymple. From those sources, he concluded that Tasman had landed on identifiable parts of Australia's north and north-west coast.[37] King, too, drew on the material collected by Dalrymple, and, on seeing Carnot Bay, he concluded that it was 'here that Tasman landed'.[38] The descriptive text quoted by Flinders and King read:

> In HOLLANDIA NOVA,... in 17° 12' S. (lon. 121° or 122° east) Tasman found a naked, black people, with curly hair ; malicious and cruel, using for arms, bows and arrows, hazeygaeys and kalawaeys. They once came to the number of fifty, double armed, dividing themselves into two parties, intending to have surprised the Dutch, who had landed twenty-five men ; but the firing of guns frightened them so that they fled. Their prows are made of the bark of trees : their coast is dangerous : there are few vegetables : the people use no houses. [39]

It is intriguing that Tasman saw watercraft whereas Dampier, when he was further north on the other side of the peninsula, saw none. Even more interesting is that Tasman recorded bows and arrows being used as weapons. His observation of that phenomenon is at odds with archaeologists' belief that bows and arrows were used on islands in Torres Strait but not on mainland Australia.[40]

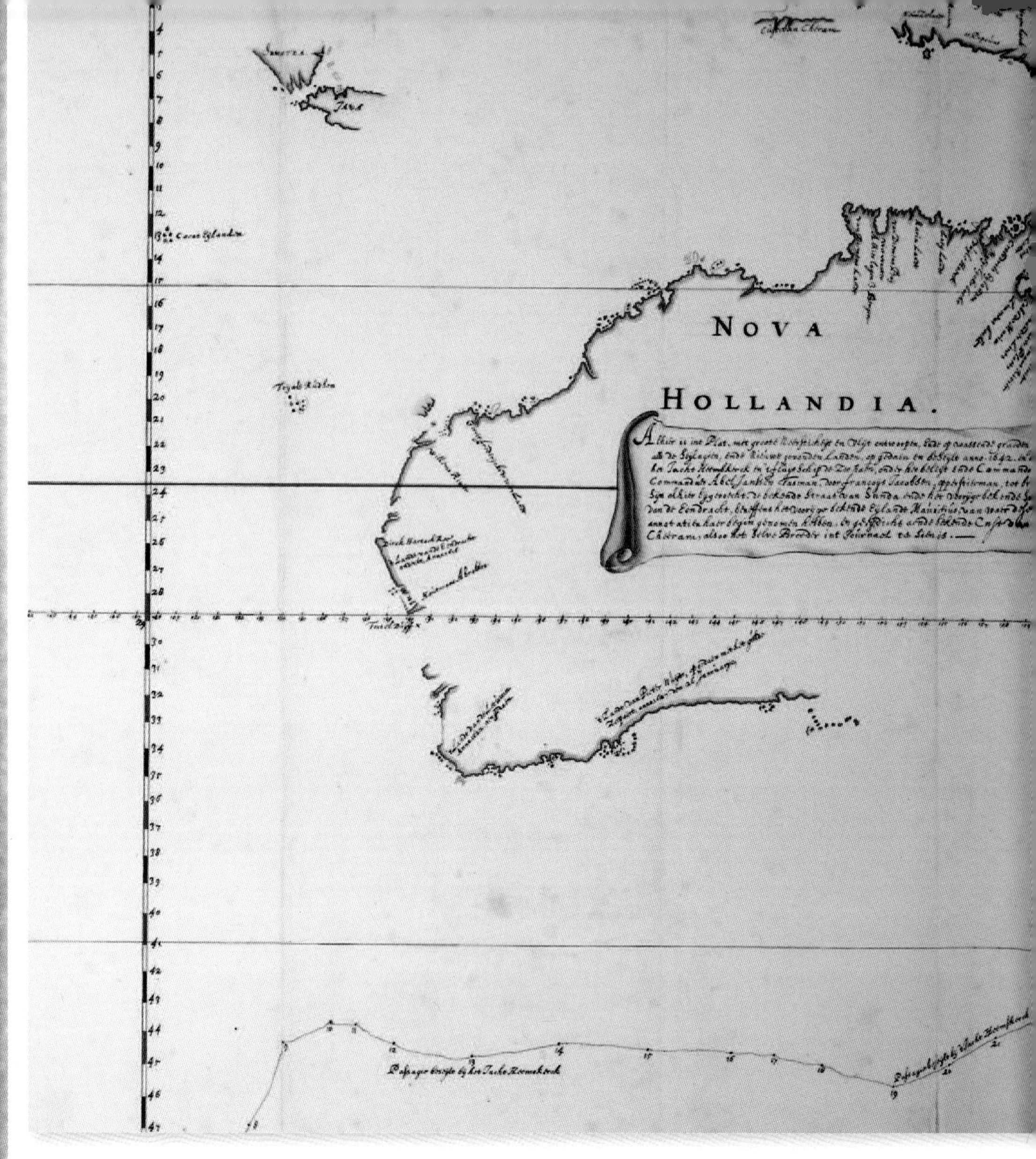

Tasman was not alone in reporting a sighting of bows and arrows in the Kimberley. In 1891, Joseph Bradshaw, who is discussed elsewhere in this volume, was exploring somewhere east of the Prince Regent River. There, he and his party saw 'about 60 dusky forms scattered along the face of the range'. He noted that 'some had what appeared to be a rude kind of bows and arrows'.[41]

It is tempting to conclude that distance could have rendered Bradshaw's interpretation somewhat fanciful. Tasman may have been closer but it could be surmised that, in referring to people with 'curly hair', he was actually writing about people from the Torres Strait or New Guinea. But adopting that approach would

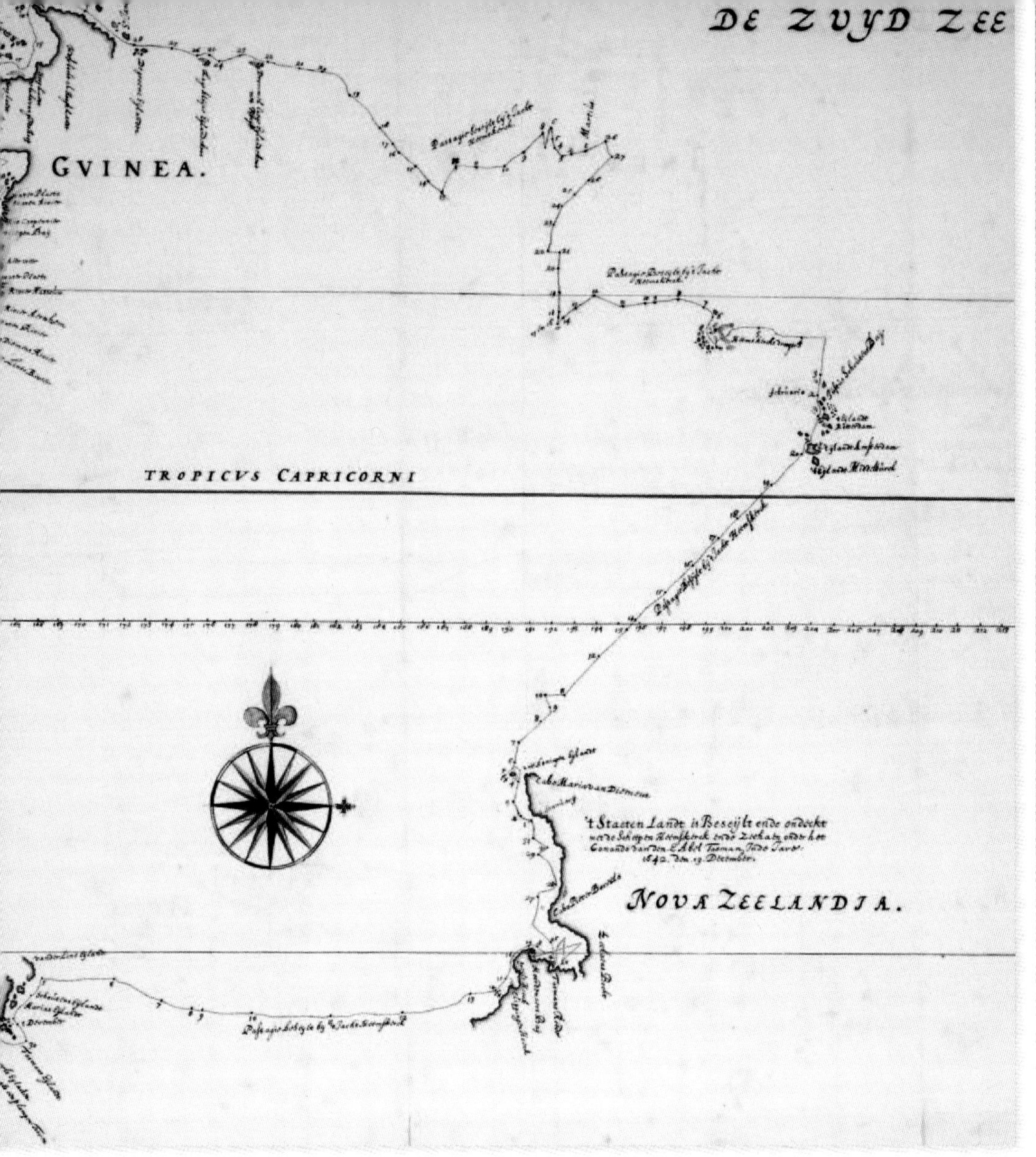

Above Portion of map showing the voyages undertaken by Abel Tasman in 1642-1643 and 1644. Courtesy of Österreichische Nationalbibliothek (Austrian National Library).

ignore the fact that Tasman provided latitude and longitude for his landing places. Also relevant is that Dampier described the hair of the people he saw as 'short and curled like that of the Negroes'. [42] Dampier went further in his manuscript version, where he wrote: 'I belive their haires would be long, if it was comed out but for want of Combs it is matted up like a negroes haire'.[43]

There is also Baudin's comment about the first Asian fishermen seen by his men on the Kimberley coast:

> Their canoe was long and raised at both ends and was very neatly kept, as well as being freshly painted in black and white. In the stern end hung some bows, 4 or 5 feet long, and several wooden boxes containing arrows.[44]

That comment, despite being made long after Tasman's visit, confirms that bows and arrows were taken to the Kimberley coast. It is not a giant leap to think that some of those items could have found their way into Aboriginal hands. Also possible is that the people seen by Tasman, and possibly those seen by Bradshaw, manufactured their own crude bows and arrows. While that possibility is remote, stone points 'small enough to have been arrow tips' have been found in the Yarar rock-shelter on the mainland east of Joseph Bonaparte Gulf.[45] It must be conceded, however, that if small stone points had a long history of being used as arrow tips, their use would probably have been recorded in the local rock art. No such art is known to have been found in Australia.[46]

The Yarar rock-shelter is not all that far from a second locality that King, in 1819, thought was probably one of Tasman's landing places. The evidence, taken from Dalrymple's work, read:

> In lat. 13° 8', and longitude 146° 18' 6" E. (probably about 129½° E. of Greenwich, and answering to this part), the people are bad and wicked, shooting at the Dutch with arrows without provocation, when they were coming on shore. It is here very populous.[47]

It is unlikely that a mariner of King's calibre would have erred in identifying a locality described by another mariner. Indeed, on the very day he mentioned the attack on the Dutch, he used the peak on Peron Island to compare his longitude, for the first time, with that of Baudin. The difference was minimal.[48]

So, what can we conclude about the information preserved from the time of Tasman's voyage? The various maps show that Tasman followed the Kimberley coastline closely enough to chart its approximate shape. Dalrymple's material, coupled with King's assessment of the latitude and longitude in the quotations, indicates that Tasman received a hostile reception from Indigenous people at Carnot Bay and somewhere near Peron Island. It appears that those people used bows and arrows but we know nothing about the origin of those weapons. The weapons could indicate the presence of outsiders on the north Australian coast prior to 1644 but, for now, that possibility must remain in the realm of speculation.

Opposite
A typical sandy embayment on the west side of the Dampier Peninsula.
Photo – Kevin Kenneally

Before Tasman

Many people have debated whether the Dutch were the first non-Aboriginal people to land on the Australian coast. While those debates relate mostly to Willem Jansz landing on Cape York Peninsula in 1606, they also embrace the question of whether Tasman was the first non-Aboriginal person to see the Kimberley coast. Some writers argue that he was not, and they cite varying pieces of evidence to support their assertions.[49] Others reject that evidence and, where it relates to maps, they say that misinterpretation of words on those maps dates from Dalrymple's 1786 assertion that mid-sixteenth century French maps carried Portuguese placenames and inscriptions.[50]

Some writers who believe in pre-Dutch visits cite amongst their evidence the Wandjina paintings seen and publicised by George Grey.[51] One writer claimed that Grey 'found a realistic (as distinct from symbolic) representation of a man, which he took to be a priest in cassock and cowl'. Then, having taken that liberty with Grey's writing, he speculated that a 'man in holy orders' might have accompanied a Portuguese expedition to the Kimberley in 1599 or 1600.[52] Another writer stated that 'Captain Grey's description fits precisely with the picture drawn by the native Mexican tribes at Jucutácato ... of the Chinese arriving in their red robes reaching to their ankles.' Keen to show that the Chinese mined lead in Australia in the early 15th century, he blithely transposed the Glenelg River, and the Wandjina that Grey saw, to Arnhem Land – more than 800 kilometres away.[53]

The further back we go, the more wondrous the assertions become. There are, however, interesting matters on which light might yet fall. This paper, for example, mentions the 'Substantial Native Hut' that Stokes saw on Bathurst Island. Archaeological work done on High Cliffy Island near the Montgomery Reef (east of Bathurst Island) has revealed hundreds of stone structures, some of which appear to have been used for houses. At least twelve other islands between High Cliffy Island and Cape Leveque were checked for such structures in 1985 without any being found. Of interest, however, is that Aboriginal people in 1972 spoke of the High Cliffy structures as 'house bases whose walls had been formed by wooden uprights with bark coverings'.[54] That description bears some resemblance to the one recorded by Stokes: 'Stout poles from 14 to 16 feet [4.3 to 4.9 metres] high formed the framework of these snug huts ... brought together conically at the roof; a stout thatching of dried grass completely excluded both wind and rain'. Why were those island shelters so different from others on the mainland only kilometres away?

Today, just like the early mariners who perused, corrected, and augmented their predecessors' charts, we are well positioned to learn more about our unique Kimberley coast. A great deal of information is out there but it needs to be tracked down, analysed and integrated. For that to occur, Indigenous people, anthropologists, archaeologists, ethnographers, historians, and other researchers need to continue tapping into, and supplementing, one another's knowledge. The opportunities for doing that are unlimited and will ultimately produce some fascinating results.

Below
South-east corner of Nova Totius Terrarum Orbis Geographica Tabula, drawn by William Blaeu, Amsterdam, after 1629.
Courtesy of Leen Helmink, Antique Maps (http://www.helmink.com).

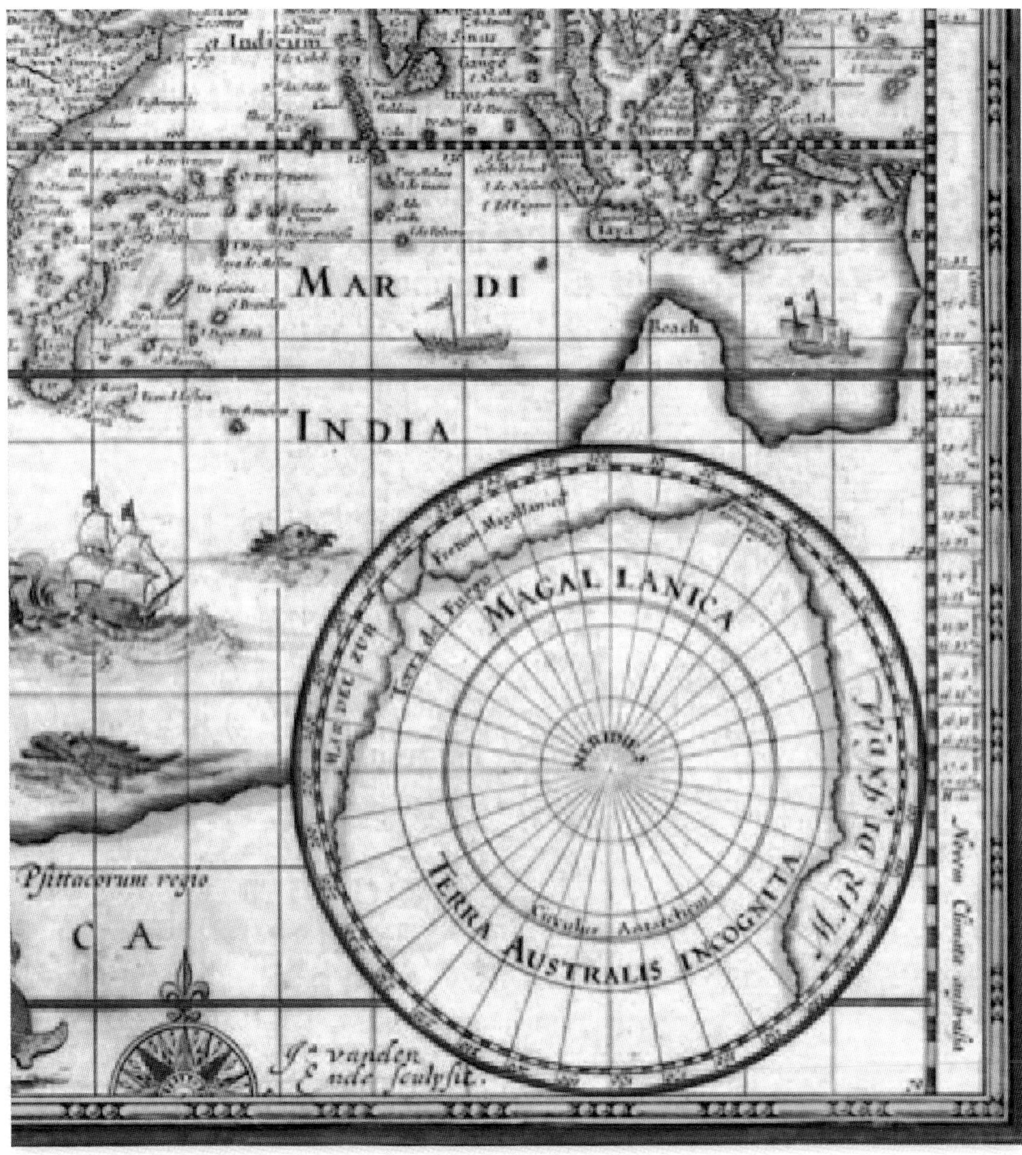

Notes

1 The primary sources cited in this paper refer to the Indigenous people as 'Aborigines', 'Indians' or 'natives', with an unstated implication that they formed part of a single population spread across the continent. To provide those people with regional identities, these footnotes record the native title claim areas that encompass places mentioned in the text. The claim areas have been taken from a map titled 'Kimberley Native Title Applications and Determination Areas As per the Federal Court (31 March 2010)', www.nntt.gov.au/Publications-And-Research/Maps-and-Spatial-Reports/Documents/Quarterly%20Maps/WA_Kimberley_NTDA_schedule.pdf, which was accessed on 26 April 2010. At the time of going to print, that map was not evident on the NNTT website.

2 Most major Australian libraries hold original or facsimile editions of the mariners' journals. Scanned copies of some can be viewed through Project Gutenberg (www.gutenberg.org/catalog/) where scope exists to search for a book by its author. A similar search on Google Books (http://books.google.com/) will often reveal the existence of facsimile or digitised editions and may lead to other books about the mariners and their work.

3 J. Cameron, 'The Northern Settlements, Outposts of Empire', in P. Statham (ed.), *The Origins of Australia's Capital Cities*, Cambridge University Press, Cambridge, 1989, p. 275.

4 J. H. L. Cumpston, *The Inland Sea and the Great River: The Story of Australian Exploration*, Angus and Robertson, Sydney, 1964, pp. 77–82, 102–3, and 121–2.

5 J. Lort Stokes, *Discoveries in Australia; with an account of the coasts and rivers explored and surveyed during the voyage of H.M.S. Beagle, in the years 1837-38-39-40-41-42-43*, 2 vols, London, 1846, facsimile edition, Libraries Board of South Australia, Adelaide, 1969, vol. 1, pp. 113–4 and 132. For a convenient source of information about mariners naming Kimberley places, see I. Murray with M. Hercock, *Where on the Coast is That?*, Hesperian Press, Carlisle (WA), 2008.

6 Stokes, *Discoveries in Australia*, vol. 1, pp. 115–16. Skeleton Point, which protrudes into the northern portion of Cygnet Bay, is within the Bardi and Jawi Native Title Determination Area.

7 Stokes, *Discoveries in Australia*, vol. 1, p. 116.

8 Information about programs for the repatriation of skeletal remains and artefacts can be seen at www.arts.gov.au/indigenous/repatriation/return, accessed 21 September 2011, while www.abc.net.au/news/2010-08-25/sacred-re-burial-of-aboriginal-remains/956934, accessed 25 August 2010, discusses an instance specific to the Kimberley.

9 Stokes, *Discoveries in Australia*, vol. 1, p. 101.

10 ibid., pp. 172–3. Bathurst Island is within the Mayala Native Title claim area.

11 P. P. King, *Narrative of a survey of the intertropical and western coasts of Australia. Performed between the years 1818 and 1822*, London, 1827, facsimile, Libraries Board of South Australia, Adelaide, 1969. For examples of King's comments on the construction of shelters, see vol. 1, pp. 43, 72, 175–6, 197, 313–14, 376, and 431–2. For an overview of King's voyages and their place in Australian maritime exploration, see M. Hordern, *King of the Australian Coast: The Work of Phillip Parker King in the* Mermaid *and* Bathurst *1817–1822*, Melbourne University Press, Melbourne, 1997, or R. Tiley, *The Mermaid Tree*, ABC Books, Sydney, 2006.

12 King, *Narrative of a survey*, vol. 1, p. 431. Careening Bay is within the Uunguu Native Title claim area.

13 King, *Narrative of a survey*, vol. 1, pp. 313–5. Vansittart Bay, which is west-north-west of Kalumburu, is within the Uunguu Native Title claim area.

14 C. C. Macknight, *The Voyage to Marege': Macassan trepangers in northern Australia*, Melbourne University Press, Carlton, 1976, pp. 1–2 and 6–8.

15 King, *Narrative of a survey*, vol. 1, pp. 37, 73–83, 135–9, and 315.

16 ibid., pp. 316–21 and 324–5.

17 N. Baudin, *The Journal of Post Captain Nicolas Baudin, Commander-in-Chief of the Corvettes Geographe and Naturalist* ... Translated from the French by Christine Cornell, Libraries Board of South Australia, Adelaide, 1974, pp. 530–41; Macknight, *The Voyage to Marege'*, p. 27. See Michael J. Morwood, 'Archaeology of the Kimberley, Northwest Australia', this volume, for further discussion.

18 The assistance of Johanneke Braam, Project leader Atlas of Mutual Heritage, is acknowledged with regard to the provision of a precise translation of the map's inscription.

19 C. R. Boxer, *The Dutch Seaborne Empire 1600-1800*, Penguin Books, Harmondsworth (UK) and Ringwood (Vic.), 1973, pp. 101–25, 209–24, 231, 262–3, 282, 313–20, and 336; J. H. Parry, *The Spanish Seaborne Empire*, Hutchinson & Co. Ltd, London, 1966, pp. 251–71, 285–306, 316–18, and 361; L. R. Marchant, *An Island Unto Itself: William Dampier and New Holland*, Hesperian Press, Carlisle (WA), 1988, pp. 42–9.

20 H. T. Fry, *Alexander Dalrymple (1737-1808) and the Expansion of British Trade*, University of Toronto Press for the Royal Commonwealth Society, Toronto, 1970, pp. 11–12, 15–23, and 47–51. See also 'Dalrymple, Alexander (1737–1808)', *Australian Dictionary of Biography*, National Centre of Biography, Australian National University, http://adb.anu.edu.au/biography/dalrymple-alexander-1949/text2341.

21 Fry, *Alexander Dalrymple*, pp. 102–16.

22 W. Dampier, *A New Voyage Round the World: The Journal of an English Buccaneer*, James Knapton, London, 1697, edited and revised edition, hummingbird press, London, 1998, pp. 41–2, 49, 56–8, 73–102, 109–18, 123–6, 140, and 159–218.

23 Marchant, *An Island Unto Itself*, pp. 77–87.

24 See, for instance, A. S. George, *William Dampier in New Holland: Australia's first natural historian*, Bloomings Books, Hawthorn (Vic.), 1999.

25 This locality, on the western side of the entrance to King Sound, is within the Bardi and Jawi Native Title Determination Area.

26 Dampier, *A New Voyage Round the World*, pp. 218–9.

27 Stokes, *Discoveries in Australia*, vol. 1, p. 112.

28 ibid., pp. 173–4.

29 Dampier, *A New Voyage Round the World*, p. 221.

30 ibid., pp. 11, 12 and 213. Striking involved the use a spear or a dart in hunting.

31 King, *Narrative of a survey*, vol. 1, pp. 245–6, quoted Cook's description of the canoes and harpoon-like implements used by 'the natives of Endeavour River' for 'striking turtle'.

32 I. Crawford, *We won the victory: Aborigines and Outsiders on the North-West Coast of the Kimberley*, Fremantle Arts Centre Press, Fremantle, 2001, p. 86.

33 G. Schilder, 'New Holland: The Dutch Discoveries' in Terra Australis *to Australia,* ed. by G. Williams and A. Frost, Oxford University Press in association with the Australian Academy of the Humanities, Melbourne, 1988, p. 103; G. Williams, 'New Holland to New South Wales: The English Approaches' in Terra Australis *to Australia*, pp. 117–18. See that volume for additional maps showing Tasman's findings, and see www.atlasofmutualheritage.nl/detail.aspx?page=dafb&lang=en&id=5972 for the full version of the map on pp. 52-53. Marlies Rahm, Österreichische Nationalbibliothek, is acknowledged for assisting with my acquisition of a copy of the map.

34 Dampier, *A New Voyage Round the World*, pp. 216–17.

35 Williams, 'New Holland to New South Wales', p. 122.

36 ibid., p. 126; Marchant, *An Island unto itself*, p. 78.

37 M. Flinders, *A Voyage to Terra Australis*, G. and W. Nicol, London, 1814, Libraries Board of South Australia, facsimile edition, 1966, volume 1, pp. vii and lv–lvii.

38 King, *Narrative of a survey*, vol. 2, p. 93. Carnot Bay is within the Djabera-Djabera Native Title claim area.

39 Flinders, *A Voyage to Terra Australis*, pp. lvi–lvii; King, *Narrative of a survey*, vol. 2, p. 93.

40 J. Flood, *Archaeology of the Dreamtime: The story of prehistoric Australia and its people*, Angus & Robertson, Sydney, 1983, revised edition, 1999, p. 257. See J. Singe, *The Torres Strait: People and History*, Queensland University Press, St Lucia, 1979, pp. 17, 18 and 21–3 for coverage of Cook, Bligh, Flinders, and others seeing bows and arrows on Torres Strait islands.

41 J. Bradshaw, 'Notes on a Recent Trip to Prince Regent's River', *Transactions of the Royal Geographical Society of Australasia (Victorian Branch)*, vol. 9(2), 1892, pp. 98–9. For further comment on encounters involving Bradshaw and his men, see Kevin F. Kenneally, 'Under A Regent Moon. Part 2: Frontier Conflict at Marigui', this volume.

42 Dampier, *A New Voyage Round the World*, p. 218.

43 Williams, 'New Holland to New South Wales', p. 124.

44 Baudin, *The Journal of Post Captain Nicolas Baudin*, p. 540.

45 Flood, *Archaeology of the Dreamtime*, p. 221.

46 P. Bindon, 'Kimberley Aboriginal art in the Australian and world context', in K. F. Kenneally, M. R. Lewis, M. Donaldson and C. Clement (eds), *Aboriginal Rock Art of the Kimberley*, Kimberley Society, Perth, 1997, p. 11.

47 King, *Narrative of a survey*, vol. 1, p. 272. King's recalculation of the longitude in this quote reflected his awareness that mariners determined the longitude of their ships by using a variety of starting points, e.g. their country's capital or some other significant location.

48 King, *Narrative of a survey*, vol. 1, p. 272.

49 See, for instance, P. Trickett, *Beyond Capricorn: How Portuguese Adventurers secretly discovered and mapped Australia and New Zealand 250 years before Captain Cook*, East Street Publications, Bowden (SA), 2007; and N. H. Peters, *EREDIA, OURO* and *LUCA. ANTARA ISLANDS* and *NOVA GUINEA: A case for determining that Nova Guinea shown on the Insulae Moluccae Map is a map of segments of mainland Australia and is the first known map of Australia*, undated, http://home.exetel.com.au/noelpeters/main.html.

50 See, for instance, W. A. R. Richardson, *Was Australia Charted before 1606?: The Jave la Grande inscriptions*, National Library of Australia, Canberra, 2006, and H. Wallis, 'Did the Portuguese Discover Australia?', *History Today*, vol. 38, Issue 3, March 1988, pp. 30–5.

51 G. Grey, *Journals of two expeditions of discovery in North-West and Western Australia during the years 1837, 38, and 39*, London, 1841, facsimile edition, Hesperian Press, Victoria Park (WA), 1983, vol. 1, pp. 201–6, 213–16 and 261–4.

52 K. G. McIntyre, *The Secret Discovery of Australia: Portuguese Ventures 200 Years Before Captain Cook*, Souvenir Press, London, 1977, pp. 76–81.

53 G. Menzies, *1421: The Year China discovered the World*, Bantam Press, London, 2002, pp. 188–90.

54 S. O'Connor, 'The Stone House Structures of High Cliffy Island, North West Kimberley, WA', *Australian Archaeology*, No. 25, Dec 1987, pp. 30–9. High Cliffy Island is within the Dambimangari Native Title Determination Area, which adjoins the Mayala Native Title claim area around Bathurst Island.

George Grey's expedition 1837–1838; first European penetration of the Kimberley interior

Hamish McGlashan

When the news of Lieutenant Colonel George Grey's heroic death while leading his regiment at the Battle of Badajoz in the Peninsular War against Napoleon reached his wife Elizabeth, she fainted and went into labour producing a son (named inevitably) George.[1] Young George was raised by his extended family with the expectation of being a hero himself. In due course he became one of Queen Victoria's most prominent subjects. By any reckoning he had a remarkable career. A brief *curriculum vitae* would read as follows:

- Age 25 leads the first major expedition by Europeans into North West Australia.
- Age 27 appointed Government Resident in Albany, Western Australia after the death of Sir Richard Spencer (formerly one of Admiral Lord Nelson's cherished captains). Marries Spencer's 16-year-old daughter Eliza and lives at the Old Farm, Strawberry Hill.
- Age 28 appointed the second Governor of South Australia.
- Age 29 publishes *Journals of two expeditions of discovery*; a best seller.
- Age 33 appointed Governor of New Zealand, replacing Sir Robert FitzRoy, the commander of the *Beagle* on Darwin's voyage.
- Age 36 knighted.
- Age 42 appointed Governor of Cape Colony, South Africa, and publishes book on *Maori Myths and Language* (he was both a brilliant linguist and an accomplished naturalist).
- Age 49 appointed to second Governorship of New Zealand.
- Age 55, elected Premier of New Zealand.
- Age 86 died and was buried in St Paul's Cathedral close to Lord Nelson; a rare accolade bestowed on only the most prominent stars of British public life.

Around the time of his death this was written of him:

> There are in this world only two human beings, and two only who from the month of June 1837 till the present day have been ceaselessly and intimately connected with the progress and development, the happiness and welfare of the colonial portion of the Empire on which the sun never sets; whose sole interest in the colonies has never ceased, and who have occupied without intermission, trust and responsibility in relation to them. The first is Her Gracious Majesty the Queen – the second is her servant Sir George Grey.[2]

Opposite
(Top) Young George Grey. Courtesy of Auckland City Libraries (N.Z.), Sir George Grey Special Collections, item 7-A3952.
(Bottom) 'Sandstone cave with paintings near Glenelg River', as depicted by George Grey in *Journals of two expeditions of discovery*, vol 1. Seen by Grey on 26 March 1838. Courtesy of Hesperian Press.

He must have been a persuasive talker when, with his friend Franklin Lushington (both 24-year-old army lieutenants), he convinced Sir John Barrow, the President of the Royal Geographical Society, and Lord Glenelg, the Colonial Secretary, to fund a major expedition which set out in 1837.[3] Grey and Lushington, having just finished a course at Sandhurst, were looking for heroism and adventure. There being no suitable wars on at that time, they were looking for an interesting "gap year" and offered themselves as explorers in Australia; anywhere in Australia.

At that time it was thought that rivers drained to a great inland sea: this was still thought likely nearly forty years later when John Forrest mounted his third exploration.[4] Alternately there was thought to be a great river system, similar to the Murray in the south east, debouching somewhere in the vicinity of King Sound or the Prince Regent River. A settlement in this area would support and protect the trade route to China, a significant consideration in view of the failed settlements at Melville Island and Raffles Bay. It was felt that foreign (i.e. non-British) occupation of northern Australia would be a threat to Australia-China trade.Thus there were both geographical and political motives to back the adventure. It took a year of negotiations and planning before the *Beagle*, recently returned from round the world with Charles Darwin, was refitted for the voyage to the Kimberley.[5]

In the end the expedition was a joint venture of the Colonial Office (land-based) and the Admiralty (coastal survey). Thus started the first European land exploration in the north-west of Australia and George Grey's climb to fame and heroism.

The assistant surveyor on the *Beagle* was John Lort Stokes who had shared a cabin with Darwin on the famous voyage. The expedition picked up another vessel, the *Lynher*, in Cape Town on the way. It was to support the land-based work while the *Beagle* surveyed the coast.

Grey's instructions from the British Government were to examine 'the country about Prince Regent's River' and then 'use the utmost exertions to penetrate from thence to the Swan River'.[6] The main objects of the expedition were:

> To gain information as to the real state of North-Western Australia, its resources, and the course and direction of its rivers and mountain ranges; to familiarise the natives with the British name and character; to search for and record ... the natural productions of the country, and all details that might bear upon its capabilities for colonization or the reverse; and to collect specimens of its natural history.[7]

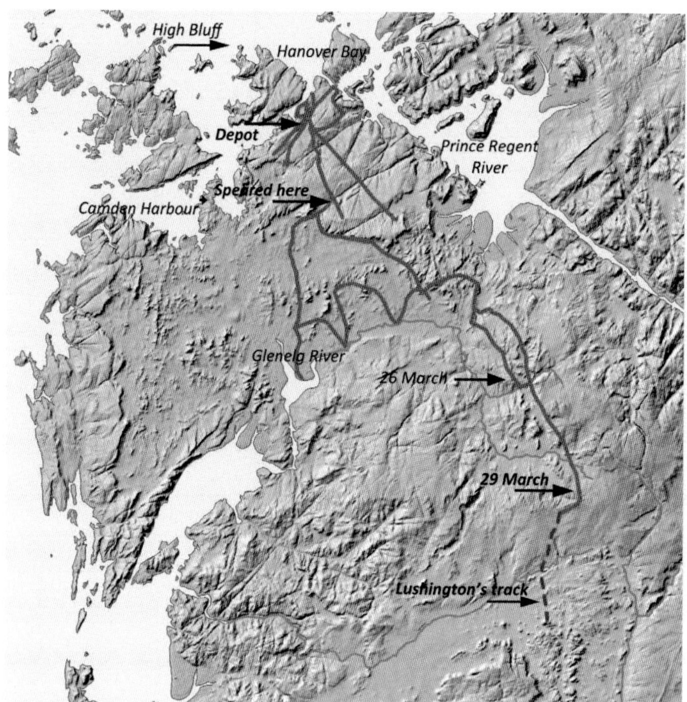

His first landing at High Bluff Point was nearly fatal. Within a few hours, he and the rest of the landing party nearly died of heat exhaustion, dehydration and drowning. He only took two pints of water for five men and three dogs; his dogs did not survive. Then, after looking at the Prince Regent River, he decided on Hanover Bay to unload his supplies, which included sheep and goats. The livestock did not fare well.

On 9 December 1837 at Hanover Bay, 'We here first hoisted the British flag, and went through the ceremony of taking possession of the territory in the name of Her Majesty and her heirs for ever.'[8] This ceremony was probably watched with interest by Aboriginal (Worora) warriors, who were no doubt on the cliffs above.

Grey's preliminary instructions stated:

> The greatest forbearance and discretion in treating with the Aborigines is strongly impressed and urged upon the travellers – it should be distinctly borne in mind that as all exploring expeditions in this country are sent out with a view to future colonization it is of the utmost importance to make friends with the natives; – to avoid familiarity with the females, a common source of quarrels; – never to allow a fancied insult to provoke retaliation, rather to submit to trifling vexation than risk creating ill will and perhaps bloodshed by hasty conduct towards the aborigines; **it should be remarked that their's is the right of soil, – we are the intruders.**[9]

Above Map of Grey's route, showing places mentioned in the text.

The *Lynher* went to Timor to pick up more stores and horses (which did not do well either!) while the land-based party explored the countryside, noting for example that a good road could be made to Camden Sound.[10] With regard to the land between Port George the Fourth and Hanover Bay, Grey wrote:

> ... its soil is, moreover, highly fertile. I conceive that a point nearer Camden Bay would be of greater consequence to the mother country; but, after such a spot, this neck of land is the most important position on the North-west coast of Australia.[11]

Grey also moved a supply depot to the head of what he named Walker's Valley, where he left some stores behind. Passing this area on our journey to retrace Grey's footsteps in 1988, we came across an old chain which may well have been left behind by Grey. As there were no volunteers to carry the extra kilos it probably remains atop a rock to this day.

Eventually Grey's party set out for the interior in early February 1838 intent on examining the hinterland of the various harbours before heading for faraway Perth. Hampered by the heat, flies, mosquitoes, harsh terrain, recalcitrant animals and daily torrential rain, he was in the middle of an unusually wet monsoon season.

A week later, surrounded by hostile Aborigines, he was struck by several spears, one of which caused a bad wound in his hip. In self defence he shot and killed one of them. In his diary he dilates on his remorse and regret; the cynical might think that in view of his instructions (above) this was written to deflect criticism. However in his subsequent career he was usually sympathetic and supportive of Aboriginal or Maori wellbeing so perhaps we should give him the benefit of the doubt. His wound compelled him to rest for two

Above Kevin Coate, 1988 expedition leader, holding a chain which may have been left at Grey's stores depot. Photo – Hamish McGlashan

Above right Sketch titled 'Attack of Natives Near Hanover Bay' from *Journals of two expeditions,* vol. 1, p. 106. Courtesy of Hesperian Press.

weeks before he was helped onto his horse and the party proceeded. The long term effects remained with him throughout his life; the persistent pain led him to Laudanum addiction.

On 27 February 1838 he writes in his diary:

> About 2 P.M. we reached the extremity of the sandstone ridges, and a magnificent view burst upon us. From the summit of the hills [MacDonald Range] on which we stood, an almost precipitous descent led into a fertile plain below; and from this part, away to the southward, for thirty to forty miles, stretched a low luxuriant country, broken by conical peaks and rounded hills, which were richly grassed to their very summits. The plains and hills were both thinly wooded, and curving lines of shady trees marked out the courses of numerous streams.
>
> Since I have visited this spot, I have traversed large portions of Australia, but have seen no land, no scenery to equal it.[12]

This was only 15 kilometres from Camden Harbour.

Top Looking south along Grey's route.

Above The Glenelg River in May 1988 when it was narrower than when Grey traversed the area in March 1838. Photos – Hamish McGlashan

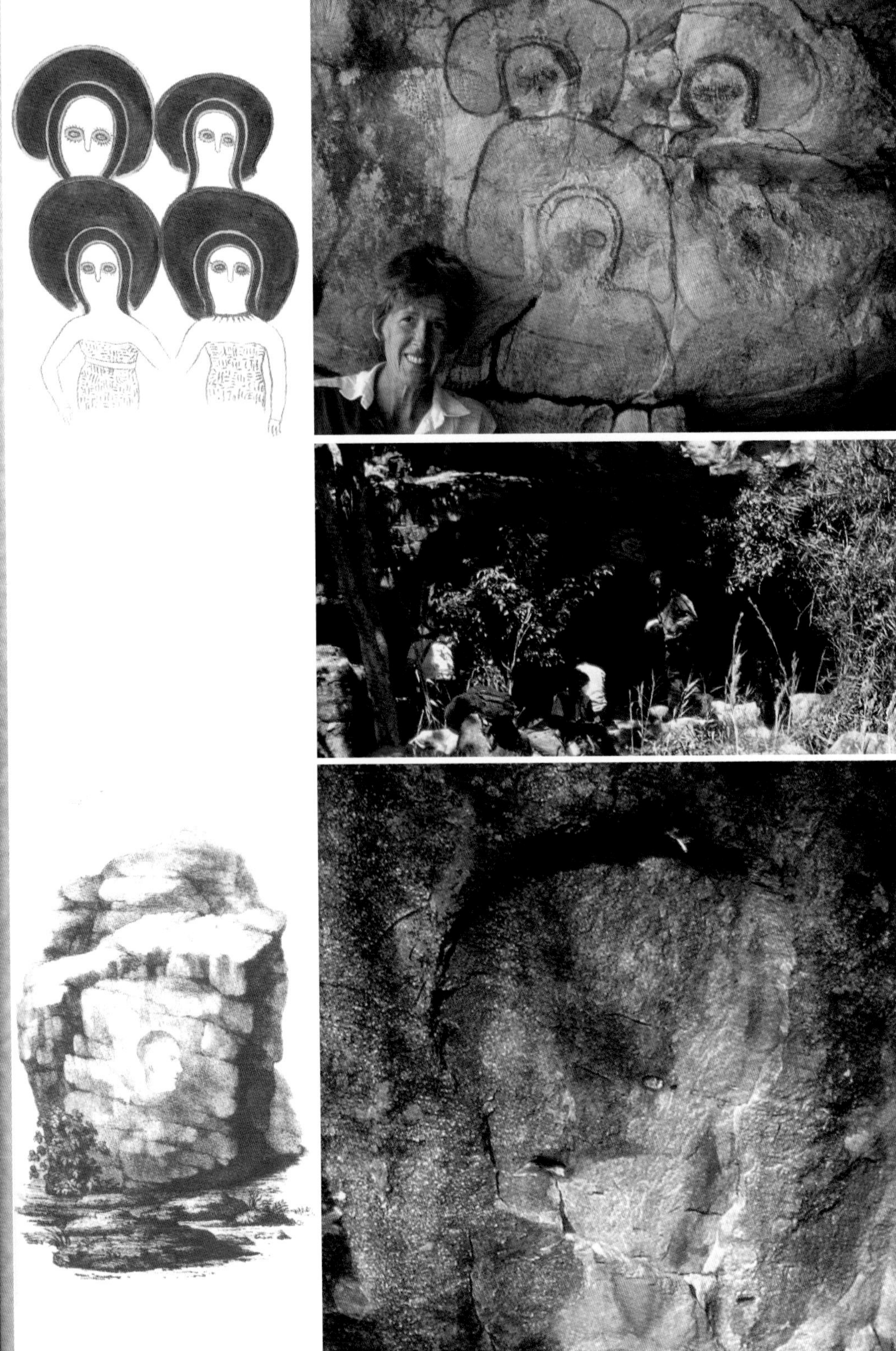

March 2nd 1838

> ... there burst upon the sight a noble river, running through a beautiful country, and where we saw it, at least three or four miles across, and studded with numerous verdant islands. I have seen many Australian rivers, but none to equal this either in magnitude or beauty...
>
> I at once named it the Glenelg, in compliment to the Right Hon. Lord Glenelg, to whom we were under great obligations...[13]
>
> ... nor would I hesitate to say, that, with the exception perhaps of the Murray, it will be found the most important on that continent; and taking into consideration its geographical position, the fertility of the country on its banks, as far as it is yet known, and the rise and fall of the tide, it may perhaps not yield in consideration even to the Murray.[14]

In the meantime John Lort Stokes on the *Beagle* was endeavouring (unsuccessfully) to find the outflow to the sea. It seems likely that Grey thought he had discovered the great northern river. Later visitors would disagree with Grey's fulsome description. Charles Kingsford Smith crash landed on the shore in 1929 and both he and Kimberley Society member Peter Knight's party in 1990 ran dangerously short of finding even any water to drink.

On 26 March, Grey was the first European to sight the now well known Wandjina paintings.

> I suddenly saw... a most extraordinary large figure peering down upon me... at the entrance to a cave, which, on entering, I found to contain, besides, many remarkable paintings.[15]

Close to the cave was what he thought was a carved head. And on 29 March another site, the subject of erroneous interpretation and attribution by writers who range from scholars of the Victorian era to von Daniken.[16]

Struggling on, they found the country impenetrable to horses and Grey's 'wound was still open and very painful'. Lushington pushed on for a few days, but the country remained ruggedly inhospitable. The whole party was forced to turn back to Hanover Bay where Grey was relieved to find the *Lynher* was still in the vicinity. The *Beagle*, with Stokes as surveyor, had explored the coast and he remarked on the luxuriant country around Camden Sound, albeit the ground underfoot was stony. Grey then sailed to Mauritius, where he recuperated and titillated his diary. Thence to the Swan River whence he made a second expedition to Shark Bay. If his first expedition was a heroic failure the second was close to a complete disaster.

Opposite
(Top far left) Sketch of female spirits from Grey's *Journals*.
Courtesy of Hesperian Press.
(Top left) Photograph of Rosemary McGlashan in front of the "26th March" cave painting taken in 1988 by Hamish McGlashan.
(Centre) Entrance to the "26th March" cave in 1988.
Photo – Hamish McGlashan

(Bottom far left) Sketch from Grey's *Journals*.
Courtesy of Hesperian Press.
(Bottom left) The "carved head" in 1988, which is, in fact, a natural flaking of the sandstone rock.
Photo – Hamish McGlashan

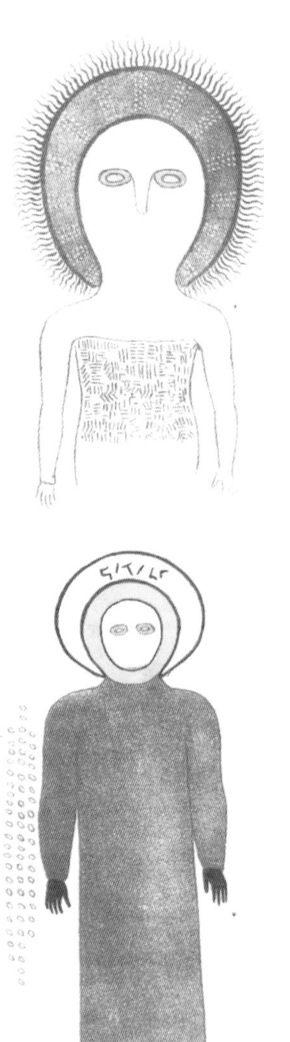

Journals of two expeditions was published in 1841, his literary masterpiece and influential best seller. It made him a hero and celebrity of his time.

Grey's later career was not without controversy or mistakes, not that he would have admitted to them, for he was a master of self-justification. In New Zealand he ignored directives from the Colonial Office, was eventually sacked from his second Governorship, and his stint as premier was riven by dissension and failure of progress. Some biographers think that the personality traits that led him into difficulties later in life were nascent in his early explorations. He certainly had great confidence, some would say overconfidence, in his own abilities and judgements, which fortunately did not lead to any deaths of members of his party on his first expedition. However, as we shall see, the fatalities came twenty-eight years later, at Camden Harbour.

Notes

1 E. Bohan, *To Be a Hero: a biography of Sir George Grey*, HarperCollins (New Zealand), Auckland, 1998, p. 16.

2 W. L. Rees and L. Rees, *The Life and Times of Sir George Grey*, K.C.B, H. Brett, Auckland, 1892, vol. 1, p. ix, quoted by J. M. R. Cameron in 'George Grey Goes Exploring – the Interplay of Personality, Politics and Place', *Journal of the Royal Australian Historical Society*, June 1992, vol. 78 (1 & 2), p. 49.

3 Cameron, 'George Grey Goes Exploring', p. 50.

4 C. Ayris, *John Forrest: Man of Legend*, Cyril Ayris Freelance, Perth, 1996, p. 25.

5 Cameron, 'George Grey Goes Exploring', p. 53.

6 G. Grey, *Journals of two expeditions of discovery in North-West and Western Australia during the years 1837, 38, and 39*, 2 vols, London, 1841, facsimile edition, Hesperian Press, Victoria Park (WA), 1983, vol. 1, p. 3.

7 ibid., p. 4.

8 ibid., p. 89.

9 J. Washington, "Sketch of Instructions for the Expedition Into Australia", Grey and Lushington Papers, (j), quoted by Cameron in 'George Grey Goes Exploring', p. 63, emphasis added.

10 Grey, *Journals of two expeditions*, vol. 1, pp. 109–11. After visiting this area on foot in 2000 we were forced to conclude that the construction of a road was absurdly improbable, as was Grey's assessment of the fertility of the soil.

11 ibid., p. 111. It is noted that Captain P. P. King applied the name Camden Bay to the water that extends from Byam Martin Island eastward to Rogers Strait. In his journal, Grey appears to have used the names Camden Bay and Camden Sound interchangeably. After the 1837–1838 expedition, the western portion of Camden Bay was known as Camden Sound and the eastern portion as Brecknock Harbour. On the maps of today, the names Camden Harbour and Brecknock Harbour tend to be used interchangeably.

12 ibid., pp. 161–2.

13 ibid., p. 166.

14 ibid., p. 182.

15 ibid., p. 201.

16 For discussion of writing about the possible origin and meaning of the Wandjina figures, see I. J. McNiven and L. Russell, *Appropriated pasts: Indigenous peoples and the colonial culture of archaeology*, Rowman Altamira, 2005, pp. 134–7.

Above Walking through 'a luxuriant country'. Grey's first impressions proved to be deceptive. Photo – Hamish McGlashan

Opposite
(Top far left and left) Sketch of a Wandjina from Grey's *Journals*. Courtesy of Hesperian Press. Photograph of the "26th March" cave painting taken in 1983 by Hamish McGlashan.

(Centre far left) Sketch from Grey's *Journals*, 29 March. Courtesy of Hesperian Press.

(Bottom left) Photograph of Wandjina recorded by Grey, 29 March, taken in 1983 with Hamish McGlashan seated. Photo – Hamish McGlashan

R.Bruce Sc.

1865 – Camden Harbour – The Quinlan Connection

Tony Quinlan

On 15 August 1821, Captain Phillip Parker King RN in the *Mermaid* anchored in a bay in the west Kimberley, south of latitude 15 degrees. He named the bay 'Camden' after the first Marquess of Camden who had been a Secretary of State for War and the Colonies in England. John Jeffreys Pratt, son of the first Earl Camden, had been created Marquess Camden and Earl of Brecknock in 1812. He was elected to the House of Commons twice, serving from 1780 to 1801 and from 1804 to 1805.

The water identified by King as Camden Bay extended from Byam Martin Island eastward to Rogers Strait and covered an area 19.2 kilometres deep and 12.8 kilometres wide. In 1838, after the western portion had become known as Camden Sound, Captain Wickham and John Lort Stokes named the eastern portion Brecknock Harbour. The map in George Grey's *Journals*, published in 1841, showed those names but a British Admiralty chart of the same year (available online through the National Library of Australia) showed the name Camden Harbour where Grey showed Brecknock Harbour. The two names tend to be used interchangeably on more recent maps and charts. As the map in this paper shows, the locality occupied by the settlement known as Camden Harbour is located off the south-eastern portion of Brecknock Harbour.

On 27 February 1838, Lieutenant George Grey of the 83rd Regiment arrived at a sandstone ridge and saw the 'magnificent view' of country that stretched inland from Camden Bay. He recorded a 'low luxuriant country, broken by conical peaks and rounded hills, which were richly grassed to their very summits'. Grey had travelled from England on the *Beagle* to explore the country around the Prince Regent River, which had been named by King.

However, on 8 April 1838, Lieutenant John Lort Stokes RN, Assistant Surveyor on the *Beagle*, came ashore on an islet at the southern end of Rogers Strait leading to Camden Harbour. He was not so enthusiastic.

Opposite
The 'Camden Harbour Settlement, Western Australia.'
Courtesy of State Library of Victoria (Accession no. IMP 25/02/67/29).

This engraving is based on photographs taken on 31 May 1865 (see page 76) and mentioned by H.A. Willis in 'The colour of blood'.

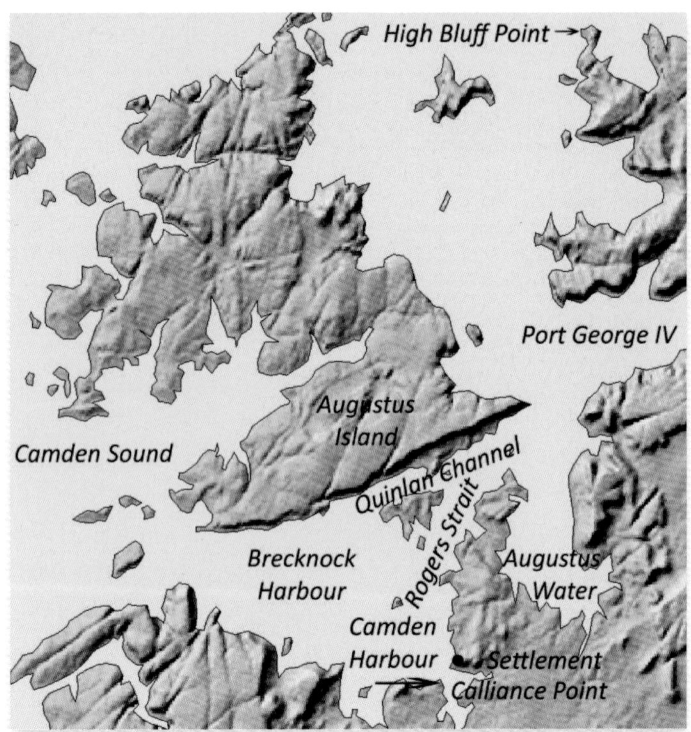

> The islet looked truly inviting, being clothed with long, rich grass, which to our cost, we found concealed boulders of granite ... and from the colour of the surrounding heights it was evident we were in an old red sandstone region.

The observations of Stokes in relation to the underlying rocky nature of the area were glossed over by other explorers combing through his notes 25 years later. Nor was it well understood that the lush growth followed each wet season's rains but withered and died at the onset of the dry season.

On 25 June 1863, surgeon James Martin, an observer in a private expedition of ten, investigated the land adjacent to Camden Harbour and the Glenelg River, having landed in George Water, which they named after Grey. It was Martin's description of the land – '300,000 acres [121,500 hectares] of the finest quality for grazing,' and 'the lowest estimate of the carrying power of this district is a sheep to an acre', plus 'a district of unsurpassed fertility', that led Governor Hampton to send a copy of Martin's report to London in 1864.

Above Map of the Camden Harbour Area. Courtesy of Hamish McGlashan

A further expedition to Camden Harbour sailed from Fremantle on 2 March 1864. It was made by Inspector of police, Frederick Kennedy Panter and included James Martin. Following the enthusiasm shown by these people and others, a Victorian named

William Harvey convened meetings of the Camden Harbour Pastoral Association in Melbourne on 28 July and 8 August 1864. The Association offered members the right to occupy land around Camden Harbour for twelve years, with a right to purchase any portion of a lease above 40 acres for ten shillings an acre. The right of occupation depended on the members first stocking the country at a rate of 100 cattle or 500 sheep for every 100,000 acres [40,500 hectares].

Such was the enthusiasm generated from these meetings that more than 100 men, women and children were embarked from Victoria on three ships. *Stag* of 400 ton sailed on 16 November 1864 and arrived at Camden Harbour on 13 December, carrying 23 settlers, 34 mares, 80 rams and 120 ewes etc. *Helvetia* of 700 ton sailed on 19 November 1864 and arrived on 14 December, carrying 33 settlers, women and children and more than 1,500 sheep. The third ship *Calliance* of 823 ton sailed on 24 November 1864 and arrived on Christmas Day, carrying 58 or more settlers and family members, including 12 women, and at least 2,580 additional sheep etc. One can readily imagine the shock of arrival, with the heat, humidity, flies and the isolation that awaited the newcomers. The average age of the men and women was 32 years and there were 25 children and babies. All were from Victoria.

Above View of Camden Harbour from Mt Lookover.
Photo – Kevin Coate

The grim faces of the settlers, their wives, and the crew of the *Stag* and the *Helvetia*, that all on the *Calliance* observed when they had dropped anchor on Christmas Day, revealed the great disappointment of the earlier arrivals. The Reverend Edward Tanner, the Chairman of the Pastoral Association, who had just arrived on the *Calliance* was later to state: 'The soil is not rich. It has the appearance and consistency of well burnt brick earth'. The aspect of the country was 'that of a dry, barren, scorched up desert'. Stones, covered by seemingly luxuriant grass after rain, covered the land 'as if they had been ejected from a volcano'. Finding drinking water was a major problem. Not only did the sheep die by the hundreds, but so did several of the horses. After two months, only 1,300 sheep were still alive, the causes being the heat, the rugged country, the grass being too dry and hard for them, and blowflies.

As soon as the *Stag* and *Helvetia* had unloaded their cargoes, they set sail, but not before 27 people comprising five families and four single men had boarded the *Stag* to return to Victoria, disillusioned. This left only the *Calliance* which had been damaged running onto a reef, when three days out from Camden Harbour near Adele Island.

On 5 January 1865, in order to inspect the damaged keel, the ship's captain Brown selected a shell and sandy beach towards which he had the crew haul the 823 ton vessel. While they were using the swiftly-moving tide to aid their exertions, a sea breeze came in, pushing the ship too quickly ashore. A dropped anchor could not take hold and the ship ran onto a large rock over which the *Calliance* was stranded as the tide ran out. Peak tides are in excess of 11 metres in these waters. As the tide fell, the ship rolled onto its side, with the weight crushing the sides and further cracking the damaged keel. The incoming tide then flooded the stranded ship causing it to be largely submerged. Many stores were salvaged over the coming days, but the ship was a write-off.

However, some help was shortly at hand. On 17 February 1865, Robert John Sholl arrived on the *Tien Tsin* having been appointed by Governor Hampton as Resident Magistrate and government representative at Camden Harbour in January. He had arrived at Fremantle in 1840, at the age of 21, with his mother, sister and a younger brother, to join another brother, William, already settled in Perth. He had married in 1844, and the first born of seven children was named Trevarton (Trevy, later to feature in the northern venture). Robert Sholl had worked his way up the ladder as a teacher, clerk of the courts, newspaper editor and later joint-owner, and as a registrar in the Wellington district. His newspaper the *Inquirer* was known to follow 'a staunchly pro-administration line in its editorial policy'.

Michael Quinlan

The government party that set sail for Camden Harbour from Fremantle on 26 January 1865 included the following 46 persons: Resident Magistrate Robert Sholl, his 19-year-old son Trevy (clerk, postmaster and tide-waiter), and a servant; three Police, including Constables Walter Gee and Jackaman, and two Native Police constables, Jimba and Billy; 13 Pensioner Guards, comprising Sgt. Ahern, Cpl. Henry Cowen and eleven Privates. Three of the guards and one police constable had their wives with them and there were nine children. There were two Assistant Surveyors, plus three chainmen and one stores Quartermaster. Finally there were the tradesmen, each with an assistant labourer. The tradesmen were a mason, a carpenter, and a blacksmith named Michael Quinlan, the latter aged 25.

Michael Quinlan had arrived, from the town of Borrisokane, Co. Tipperary, at Fremantle on the SS *Palestine* in 1863, with a young wife Maria and two children aged two and less than a year. They were part of a group that settled on small holdings in Toodyay (Newcastle as it was then called) out of Perth. When Michael joined the expedition to Camden Harbour in January 1865, as a replacement taken on at the last moment, the family's worldly possessions comprised three cows and a few horses, a hut, an iron plough, one bedstead, one sofa, one table and some cooking utensils. No doubt, the reason to join was to save money for the growing family, as he left behind a pregnant wife.

Above View of the first landing and unloading place for the settlement with Mount Lookover in the background.
Photo – Tony Quinlan

It was not until the *Tien Tsin* reached Camden Harbour and the party had disembarked was the enormity of the problem facing the earlier arrivals revealed. Everywhere, sandstone rocks were found, covered by lush green grass (but poor feed for stock), with little water available. The humidity was obviously debilitating for the settlers who had arrived from Victoria at the worst time of the year. Of the 4,500 sheep which had been landed, only 1,354 were then alive.

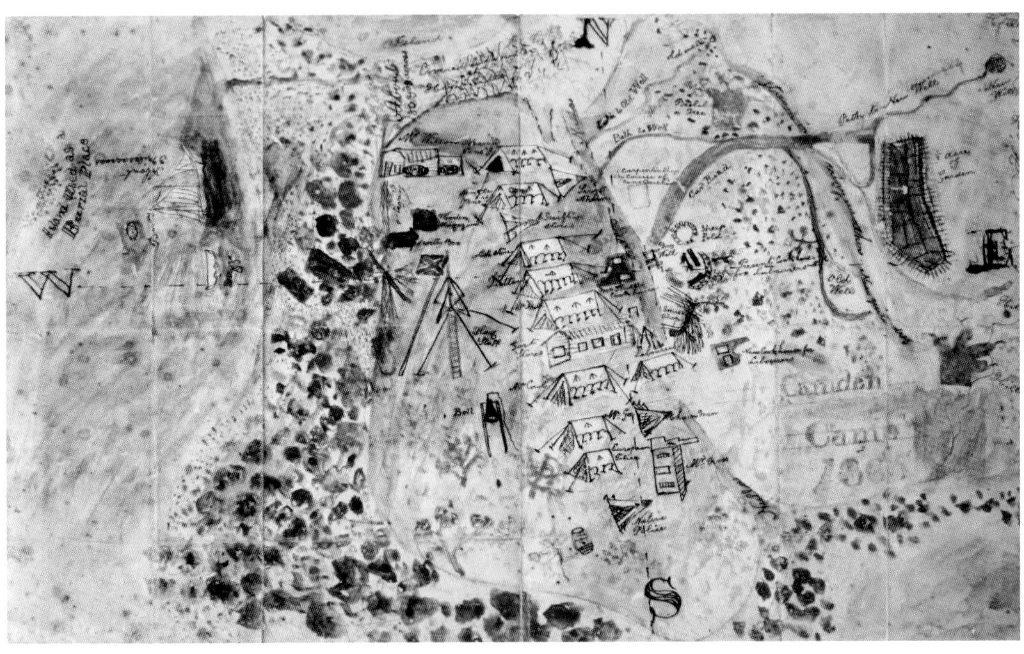

Above Sketch of Government Camp. Courtesy of Museum of Western Australia (WINC 2066).

Right Photo of Government Camp. Courtesy of State Library of Western Australia (21412P, 6909B/27, Alfred Hawes Stone Collection) and Mrs D. Croft.

Disillusion

So disillusioned were many of the settlers that, when the *Tien Tsin* sailed south on 18 March 1865, 53 members of the Camden Harbour Pastoral Association were on board. Even the chairman of the Association, the Rev. Edward Tanner, was one of those who booked a passage to Fremantle on the departing ship. Robert Sholl and the other members of the government party were effectively to now become a recovery expedition, with the task of safely extricating the remaining Association settlers from the trials of the failed venture. The settlers believed that they had been misled by the Western Australian authorities, in statements contained in several pamphlets sent to the Association in Victoria, prior to making their commitment to join the settler group.

Governor Hampton was made aware, by Robert Sholl and others, of the problems being faced and he offered to change the conditions of securing other land in the north-west of the State. Anyone taking 200 sheep or 100 cattle there would be entitled to 100,000 acres. This did not resolve the problem faced by those who had lost all or the majority of their sheep but the fact that they had originally brought sheep with them was accepted as fulfilment of one of the conditions of securing land.

Over the next months, commencing in April, Robert Sholl and others made several exploration journeys into the country backing Camden Harbour, particularly south-east towards the Glenelg River. He ventured a few miles south of Grey's furthest point of exploration. The party battled the rock-strewn hills and gullies, referring to it as being 'fearful country'. Not the least of their concerns was the bites of the green bush ants that frequented the area.

Aboriginal Attacks

A typically callous indifference to the invasion of Aboriginal land and sacred sites resulted in numerous clashes and cases of wanton slaughter of the Indigenous inhabitants of the area, even before the settlement at Camden Harbour. The diary of Trevy Sholl records several incidents where unjust and cruel treatment of the Aborigines took place. The Aborigines were not happy at the increasing encroachment by the white invaders. By the same token, the settlers were not happy with the spearing and the theft of stock carried out by the local people. There was serious tension created. At Camden Harbour, the Aborigines had taken a liking to trying, and succeeding, to steal the surveyor Cowle's boat. In searching for the boat, confrontation with a group of 100 Aborigines saw the whites retreating, firing as they went. The search would soon lead to tragedy.

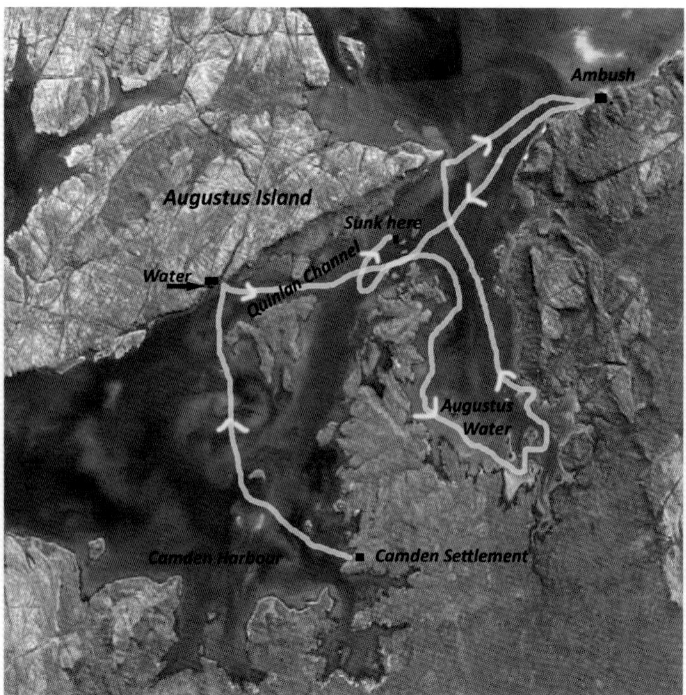

Michael Quinlan's Death

In late August 1865, Gov. Hampton had agreed to the closure of the settlement and a boat was to be chartered to take away the last of the settlers and Sholl's party. By 4 September 1865, Sholl had commenced packing for the departure. With time on their hands, a further search was to be made for Cowle's missing boat.

The government pinnace was prepared and set off early on that day with Robert Sholl, Trevy Sholl, Thomas Thomkinson, Michael Quinlan, Walter Gee and Daniel Coffey. They followed Cowle's party who sailed in another boat and carried seven days' provisions. They sailed and rowed to Augustus Island to fill breakers with fresh water and then proceeded to sail around Augustus Water looking for the stolen boat, to no avail.

That evening, they anchored offshore from a sandy beach on the eastern shore of Port George IV. Early on 5 September, they sailed around the bays and inlets looking for the boat. They encountered an Aboriginal man standing on a rocky ledge trying to entice them to come ashore. Fearing an ambush, having noticed others and their spears concealed behind some rocks, they moved further along to a safer spot, so they thought. They hoped to entice the man with some bread. Robert Sholl, Trevy, Quinlan and Thomkinson went ashore, but the man wouldn't come closer. Fearing trouble, Sholl

Above Route of the search for the pinnace. Courtesy of Google, with route marked by Hamish McGlashan.

ordered the party back into the boat. Trevy lingered. As the others got into the boat, a shower of spears and clubs was launched from behind the rocks. Constable Gee was stuck by a blunt ended spear in the left shoulder. He pulled out the spear while Trevy and others fired on the Aborigines. Trevy then dived into the boat, being struck on the way in by a dowak or club that caused a severe wound to his shoulder and arm. With Gee also in considerable pain, they pushed off with the oars and managed to get away, clear from the spear throwing distance. Having got near to Rogers Strait, but exhausted by rowing against the outgoing tide, they decided to drop anchor in shallow water. However, the anchor dragged into the deeper water and snagged on a rock. Immediately, the bow of the boat was dragged underwater and the boat foundered. Quinlan, who was standing in the bow, must have been entangled in the rigging or jib sheets. He went down with the boat and never surfaced.

The others were swept either onto islands at the head of Rogers Strait or past Augustus Water and finished back in Port George IV, near where they had set out that morning. Robert and Trevy Sholl managed to struggle back to Camden Harbour by walking around Augustus Water, arriving there two days later after walking at night and partly by day, with some fitful sleep and finding little water. Gee was rescued from an island by a boat sent from the camp. Thomkinson struggled back to the camp, minus his clothes but wearing his boots, having lost his bundled clothing when struggling to swim ashore. Likewise, Coffey was found without trousers and was considerably sunburnt.

Constable Walter Gee succumbed to his wound and other complications, on 17 September 1865, and was buried on Sheep Island, the ninth person to die since the settlement commenced. He left his pregnant wife and four young children to mourn his passing.

Unbeknown to Michael Quinlan in Camden Harbour, Mrs Quinlan had given birth to twins in Toodyay on 13 June 1865. Both mother and a girl died on the day of the births. The twin boy died some six months later. The elder children, Timothy and Mary aged 4 and 2, were reared and educated within the Perth family of Joseph Thomas Reilly. Timothy was my grandfather, who subsequently became the MLA for West Perth and then Toodyay, Speaker of the House from 1905 to 1911, Papal Knight and Trustee of the University Endowment Act (UWA). But that is another story.

Top The grave of Mary Jane Pascoe, one of the early settlers, on Sheep Island in Camden Harbour.
Photo – Tony Quinlan

Above Timothy Quinlan

Finale

The Camden Harbour settlement was finally abandoned with the arrival and departure of the government chartered ship *Kestrel*, 170 ton. All remaining Pensioner Guards, police, Resident Magistrate Robert Sholl and his party, together with about 16 settlers, sailed south on 29 October 1865. Sholl had been appointed Resident Magistrate at Port Walcott, where he departed the *Kestrel* in Tien Tsin harbour on 24 November.

The last entry in Trevy Sholl's diary, recorded at Camden Harbour, read; "Goodbye, land of Camden, I am not sorry to leave you".

Opposite
Looking to Sheep Island from landing site of Camden Harbour settlement.
Photo – Mike Donaldson

References

Australian Dictionary of Biography. See http://adbonline.anu.edu.au/biogs/A010182b.htm for 'Camden, first Marquess (1759 – 1840)', or, in print, vol. 1, 1966, p. 196.

Erickson, R. *Old Toodyay and Newcastle.* Toodyay Shire Council, [Toodyay, WA], 1974.

Forrest, K. *The Challenge and The Chance: The Colonisation and Settlement of North West Australia 1861-1914.* Hesperian Press, Carlisle (WA), 1996.

Grey, G. *Journals of two expeditions of discovery in North-West and Western Australia during the years 1837, 38, and 39.* T. and W. Boone, London, 1841, facsimile edition, Hesperian Press, Victoria Park (WA), 1983, vol. 1.

King, P. P. *Narrative of a survey of the intertropical and western coasts of Australia. Performed between the years 1818 and 1822.* John Murray, London, 1827, facsimile edition, Libraries Board of South Australia, Adelaide, 1969, two volumes.

Quinlan, L. *Undaunted Spirit, The Life and Times of Joseph T. Reilly.* Polding Press, Melbourne, 1980.

Reilly, J. T. *Reminiscences of Fifty Years' Residence in Western Australia.* Sands & McDougall Ltd., Perth, 1903.

Richards, C. *There Were Three Ships.* UWA Press, Nedlands, 1990.

Sholl, Robert John. Journal, 1865. State Records Office of Western Australia, Series 1750, Item 25, available on microfilm.

Willis, H. A. 'The colour of blood'. *Eureka Street*, vol. 7, no. 1, January-February 1997, pp. 20–5.

Guano Mining: Kimberley's first extractive industry

Tim Willing and Alison Spencer

The word guano, the droppings of countless seabirds accumulated over centuries, derives from a Peruvian word 'huano', meaning dung.[1] The value of guano as an agricultural fertiliser had been known since the time of the Inca Empire, but it was scarcely appreciated outside Peru. In 1835 the first shipment of Peruvian guano reached England. Experiments on wheat and turnip crops proved so successful that commercial interest was rapidly aroused.[2] In 1842 a Liverpool merchant and shipowner, John Rae, dispatched three vessels amidst great secrecy to a tiny island off the coast of southwest Africa – present-day Namibia. An American sea-captain had reported seeing guano there 25 feet (8 metres) in depth. The island was Ichaboe, but word was soon out and an anarchic boom ensued.[3] By December 1844 there were 300 British and five American vessels anchored, awaiting loading, with 2,000 labourers toiling ashore.[4] The boom peaked in January 1845 when 450 ships were reported in its anchorage. In all it was estimated that 'about 300,000 tons of guano were shipped from Ichaboe to Britain and sold at an average price of £7 per ton... Ichaboe saved British shipping ... [and] ... great firms sprang to life in Liverpool as a result of the reeking riches of Ichaboe'.[5] During the 1850s, there was a massive expansion in the guano trade from islands off the coast of Peru, particularly to the United States, but it was characterised by appalling labour conditions.[6] Peru's near monopoly lead to increasing interest by other countries in finding and controlling alternative sources of guano. American annexation of islands in the Pacific was one result.

Opposite
Browse Island. Detailed view in late March 1878 showing flocks of seabirds, guano camp and trolleys on central tramway. Shipwrecks: rib remains of *Matterhorn* (left) with barque *Carleton* (right). Original painting in the collection of the Yarmouth County Museum and Archives.
Photo courtesy of the Yarmouth County Museum and Archives, Yarmouth, Nova Scotia, Canada.

Early Guano Mining in Western Australia

Mike McCarthy noted that the guano industry of Western Australia 'is of particular interest as it set the historical precedents for the granting of mining leases in Western Australia'. It also 'helped set the scene for the interaction between government and entrepreneur which is a feature of mining in this state'.[7]

By the 1840s small quantities of guano were being opportunistically removed from the Abrolhos Islands and shipped to Fremantle. In the trade, there was an important distinction between 'live' or fresh guano and 'dead guano' or rock phosphate. The latter, 'a limestone, converted in part to tri-calcic phosphates', required experienced judgement to determine its quality and market value. By the 1850s substantial guano deposits were identified at Shark Bay and the first formal guano lease was granted for an islet near Dirk Hartog Island. Cargoes were shipped principally to England and Mauritius.[8]

Discovery of Browse Island Guano

In May 1872 the stockowner and entrepreneur George Howlett, of Roebourne, purchased the brig *Wild Wave* (180 tons) and went into partnership with George Crouch. As the Hendersons relate:

> On her first visit to the west coast, in 1872, the *Wild Wave* sailed to Fremantle from Port Darwin via Port Walcott and Champion Bay. Calms detained the vessel on the voyage past the Kimberley coast. Howlett was on board, and to occupy his time, he followed the immense flights of sea birds, which seemed to be converging on a particular point. The birds led him to Browse Island, where he took guano samples.
>
> Howlett sent the samples to Melbourne on the *Wild Wave* for testing, and they proved to be extremely rich in phosphates. With thoughts of exploiting the deposits, he sent the *Wild Wave* back to Fremantle in July 1873, and arranged for a voyage to Singapore via Port Walcott, under the command of Captain Edward Fothergill.[9]

The *Wild Wave* sailed from Fremantle on 25 August 1873, loaded with sandalwood and mining equipment, but was wrecked a few days later on the Montebello Islands with Howlett aboard. Although no hands

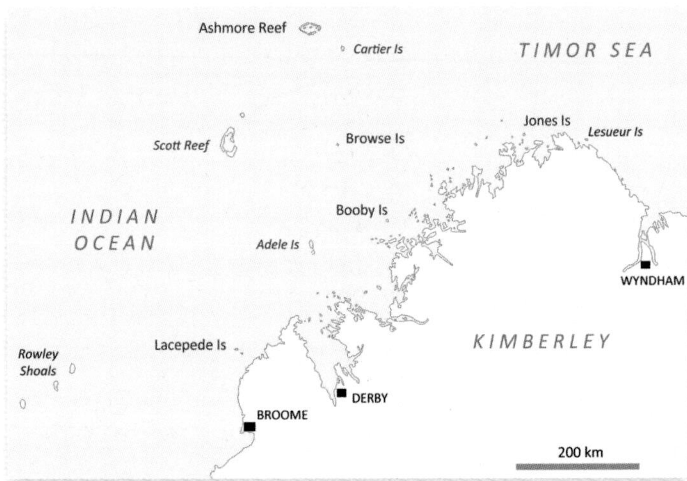

Right Map of the Kimberley offshore islands.

were lost, it was a cruel blow for Howlett, effectively preventing him from financing the guano venture alone. In August, he had applied to the Surveyor-General on behalf of Crouch Brothers, merchants of Roebourne, for a lease of Browse Island,[10] and in December, Crouch Brothers specifically sought a ten-year lease.[11]

Word of Howlett's discovery of the Browse Island guano probably passed – like a Chinese whisper – from one sailor to another. Unbeknown to anyone in Western Australia, William Fisher and Peter Facy's brig *Prairie* (139 tons) left Port Darwin in June 1874 and sailed for Browse Island to load a surreptitious cargo of guano.

On the second day of guano loading, 2 July 1874:

> ... a boat belonging to the brig was returning ... having on board the captain [McFarlane], Mr. Farr, chief officer, Mr. Clarke, of the Marine Hotel, Lower Murray-Street, Hobart Town; Hans Martin, Thomas Burgess, and William Harburgh, all seamen; and Charles Johnson and Henry Warby, apprentices. After shoving off from the island, the boat suddenly filled in the surf, and shortly afterwards was swamped. The captain struck out for the shore, but owing to the heavy surf, his strength failed him, and he went down to rise no more. Mr. Farr, who swam with him, was more successful. He managed to cling to a rock, and subsequently succeeded in gaining the shore. Nothing was afterwards seen or heard of the Captain, Mr. Clarke, or the three seamen and two apprentices. Mr. Farr remained on the island for one day and two nights without either food or water.[12]

Above Browse Island. Anchored barques in foreground are probably *Marion, Flora, Cleveland* and *Niphon*. Original painting in the collection of the Yarmouth County Museum and Archives. Photo courtesy of the Yarmouth County Museum and Archives, Yarmouth, Nova Scotia, Canada.
For details, see E. Ruff, 'Browse Island: the painting', *The Great Circle,* vol. 32, no. 2, 2010, pp. 52-62.

In a more detailed account, Farr reached the shore, half dead with fatigue, about nightfall:

> Mr. Farr then collected a number of [guano] bags, and lay down to rest himself in one of the numerous turtle holes about the beach, covered up with bags, and in that way passed his first night on this deserted island. When he awoke in the morning he found the yellow retriever dog belonging to Captain Macfarlane lying alongside of him.[13]

By daybreak on 4 July 1874 the surf had moderated sufficiently for the steward aboard *Prairie,* Joseph Campstey, accompanied by four apprentices to rescue James Farr and the retriever. Forced to slip the *Prairie*'s anchors, there being insufficient manpower to weigh them, Farr successfully navigated for Cape Leeuwin, blessed by favourable winds. The *Prairie* finally reached Hobart on 30 August still under Farr's command, with 15 tons of guano.

In July 1874, George Howlett wrote to the Commissioner of Crown Lands from Adelaide, advising that Crouch Brothers had been dissolved, but that he still sought a lease of Browse Island to ship guano and had appointed J. G. Anderson to negotiate in Perth on his behalf.[14] In August, Anderson was informed that Howlett's application had been accepted.[15] In December Howlett wrote from Adelaide advising the Commissioner that he was prepared to outlay £2,000 to send a vessel to Browse Island for 300 tons of guano 'by way of experiment'.[16] In March 1875, William Bentham Neales, a wealthy mining surveyor of Adelaide, advised Howlett that he was prepared to finance the venture, subject to the lease including his name.[17] On 1 May, Malcolm Fraser, Commissioner of Crown Lands, advised Howlett that he and Neales had to commence working Browse Island within six months. He was prepared to grant them a joint lease at £10 per annum with a monopoly for ten years; a minimum of 400 tons of guano was to be exported annually with a royalty of 2s. 6d. per ton shipped.[18]

In July 1875, the Adelaide solicitor, Paul Frederick Bonnin, acting for Howlett and Neales, wrote to the Commissioner advising that the ketch *Tasman* had sailed from Adelaide to load a sample cargo at Browse Island. He further advised that Howlett and Neales had formed a 'co-partnership' with William Trevett Dalwood, William Knox Simms and William Adolphus Paqualin, gentlemen of Adelaide, to share the cost of the guano testing.[19]

Above At left, James Farr, Chief Officer of the brig *Prairie*.
Courtesy of Maritime Museum of Tasmania.

The Browse Island Guano Company Limited of Adelaide (1876-1887)

The Articles of Association, founding the Browse Island Guano Company Limited (BIGCL) in Adelaide, were signed on 26 February 1876.[20] On 15 May a party of BIGCL directors and shareholders went to the Semaphore, Port Adelaide to farewell and toast Howlett and Neales, as well as inspect the three-masted American schooner *Sadie F. Caller* (414 tons), chartered to convey them to Browse Island. The BIGCL had decided to work the guano by 'coolie labour'. Howlett was to travel as supercargo and 'to superintend the loading of vessels'. The *Tasman* sampling voyage, overseen by Paqualin, had 'fully established the richness of the guano, the quantity of which lying on a base of broken coral and sand was roughly estimated at 200,000 tons, there being a depth of from 6 feet [1.8 metres] to 3 feet 6 inches'. About 150,000 tons was 'of excellent quality' with about 30,000 tons 'of very superior richness'. The BIGCL had sent guano 'to Mauritius and other places, where a market for an article containing from 70 to 80 per cent of phosphates was soon established'. It was being offered prices 'up to £6. 2s. 6d. per ton afloat', applications were 'coming in from Germany for supplies', and other vessels would 'be chartered to meet the European and home demand'. All shares in the BIGCL had been taken up.[21]

When the *Sadie F. Caller* sailed from Port Adelaide on 18 May 1876, in command of Captain Amasa Tarbox Webber, it was reported that she 'took 30 coolies, a year's provisions and materials to construct an iron jetty and tramway at Browse Island'.[22] Arriving in Port Darwin on 26 July, the schooner discharged 150 sheep and a miscellaneous cargo before departing for Browse Island on 9 August.[23] The *Sadie F. Caller* delivered 625 tons of guano to Mauritius, arriving there on 30 November.[24]

It was only in July 1876 that Bonnin wrote to the Commissioner of Crown Lands, requesting that the lease of Browse Island be transferred to the BIGCL owing to the need to raise the very large amount of capital required to work the Island.[25] The BIGCL then began advertising in Melbourne that it was desirous of receiving offers from shipowners willing to load guano at Browse Island for the European Market.[26]

In May 1877, Howlett and Webber discovered guano deposits at West Island, Ashmore Reef during another voyage of the *Sadie F. Caller.* Their subsequent bitter feud and efforts to establish ownership has been well documented elsewhere.[27]

Following the initial guano shipment aboard the *Sadie F. Caller* in 1876, numerous shipments were made by the BIGCL for about three years. However, low guano prices at Hamburg in 1880, resulting from new phosphate discoveries in Florida, discouraged the BIGCL from resuming significant exports until 1885. In that year, George Warland, BIGCL's island manager, reported on the practical difficulties of loading guano:

> ... it has to be boated off during calm weather, and even then it wants very skilful handling to take a boat through the surf. The least hesitation or error of judgement on the part of the steersman, and if the sea catches the boat at all on one side, it turns her over and over like a straw, and tosses her up high and dry on the beach, *minus* men, oars, and guano. The men and oars are generally saved, and make the attempt again with another load.

Warland ended his account by writing:

> At one time the island had at least twenty-three different races or nationalities represented amongst its population, of all shades of colour, from the European to the South African. Of the coloured contingent, the Japanese were far and away the best workers.[28]

The years 1878 and 1879 were particularly bad for shipwrecks – with the loss of *Carleton, Runnymede* and *Sulina*. Additionally, the captain and 16 crew of the German ship *Matterhorn* were drowned when that vessel foundered off Browse Island in March 1878.[29] Sea captains complained that the BIGCL had chartered an excessive number of vessels, inadequately provisioned them with stores and supplied insufficient bags for guano loading. They alleged that waiting barques almost circled the island, sometimes queuing for five months to obtain a cargo, and were cutting up spare sails to make guano bags![30] Not surprisingly, some captains chose to cut their losses and depart empty. One example was Captain Hughes of the British iron barque *Cambrian Monarch*, who proceeded instead to Java.[31]

On 5 March 1883, the annual meeting of the BIGCL was held in Adelaide. The directors submitted a 'somewhat meagre report' to the shareholders. They had received £1,205. 6s. 4d. from the sale of guano stored in London. About £1,500 had been spent chartering the ship *Condoren*, which was to sell its guano cargo in Hamburg at 'the satisfactory price of 2s. per unit'. As the insurance quoted on the cargo was exorbitant, the directors decided to risk making the shipment with no insurance. The W.A. Government was paid royalty payments amounting to £289. 2s. 3d.[32]

In early March 1885, a meeting of BIGCL shareholders was held in Adelaide with the banker John Brodie Spence presiding. The directors 'regretted that they had little to report since the last general meeting'. Information had been received that *Karnan* and *Alert* had arrived in London and that their cargoes had been sold. Unfortunately, the *Risoe* 'had foundered at sea some weeks after leaving Browse Island' and the BIGCL had claimed £300 insurance in respect of the cargo. The balance sheet revealed that expenditure was approximately £100 in excess of receipts.[33]

During 1885 and the early part of 1886 ten barques are recorded to have shipped guano from Browse Island.[34] According to the Government Geologist, A. Gibb Maitland, these vessels shipped a total of 6,562 tons of guano from the island, mainly to Hamburg. However, there are some doubts as to the accuracy of these figures as the BIGCL almost certainly understated the total tonnage shipped to reduce royalty payments.[35] Given the figures quoted by Maitland, it can be surmised that the total amount of guano removed from Browse Island, from the time Howlett took his first samples in 1873 to the cessation of formal mining activities in 1887, amounted to less than 40,000 tons.

On 7 March 1887, an extraordinary general meeting of the BIGCL in Adelaide resolved to wind up the company voluntarily. J. B. Spence and L. S. Wicksteed were appointed liquidators with their remuneration fixed at £40.[36]

Although all significant mining activities had ceased at the island in July 1886, it was not the end of endeavours to mine guano from Browse Island.

Above The iron barque *Cambrian Monarch* painted on a sailor's sea chest.
Courtesy of Vallejo Gallery (http://vallejogallery.com/).

Captain Schutt and the Browse Island Company Pty Ltd (1912-1936)

Captain Louis John Daley Schutt was the master of the iron barque *Yarra* when it was wrecked on Scott Reef in January 1884 during a cyclone. Schutt and his crew fabricated a raft from the wreckage and made a hazardous, five-day, 160-kilometre voyage to Browse Island. He and his crew then spent five days assisting the loading of guano on to two Scandinavian vessels, in return for passages for his family and crew to nearby Australian ports.[37] This must have made a profound impression on him because in 1912 Schutt secured a ten-year Special Lease on Browse Island 'for obtaining and removing guano' at an annual rent of £25, subject to the payment of one shilling per ton royalty on all guano removed in excess of 500 tons. This lease was surrendered in 1915, in consideration of a new lease being granted for a term of 21 years under the same conditions.[38]

On 11 June 1917, Schutt wrote to the Pacific Phosphate Co. Ltd. of Melbourne, enclosing a copy of his Browse Island lease as well as 'a memorandum giving particulars of the Island, results of analyses of 9 samples of Browse Island Guano and a book of 24 photographs taken on the Island'. Schutt's letter advised:

> I am prepared to transfer my rights and interests in the lease to your Company for the sum of Fifteen thousand pounds, payable in a lump sum or by instalments of One thousand pounds per annum, interest at five per cent per annum to be allowed on the balance unpaid. Although there is no provision in the lease for subletting I am given to understand that this would be allowed to an approved person or corporation. If your Company is prepared to do business I shall be glad to assist as far as I can in completing arrangements to develop the Island and would give my services free of cost.

A. J. King, representative of the Pacific Phosphate Co. Ltd. in Melbourne, wrote to the firm's Secretary in London on 9 July 1917, enclosing Schutt's correspondence, lease documents and photographs. However he had, very sensibly, taken the precaution of seeking out and conferring with members of the Victorian Fertiliser Association first. They informed him that, in October 1915, an expedition had been sent to Browse Island under the auspices of the Victorian Superphosphate Manufacturers. The expedition, which had included Schutt, a surveyor, an analyst and a boring master, cost £1,400. King reported that he had sighted the reports made by the surveyor and analyst , but they advised that only 6,000 tons of high grade rock phosphate (80.5% P, dry weight) remained.[39]

King's letter advised that the Victorian Fertiliser Association had, understandably, declined Schutt's offer to dispose of his Browse Island interests. King correctly surmised that 'owing to the nature and limited extent of the deposit', it was extremely unlikely that the Directors of the Pacific Phosphate Co. Ltd. would be prepared to entertain Schutt's current proposition.

The Browse Island Company Pty Ltd (BICPL) of Melbourne was incorporated on 9 October 1920 with its office at Aberdeen House, 528 Collins Street. Its Directors were Richard Dodds and William Bendixsen, with Charles William Cowper as Company Secretary. In March 1921 Schutt transferred his lease on Browse Island to the BICPL.[40]

In the same year Schutt had purchased an old brigantine *Rachel Cohen* (170 tons), fitted with an 80 horsepower auxiliary engine for £5,449. In August 1921, under Captain Richard Gould, the vessel was nearly wrecked at Browse Island. One month later, having loaded only 26 tons of guano, the crew went on strike and the *Rachel Cohen* proceeded to Broome. While this enterprise proved financially disastrous for both Schutt and the BICPL, their losses compounded when the vessel sank at Darwin in 1924, voiding its insurance policy![41]

The BICPL's lease of Browse Island was finally cancelled in 1936 for non-payment of rent.[42] In the meantime, Captain L. J. D. Schutt, aged 84, had died on 14 May 1934 at his home in Brighton, Victoria.[43]

Above Stacked rock phosphate at the southern end of Browse Island in 2005.
Photo – Tim Willing

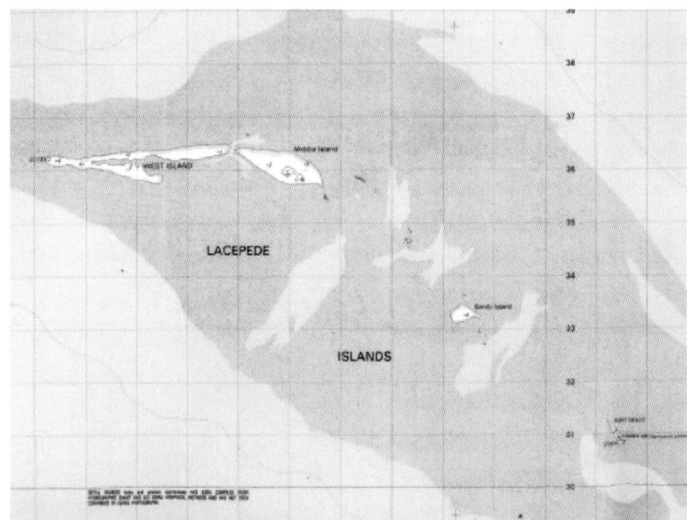

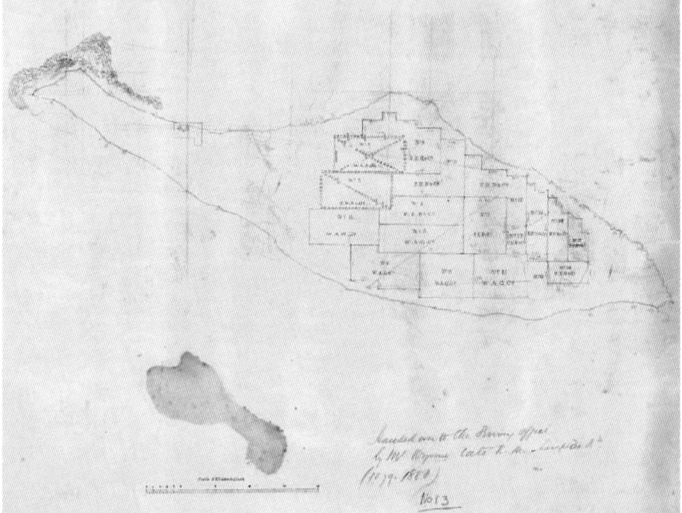

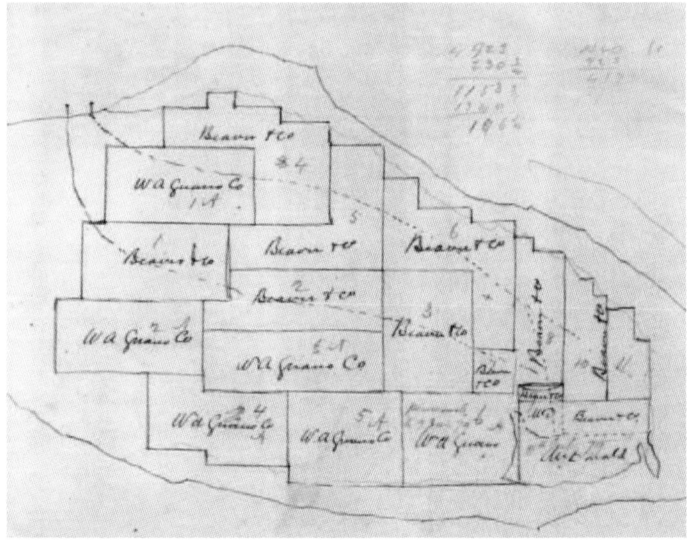

Top Lacepede Islands (Crown Copyright reserved).

Above Map of Middle Island, illustrating guano allocations to contractors. Courtesy of State Records Office of Western Australia, 237 Survey Plans, Cons 3846, item 124.

Right Map showing route of tramways and allocated guano sections at Middle Island. Courtesy of State Records Office of Western Australia, Acc 1816/12.

Guano Mining on the Lacepede Islands (1876-1879)

The Lacepede Islands lie some 20 kilometres west of the Dampier Peninsula coast, approximately 150 kilometres north of Broome. They comprise four sand cays, perched on an extensive coral reef, although the two larger islands (West Island, 107 hectares and Middle Island, 54 hectares) have significant exposures of beach rock and limestone.[44]

In May 1876 the Melbourne firm of Poole, Picken & Co. was licensed to take guano from Middle Island at the Lacepedes. Soon afterwards, the English adventurer Gilbert Carver Roberts arrived in the French barque *Forcade la Roquette* with authority from the United States Consul in Melbourne, the merchant Samuel Perkins Lord, who laid claim to the Islands under the United States Guano Act of 1856. Roberts found the barques *Alexandra* and *Nicolino* loading guano illegally for export to Mauritius. After raising the Stars and Stripes, Roberts proceeded to Roebourne, only to be fined £100 for illegal guano removal.[45] The issue of sovereignty was resolved when the United States Government rejected its consul's claim to the Lacepedes.[46]

In November 1876, the Western Australian Government appointed an Irish-born clerk, Richard Wynne, to oversee operations on the Lacepedes. He arrived with a constable, three boatmen and a Chinese cook. Wynne's responsibilities included ensuring that the guano deposits were mined in an orderly and systematic manner, royalties were paid and law and order maintained.[47] He initially lived in a tent but, after extensive communications with the authorities in Perth, a stonemason was engaged to construct a two-room limestone building, rather grandly known as 'Lacepede House'.[48]

Near the house a fifty-foot (15 metre) flagpole held a hoisted lantern at night. During daytime, signal flags were flown to assist dozens of sailing ships locate the dangerously exposed anchorage offshore.[49]

Arriving barques brought bundles of corn sacks for loading guano from open boats, a tediously slow and sometimes dangerous process. Several surviving maps (opposite page) show that the Melbourne-based rival contractors, the W.A. Guano Company and F. E. Beaver and Company, laid down tramways across Middle Island. Horse-drawn trolleys hauled the guano along lines to makeshift wooden jetties on the northern shore of the island.[50]

On 16 February 1877 a catastrophic cyclone struck the islands. The barque *Aboyne* was driven ashore and wrecked in minutes with six lives lost; *Albert Victor, Helen Malcolm* and *Isabellas* were also wrecked. Fifty-one sailors became castaways.[51]

In April 1878 Wynne wrote to Perth that there were 165 persons on the island digging guano but that they were 'on strike, insolent and drunk'. Fifty-seven vessels had loaded 24,715 tons of guano.[52] Its principal destination was Hamburg in Germany, although significant amounts were also sent to Mauritius. A typical voyage to Hamburg, via the Cape of Good Hope, took four months.[53]

The following month the government called tenders for a sole party to remove the remaining 40,000 tons of guano.[54] Wynne was placed in a difficult position, as in reality far less guano of commercial value was left. Unhappy contractors F. E. Beaver & Co. and McDonald & Mockford commenced legal proceedings against the government. By November 1879 all the commercial guano had been mined and Wynne returned to Fremantle.

According to Woodward,[55] a total of 37,226 tons of guano was removed from the Lacepede Islands in the period 1876-1879. From this, the government derived royalties totalling £18,611.

Above Wrecked shipping at the Lacepede Islands from the February 1877 cyclone. Lithograph in *Australasian Sketcher*, 9 June 1877.

However, the final cost of arbitration (£5,614 to F. E. Beaver, awarded in May 1881) and damages (£9,783 to McDonald & Mockford, awarded in August 1888) totalled £15,397.[56] If the costs for administering the Lacepedes in salary paid to Wynne and wages to his staff are added,[57] the overall financial benefit of Lacepede guano to the colony was arguably negative – largely due to poor business practice by government.

Lacepede Islands after 1880

James William Sherbrook Kelly, Wynne's boatman – widely known as "Shiner" Kelly – had barely taken office as caretaker administrator when a severe cyclone in January 1880 overwhelmed Middle Island. It washed away 'Lacepede House', which functioned variously as the harbourmaster's office, residence, police station, courthouse, jail and post office.[58]

Kelly remained on Middle Island:

> ... as a kind of "man in possession". He was, sometimes for months, without any other companionship than that of the wild sea fowl and the numberless turtle which frequent those barren islets; but he appeared to be contented enough in his Robinson Crusoe-like position; the only hardship he complained of being the scarcity of books and newspapers, which he eagerly sought from any vessel passing or approaching his lonely realm.[59]

Governor W. C. F. Robinson indicated that the rationale for retaining Kelly on the Lacepedes was essentially legal:

> On consulting the Law Officers, I was advised that it was important to retain him in charge of the deposits, pending the settlement of certain legal proceedings; and as it would be quite impossible for the Police to keep an effectual watch on the Islands from such a distance as Roebuck Bay or the Fitzroy, I do not think it would do to remove Kelly from the Islands at present.[60]

On 23 March 1884 Kelly was dismissed for accepting bribes and allowing the Lacepede Islands to be used by pearlers as a depot for kidnapped Aborigines.[61]

In 1890, the government received three applications for the sole right to remove guano for a period of five years from the Lacepede Islands. This was in spite of John Forrest's cautionary note that the quantity and quality of the guano were 'at the risk of the applicant'.[62]

The successful lessee was to pay a royalty of 10s. per ton, based on ship's register and had to ship a minimum of 1,000 tons per year. The firm of Broadhurst & McNeil secured the lease and paid the Government a deposit of £250. In 1891, Florance Constantine Broadhurst visited the Lacepedes and advised that 'after a prolonged examination' the guano deposits were found to be 'all but worthless'. The £250 deposit was forfeited.[63]

Above Richard Wynne (1834-1915). Courtesy of State Library of Western Australia (284730P).

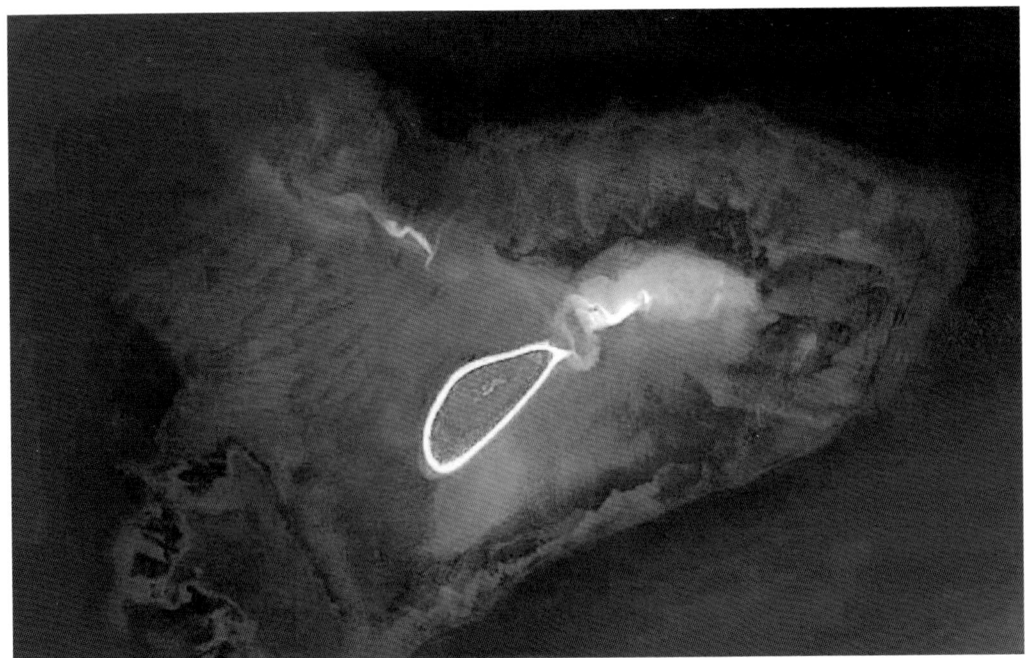

Above Jones Island, approximatley 800 metres long.
Courtesy of NASA.

Right Adult Brown Booby (*Sula leucogaster*) in flight: source of much of the guano on the Kimberley Islands.
Photo – Tim Willing

Guano mining at Jones Island (1884 and 1891-1892)

With the cessation of mining activities on the Lacepede islands in 1879, other potential sources of guano on the Kimberley coast were investigated. The government estimated in 1884 that there were deposits of 50,000 tons of guano containing 80% tri-calcic phosphate upon 'Jones, Lesueur and Stewart Islands and Black Hawk Reef', locations in the vicinity of Cape Londonderry.[64] It is recorded that 2,577 tons of guano were mined and shipped from Jones Island during 1884 by F. S. & F. E. Beaver, who traded as the Colonial Guano Co., paying royalty of £1,675.[65] Mining was carried out by 45 Chinese labourers in harsh conditions.[66] Malnutrition, dehydration, dust inhalation and perhaps opium addiction were probable factors contributing to a high mortality rate amongst the work force. Five labourers are known to have died.[67] Remaining guano on the island was deemed too low in grade to warrant extraction.

A final attempt to mine guano on Jones Island was made in 1891-1892 by Fremantle-based chemists and entrepreneurs Louis Knoop and Edward Mayhew, under the banner of the Jones Island Guano Co. They employed 25 Chinese labourers and shipped 350 tons of guano to New Zealand, before a price collapse ended the venture.[68]

Conclusion

From the first interest in mining guano at Browse Island in 1873 to the final pitiful shipment from there in 1921, a total of no more than 70,000 tons of guano was shipped to world markets from islands offshore from the Kimberley region. During the 1870s there was a marked contrast in the way the Colonial Government chose not to supervise guano mining at Browse Island, while at the Lacepedes it was closely supervised by an appointed official. Many ships were wrecked and lives lost due to the lethal combination of exposed island anchorages and a failure to cease loading during the cyclone season. Much of the labour for the actual mining of the guano was done by Asian, as well as some European, labourers (especially at the Lacepedes). Working conditions were often harsh and periodically dangerous. Guano mining was the Kimberley's first extractive industry and set the scene for the discovery of gold and further mining activity.

Acknowledgements

The authors gratefully acknowledge the assistance of Jeff Gresham in compiling this paper. Cathie Clement generously gave access to her extensive guano research notes and undertook final editing. Trish Pepper is thanked for presenting an early version of this paper to the Kimberley Society in Perth in March 2010.

Notes

1 R. Craig, 'The African Guano Trade', *Mariner's Mirror,* vol. 50, part 1, 1964, p. 25.

2 A. C. Watson, 'The Guano Islands of Southwestern Africa', *Geographical Review*, vol. 20, 1930, p. 634.

3 Craig, 'The African Guano Trade', pp. 27–31.

4 Watson, 'The Guano Islands of Southwestern Africa', pp. 639–40.

5 L. Green, *Panther Head: the Full Story of the Bird Islands off the Southern Coasts of Africa, the Men of the Islands and the Birds in Their Millions*, Stanley Paul, London, 1955, p. 96.

6 D. O'Donnell, 'The nineteenth century Pacific guano trade', *Bulletin of the Australian Institute for Maritime Archaeology*, vol. 19 (2), 1995, pp. 27–32.

7 M. McCarthy, 'Failure and Success: the Broadhursts and the Abrolhos Guano Industry', *Studies in Western Australian History,* vol. 13, 1992, p. 10.

8 ibid., p. 12.

9 G. and K-J. Henderson, *Unfinished Voyages: Western Australian Shipwrecks 1851–1880*, University of Western Australia Press, Nedlands, 1988, p. 133, with additional information on Howlett taken from pp. 131 and 134.

10 State Records Office of Western Australia (SROWA), SDUR/C6/735.

11 SROWA, SDUR/C6/745.

12 *Mercury* (Hobart), 22 August 1874, p. 2.

13 ibid., 31 August 1874, p. 2.

14 SROWA, SDUR/H3/327. Also Anonymous, 'Notes on the Early History of Browse Island', Battye Library, Research Note (RN) 217, 1951.

15 SROWA, SDUR/A1/127.

16 SROWA, SDUR/H3/336.

17 SROWA, SDUR/H3/349a.

18 SROWA, SDUR/B10/1068D.

19 SROWA, SDUR/B9/1015.

20 State Records of South Australia, Lodged company documents of defunct companies, GRS/513, File 1/1876.

21 *South Australian Register*, 17 May 1876, p. 5; *Adelaide Observer*, 20 May 1876, p. 12; *Inquirer* (Perth), 5 July 1876, p. 3.

22 *Adelaide Observer*, 20 May 1876, shipping column.

23 *Northern Territory Times and Gazette,* 29 July 1876 and 12 August 1876.

24 *Commercial Gazette* (Port Louis, Mauritius), 1 December 1876.

25 SROWA, SDUR/B10/1085.

26 *Argus*, 26 September 1876, p. 3.

27 R. E. Webber, *Yankee Captain: Amasa T. Webber 1840-1880,* Sharp and Company Printers, Rutland, Vermont, 2007, pp. 123–221.

28 *West Australian*, 23 January 1886, p. 5.

29 G. and K-J. Henderson, *Unfinished Voyages*, pp. 232–3, 255 and 256. See the image on p. 82 for a depiction of two of the shipwrecks.

30 *Northern Territory Times and Gazette*, 3 August 1878, p. 2.

31 *Newcastle Morning Herald and Miner's Advocate*, 23 December 1878, p. 2.

32 *Adelaide Observer*, 10 March 1883, p. 38.

33 ibid., 7 March 1885, p. 36.

34 *Shipping Gazette and Lloyds List.*

35 SROWA, Phosphates General, Cons 4116, item 1960/47.

36 *Adelaide Observer*, 12 March 1887, p. 28; *South Australian Government Gazette,* 12 May 1887, p. 1002.

37 L. Cairns and G. Henderson, *Unfinished Voyages: Western Australian Shipwrecks 1881–1900*, University of Western Australia Press, Nedlands, 1995, pp. 57–8. Also *North Australian*, 29 February 1884, p. 3.

38 Anonymous, 'Browse Island', Battye Library RN 600, 1951; also SROWA, Cons. 5870, item 69, p. 103, Browse Island - obtaining and removing guano, and p. 143, Browse Island Company Pty Ltd.

39 National Archives of the United Kingdom (Kew, Surrey), British Phosphate Commissioners, Reports on Various Phosphate Islands, 1882-1920, Dominions Office File 140/512.

40 SROWA, Browse Island Co Pty Ltd, Cons 1370, item 1921/017.

41 SROWA, *Rachel Cohen,* ship's logbook and crew list, 1921, AN 16/4, Acc 1056. Also *Sunday Times*, 14 December 1924, p. 13.

42 Anonymous, 'Browse Island'.

43 Registry of Births, Deaths and Marriages, District of Melbourne, Victoria, Reg. No. 3939.

44 A. A. Burbidge, N. L. McKenzie and K. F. Kenneally, *Nature Conservation Reserves in the Kimberley, Western Australia*, Department of Conservation and Land Management, Como, 1991, p. 19.

45 *Herald* (Fremantle), 30 September 1876, and *Age* (Melbourne), 9 December 1876.

46 Western Australia, *Votes & Proceedings*, 1877, Paper No. 15, p. 16, letter dated Downing Street, 31 May 1877.

47 SROWA, Guano, 12/09/1876 – 23/12/1876, Cons 36, item 829, instructions to Wynne dated 18 November 1876.

48 SROWA, 399 Plans, Cons 1647, item 152; and SROWA, Guano, 12/09/1876 - 23/12/1876, Cons 36, item 829, letter from Wynne to Acting Colonial Secretary, 10 November 1876.

49 *Government Gazette of Western Australia*, 25 June 1878, Notice No. 104.

50 SROWA, Guano. Lacepede Islands, 24/02/1877 - 03/10/1877, Cons 36, item 864, p. 105, letter from Wynne, 25 June 1877.

51 G. and K-J. Henderson, *Unfinished Voyages*, p. 213-18. Wynne's account is at SROWA, Guano. Lacepede Islands, 24/02/1877 - 03/10/1877, Cons 36, item 864, p. 15 and p. 24. For Captain Richard Wills' account, see *The Argus* (Melbourne), 26 April 1877, p. 10.

52 SROWA, Guano, 07/01/1878 - 28/12/1878, Cons 36, item 887, pp. 53–57a, Wynne letter of 10 April 1878.

53 *Inquirer*, 14 January 1880, p. 2, and 21 January 1880, Supplement, p. 1.

54 *Government Gazette of Western Australia*, 9 May 1878, pp. 118-19, notice no. 87.

55 H. P. Woodward, 'The Phosphatic Deposits of Western Australia', *Bulletin of the Geological Society of Western Australia*, vol. 74, 1917, p. 24.

56 Western Australia, *Votes & Proceedings*, 1882, Despatches 35; and *West Australian*, 20 August 1888, pp. 2-3.

57 SROWA, 1880-1888 Departmental Expenditure, Cons 1816, item 38. Wynne's budget for 1879 alone was £888, of which his salary made up £336.

58 B. Pope, 'The Quest for Two Quid! or the Postal History of the Lacepede Islands', *Black Swan*, vol. 11, no. 7, September 2004, pp. 80-2.

59 H. Taunton, *Australind: wanderings in Western Australia and the Malay East*, Edward Arnold, London, 1903, p. 189.

60 Western Australia, *Votes & Proceedings*, 1882, Paper No. 29, Minutes on the Subject of Police Protection for the Kimberley District, p. 4.

61 SROWA, Correspondence (Gribble Case), Cons 388, item 03, Government Resident Kimberley Kidnapping ..., p. 76.

62 *Government Gazette of Western Australia*, 15 November 1888, p. 708.

63 Woodward, 'The Phosphatic Deposits of Western Australia', p. 15.

64 ibid, p. 12.

65 *Government Gazette of Western Australia*, 17 July 1884, p. 379, and 14 August 1884, p. 422.

66 SROWA, Report of Police Sergeant Troy, Cons 430, item 1884/1837, 6 September 1884.

67 SROWA, Guano - General, Cons 3712, item 1898/008, letter from Louis Knoop to H. P. Woodward, 3 September 1913.

68 ibid. Also *Northern Territory Times & Gazette*, 11 September 1891, p. 3; 8 January 1892, p. 2; 15 April 1892, p. 3; 17 June 1892, p. 3.

Alexander Forrest's expedition 1879 and early development of the cattle industry

Geoffrey Bolton

At the end of the wet season in 1886 travellers in unprecedented numbers began to pass through Liveringa, then the outermost pastoral property along the Fitzroy valley in the Kimberley district. Most were prospectors, the first of hundreds attracted to the region by news of the discovery of gold at Hall's Creek, but one was significantly different. He was Willie MacDonald, who with his brother Charlie had set out three years earlier from Goulburn in New South Wales to drove cattle overland to a pastoral lease at Fossil Downs, upstream near the junction of the Fitzroy and Margaret Rivers.

It was a momentous encounter in Australian history. In 1813, little more than seventy years earlier, the first non-Aboriginal explorers crossed the Blue Mountains to launch the pastoral occupation of inland Australia. In the lifetime of one man or woman the frontier of pastoral settlement had pushed across New South Wales and Queensland, through the Northern Territory and into the East Kimberley district of Western Australia. Now Willie MacDonald, the outrider of this movement, had met up with the Western Australians who had moved north from Perth since 1829. To put it one way, the ring had closed around Aboriginal Australia. To put it another way, the two pastoral frontiers had now merged into one.

But they represented two rather different traditions. The West Kimberley leaseholders concentrated mainly on sheep, and the pioneers brought their stock by sea. A good deal of the north of Western Australia, notoriously the Ninety Mile Beach,[1] offered insufficient water and feed to support safe stock routes. The East Kimberley pastoralists were cattlemen from Queensland and New South Wales with at least half a century's tradition behind them of overlanding large mobs of stock across long distances. For this reason it became customary to speak of West and East Kimberley as two separate regions, 'the Kimberleys', although this usage is now discouraged.

Opposite
Alexander Forrest's 1879 Kimberley Expedition. Left to right starting from the back: James Carey, John Campbell, Matthew Forrest, Arthur Hicks. Front: Tommy Pierre, Fenton Hill, Alexander Forrest, Tommy Dower. Courtesy of State Library of Western Australia (66175PD, BA1741).

Editors' note: While the names applied to the men in this photo are those of the expedition members, it has not been possible to onfirm that all of the names have been correctly assigned.

As mentioned in previous papers,[2] the Camden Harbour settlement was attempted in 1864 as part of the great upsurge in interest in northern Australia that saw North Queensland occupied in the space of four years, 1861 to 1865 and the Northern Territory pass into the hands of South Australia. Camden Harbour was abandoned in 1865, but the promise of its hinterland remained to tantalise speculators.

In 1875 Alexander Forrest, a contract surveyor, was sent to the Roebourne district to map the district and assist the pastoralists in sorting out disputes about the boundaries of their leaseholds. The younger brother and loyal second-in-command of John Forrest, Alexander had shared in the glory that came of two successful transcontinental expeditions in 1870 and 1874, but understandably yearned to carve out a reputation for himself. It is very probable that while at Roebourne he picked up a hint of the promising country that lay along the Fitzroy valley beyond the inhospitable Ninety Mile Beach. He may have conversed with Aborigines; he may have taken advice from squatters such as McKenzie Grant, who became a close enough friend to serve later as godfather to one of his children; he may have consulted a less reputable source, a man named Mountain who travelled long distances to find Aborigines who could be coerced into working for the pearling fleet. All this is conjecture. What is known is that Alexander Forrest returned from the North-West with plans to conduct an expedition to the Fitzroy valley and towards Camden Harbour. By 1878 the Legislative Council was persuaded to find the money to support such an expedition. Towards the end of the wet season in February 1879 Forrest sailed from Fremantle to Cossack before overlanding north. His party consisted of Fenton Hill as geologist, John Campbell, James Carey, Arthur Hicks, a younger brother Matthew Forrest, and two Nyoongars, Tommy Pierre and Tommy Dower.

After a journey plagued by ferocious mosquitoes but otherwise uneventful they arrived at the Fitzroy in May and traced it inland to near the current site of Fitzroy Crossing, delighted with its potential for pastoral settlement and naming the geographic features as they went. In an early example of rewarding sponsorship with naming rights, Forrest christened one range of hills the Oscar Range after the King of Sweden and Norway who had contributed to the Royal Geographical Society, one of the expedition's supporters. Turning north-west with the aim of making for the Glenelg River, in the vicinity of Camden Harbour, Forrest and his party found themselves confronted with a more formidable range of mountains which he named after King Leopold of Belgium. They spent many days trying

to find a way through the range, but the country was impenetrable – in later years the old stockmen would say that you needed block and tackle to get cattle over the Leopolds – and eventually Forrest gave up. He decided instead to return to the Fitzroy and strike east across the Northern Territory border to the recently constructed Overland Telegraph Line. With no possibility of replenishing their supplies except what they could secure by way of native game, this decision was not without risk, and perhaps John Forrest would not have taken it; but Alexander was a little less careful and his gamble paid off. Following a major tributary of the Fitzroy which he named the Margaret after John Forrest's wife, he struck north-east past Mount Barrett (named for his fiancée Amy Barrett-Lennard) near the future site of the Halls Creek gold rush, discovered another large river which he named the Ord after the governor of Western Australia, and then made a dash for the Overland Telegraph, arriving near Daly Waters when their resources were all but gone.

He returned to a warm welcome. He estimated that he had discovered at least ten million hectares of good pastoral country, confidently predicted that gold would be found, and sketched the possibilities of tropical agriculture. The district – naming rights again – would be named after the earl of Kimberley, the British secretary of state for the colonies. Forrest's report came at a time when investors in Melbourne and Brisbane were looking for new worlds to conquer in northern Australia. Forrest

Above 'First arrival at the Fitzroy' (reproduced from Alex Forrest, North-West Exploration. *Journal of Expedition from DeGrey to Port Darwin*, Corkwood Press).

Top and above 'Devil's Creek, King Leopold Ranges' (reproduced from Alex Forrest, *North-West Exploration. Journal of Expedition from DeGrey to Port Darwin,* Corkwood Press) and photo of ranges from Gibb River Road.
Photo – Jeffrey Gresham

Right Alexander Forrest's 1879 route through the Kimberley.

cannily set himself up in an office in Howick Street (now the eastern half of Hay Street) and offered his services as a consultant to prospective investors. He also made sure that the attractions of the Kimberley district were advertised at the great Melbourne exhibition of 1880.

In October 1880 applications were invited for pastoral leases in the Kimberley district, attracting an immediate response. Balloting for the first allocations of leases took place on 1 February 1881. In the next three years applications were lodged for leaseholds totalling more than 20 million hectares. Many of the applicants were 'map graziers', speculators vying for a piece of land with river frontages without setting eyes on the country. Some were Melbourne investors who had burnt their fingers in the Camden Harbour project. One was a travelling English aristocrat, the Duke of Manchester. But some were members of Western Australian families who had established themselves in the South-West and were looking for opportunities for their younger generation. In a meticulous piece of detective work Cathie Clement has shown how the allocation of leases by the Survey Department sometimes worked in favour of the local applicants. It also helped applicants from outside Western Australia – mostly from the eastern colonies, but a few English – if they were thoughtful enough to employ Alexander Forrest as their agent. Gradually the scramble sorted itself out. Many investors fell away; the remainder consolidated their holdings. For instance the Duracks and the Emanuels, who were working in co-operation, reached an agreement that the Duracks would concentrate their holdings on the Ord River while the Emanuels would take up a range of leases along the Fitzroy valley including the future Gogo and Noonkanbah stations.

What was the attraction? Twenty years earlier the north of Queensland came under pastoral occupation at a similarly hectic pace, but it was relatively closer to established settlement and soon reinforced by the sugar industry using cheap indentured Melanesian labour. Even so, many pastoralists failed. The cattle industry was saved largely by the discovery of gold at centres such as Charters Towers, Ravenswood and the Palmer, thus creating a strong local demand for beef. In 1883 the outlook for the Kimberley district was less certain. An editorial in *The West Australian* put the optimistic view:

> The enterprising young pastoralist with moderate means is obliged to start for the 'Never-never.' And a 'Never-never' with, apparently, so much to recommend it as our new Kimberley district was at the time of its discovery a perfect godsend to the Eastern squattocracy, as well as to ourselves, to whom it has given a progressive spurt such as we have never experienced before.

Doubts would have been excusable. Although ports were declared in 1883 at Broome and Derby it would take time to build jetties and other facilities, and they were hundreds of kilometres from the Ord valley. The discovery of gold could not be taken for granted. With only 30,000 non-Aboriginal inhabitants in Western Australia and a much smaller number in the Northern Territory, there was otherwise not much prospect of penetrating established markets in eastern Australia. Once established in the Kimberley district the pastoralists would make several attempts to test markets in Southeast Asia, but such thinking was not common in the early 1880s. And yet the squatters came.

Assisted by closer proximity, the Western Australian investors in West Kimberley were the first to stock their leases. Indeed George Julius Brockman jumped the gun by sailing to Beagle Bay with sheep before the Survey Department had officially opened the district. Others followed, among them the Murray Squatting Company, made up as its name suggested by young men from around Pinjarra, and the Kimberley Pastoral Company whose shareholders were mainly Fremantle investors. They soon encountered their share of hazards. Alexander Forrest had reported that he experienced no trouble with the Aborigines, and maybe this was due to the diplomacy of the Nyoongar members of his party, Pierre and Dower. But when the newcomers and their sheep indicated that they wanted to stay in the Fitzroy valley permanently, the picture became less rosy. The spearing of Hamlet Cornish in 1882 initiated fifteen years of hostilities in West Kimberley that ended only in 1897 with the death of Jandamarra (Pigeon) and the end of organised Bunuba resistance. Nor were the elements friendly. As an old man George Rose, whom Alexander Forrest had sent to manage Yeeda station, recalled how in 1883 they had shorn twenty-one bales of wool and taken them to the mangrove flats which would be the future site of the port of Derby, there to await the arrival of a flat-bottomed lighter that would take the wool to a waiting ship. Suddenly a huge tsunami swept up King Sound and the year's wool vanished into the waters. He wondered what God or Nature was telling him. It was only months later that he learned of the great volcanic eruption at Krakatoa that had stirred up the ocean.

More than the Western Australian sheep graziers, the overlanders from Queensland and New South Wales have stirred the imaginations of future generations. Three large parties with beef cattle made the crossing between 1883 and 1885. First to arrive

were the veteran drovers Nat Buchanan and Bob Button in charge of stock for the Melbourne investors, Osmand and Panton, who took up Plympton St Mary, soon better known as the Ord River station. Members of the Durack family and their associates came to settle Argyle, Rosewood and Lissadell stations on the lower Ord. An even longer journey was undertaken by the MacDonald brothers of Goulburn, who were to take up Fossil Downs further west on the upper Fitzroy. All successfully completed their treks and established themselves for many years.

Questions remain about their achievement. The overlanders had to cope not only with the Aborigines through whose lands they passed, but also the established pastoralists in Queensland and the Northern Territory. 'Banjo' Paterson has summed up the issues:

> Now this is the law of the Overland, that all the West obey;
> A man with travelling stock must cover at least six miles a day.
> But this is the law that the drover makes, and it's easily understood:
> They do their stint when the grass is poor, but they camp when the grass is good.

1883 was a bad season in north and central Queensland, and feed was poor. Pastoralists in the region did not welcome the impact along the stock routes of several large herds of travelling cattle, totalling in all more than twelve thousand. This side of overlanding

Above 'Droving cattle Kimberleys'.
Courtesy of State Library of Western Australia (5458B/23, Reg Durack Collection).

does not feature prominently in *Kings in Grass Castles*, but Geraldine Byrne in her account of the Kilfoyle family, *Tom & Jack*, is more candid. She has uncovered evidence of more than one altercation between local men and travelling overlanders. One fight eventually came before the Cloncurry magistrate.

Byrne also offers some insights into the processes by which the overlanders came to terms with the Indigenous occupants of the Ord Valley. Mary Durack gave considerable credit to the mediatory role of the Duracks' Queensland Aboriginal employees. But Chris Owen, drawing on a study of contemporary police and welfare records, reports one of the Duracks as stating in 1896:

> In former years I used to treat [the bush natives] kindly, I killed bullocks and fed them: they returned my kindness by driving my bullocks over the ranges, and scattering them on the runs and now I have turned "dog" on them now.

Byrne finds grounds for believing that Tom Kilfoyle on Rosewood found it easiest to turn a blind eye to occasional stock losses. We in the early 21st century must avoid easy generalisation about the first generation of racial contact in Kimberley.

Fortune favoured the new arrivals in East Kimberley. Alexander Forrest's hints of gold-bearing country attracted the attention of several prospectors from the Northern Territory. In 1885 Charlie Hall and his party found promising traces of colour in the region that soon became known as Hall's Creek. The news provoked a short-lived gold rush in 1886.[3] Perhaps 1,500 men found their way to the new field, some overlanding, but most arriving through Derby or the hastily established new port at Wyndham on Cambridge Gulf. The cattlemen had their market. M. P. Durack all his life remembered celebrating his twenty-first birthday by selling a mob of cattle to a Halls Creek butcher who paid £13 for heifers and £17 for steers – glittering prices which would not last.

But it was enough to entrench the cattlemen in the East Kimberley. Others followed on a smaller scale, especially as economic recession began to grip the bush workers in Queensland. Several decided to try their luck in the Kimberley. An observer wrote:

> They travelled along the long, long northern trail where they were helped considerably on their journey by the hospitable cattle-stations … As to beef supplied free to travellers, that gratuity was in most cases an enforced one; many would have helped themselves to a fat steer on the run, as all were armed and usually carried salt ready for emergencies.

Family groups were rare among these travellers, making the saga of Joseph Bridge and his wife Deborah notable. Seeing no prospects in Queensland they left Normanton in 1895 in a covered van drawn by bullocks. They were accompanied by their children, the oldest of them the ten-year-old Mabel who was usually employed in leading the team. Arriving in Western Australia with his family and livestock intact, Joseph Bridge took up a small leasehold at Cartridge Springs north of Halls Creek. He was one of a number of battlers arriving in that district in the 1890s who were frequently suspected – who knows how justly? – of helping themselves to the cleanskin calves of larger neighbours. The family took root in the district. A grandson, Ernie Bridge, became a well-known performer of country and western music, a respected local businessman, chairman of the Halls Creek council, local member of parliament, and eventually entered the history books as Western Australia's first cabinet minister of Aboriginal descent.

Gradually the overlanders passed into Australian folklore. In 1949 'The Overlanders' was the name given to a popular film. It was set in the recent past and was not about the pioneers of the 1880s, but M. P. Durack, the surviving patriarch of his family, was invited to the premiere. They asked the old gentleman how he had enjoyed the film. He said he liked it very well, but one thing puzzled him: how was it that the young drovers in the story had set out with a mob of Herefords and ended up with a mob of Shorthorns?

Above 'On cattle camp, Big Lagoon, Argyle Station, ca. 1930'. Courtesy of State Library of Western Australia (061513PD, BA1222/30, Reg Durack Collection).

M. P. Durack kept diaries every day of his life from 1886 until his death in 1950. His daughter Mary Durack used these diaries, together with interviews with elderly members of the family, as the basis for *Kings in Grass Castles*, the first of an intended trilogy. It appeared in 1959. One year earlier Russel Ward achieved fame with the publication of *The Australian Legend*, portraying the nomadic bush workers of the outback as the founders of the Australian national character. Both works found instant popularity in the Australia of Robert Menzies, venturing hesitantly into an urbanising and multicultural future and ready to respond nostalgically to the epic resonances of pastoral myths. Ward's 'Legend' soon became a chopping block for historians with alternative interpretations, but *Kings in Grass Castles* remained unchallenged. The development of the Ord River scheme helped to entrench the legend. The early beginnings of the scheme owed much to the advocacy of Kim Durack, brother of Mary and Elizabeth. The huge dam created on the Ord was given the name of Lake Argyle after the Duracks' main station. While part of the homestead was drowned nine fathoms deep, the remainder was moved to a site overlooking the dam, and rebuilt as a memorial to the family, attracting hundreds of tourists each year.

In 2003 a dissonant voice was raised. In a *Quarterly Essay*, 'Whitefella jump up', largely devoted to praise of the Aboriginal mode of adaptation to the Australian environment, Germaine Greer took a gratuitous swipe at the overlander legend. She wrote:

> The ultimate purpose of a book like *Kings in Grass Castles* is to elevate the squattocracy, deservedly loathed by the Aussie battler, to heroic status. In such hagiography rank opportunists are credited with "courage" and "vision" rather than simple greed and land-hunger. Ironically, the Duracks came from the lowest of the low, at least in the estimation of British landowners, for they were aboriginal Irish, known as "black", "bog" or "wild" Irish... As soon as they accumulated spare cash they began to ape the manners of their old oppressors.

Not surprisingly this drew spirited responses from Patsy Millett and Perpetua Durack Clancy, respectively daughters of Mary and Elizabeth Durack.

It is odd that a feminist like Germaine Greer should have missed the point of Mary Durack's work. Russel Ward had given a masculine account of the outback in which women and children played little part. Not only in writing about her own family, but in recovering the story of others like the Bridge family, Mary Durack reminded us that the story of the pastoral frontier is not merely the story of the blokes. The iconic status of the overlanding tradition will probably never be dethroned, not even by such travesties as Baz

Luhrman's 'Australia', but the story of the Kimberley frontier would be incomplete without the women and children. Mary Durack's writing restored them to the historical record.

Above Granites, south west of Halls Creek. Photo – Mike Donaldson

Notes

1 Ian Murray with Marion Hercock, *Where on the Coast is That?*, Hesperian Press, Carlisle (WA), 2008, p. 95, states that the name of Ninety Mile Beach was changed to Eighty Mile Beach in 1915 but reverted to its earlier name several times before 'it was finally determined and approved as "Eighty Mile Beach" in July 1961'.

2 See Tony Quinlan, '1865 – Camden Harbour – The Quinlan Connection', this volume, for comment on the settlement and its abandonment.

3 See Phillip Playford, 'The Kimberley gold rush of 1885–1886', this volume, for further discussion.

References

Bolton, G. C. A survey of the Kimberley Pastoral Industry from 1885 to the Present. M.A. thesis, UWA, 1953.

Bolton, G. C. *Alexander Forrest: His Life and Times*. Melbourne University Press, Carlton, 1958.

Buchanan, Gordon. *Packhorse and Waterhole with the First Overlanders to the Kimberleys*. Angus & Robertson Limited, Australia, 1933, facsimile edition, Hesperian Press, Carlisle, 1984.

Byrne, Geraldine. *Tom & Jack: A Frontier Story*. Fremantle Arts Centre Press, Fremantle, 2003.

Clement, Cathie. Pastoral Leasing in the Kimberley District of Western Australia. B.A. Honours thesis, Murdoch University, 1982.

Clement, Cathie. Australia's North-west: A Study of Exploration, Land Policy and Land Acquisition, 1644-1884, Ph.D. thesis, Murdoch University, 1991.

Durack, Mary. *Kings in Grass Castles*. Constable and Company Limited, London, 1959.

Durack, Mary. *Sons in the Saddle*. Constable and Company Ltd., London, 1983.

Forrest, Alex. 'North-west Exploration: Journal of Expedition from DeGrey to Port Darwin', *Western Australia Parliamentary Papers*, No. 3 of 1880. A facsimile edition was published by Corkwood Press, Bundaberg, 1996.

Keene, Derek. *The Kimberley Bridges*. Privately published, Halls Creek, no date.

Owen, Chris. '"The police appear to be a useless lot up there": law and order in the East Kimberley 1884–1905', *Aboriginal History*, vol. 27, 2003, pp. 105–30.

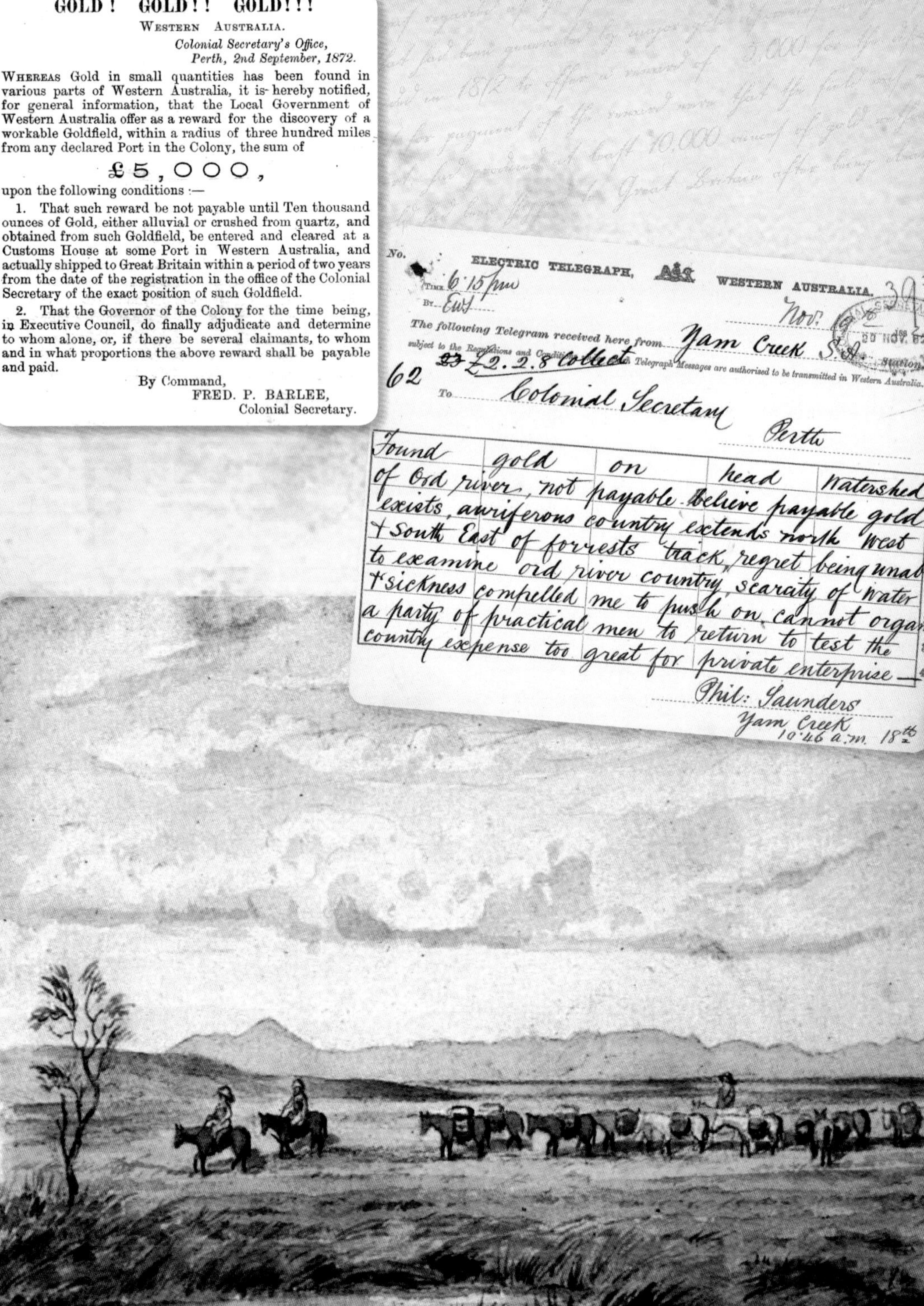

GOLD! GOLD!! GOLD!!!

WESTERN AUSTRALIA.

Colonial Secretary's Office,
Perth, 2nd September, 1872.

WHEREAS Gold in small quantities has been found in various parts of Western Australia, it is hereby notified, for general information, that the Local Government of Western Australia offer as a reward for the discovery of a workable Goldfield, within a radius of three hundred miles from any declared Port in the Colony, the sum of

£5,000,

upon the following conditions:—

1. That such reward be not payable until Ten thousand ounces of Gold, either alluvial or crushed from quartz, and obtained from such Goldfield, be entered and cleared at a Customs House at some Port in Western Australia, and actually shipped to Great Britain within a period of two years from the date of the registration in the office of the Colonial Secretary of the exact position of such Goldfield.

2. That the Governor of the Colony for the time being, in Executive Council, do finally adjudicate and determine to whom alone, or, if there be several claimants, to whom and in what proportions the above reward shall be payable and paid.

By Command,
FRED. P. BARLEE,
Colonial Secretary.

No.
ELECTRIC TELEGRAPH, WESTERN AUSTRALIA.
TIME 6.15 pm
BY EWJ
Nov. 18
The following Telegram received here from Yam Creek S.A. Station
subject to the Regulations and Conditions ... Telegraph Messages are authorised to be transmitted in Western Australia.
~~23~~ £2.2.8 Collect
62
To Colonial Secretary
Perth

Found gold on head of Ord river, not payable. Believe payable gold exists, auriferous country extends north West & South East of Forrests track, regret being unable to examine Ord river country, scarcity of water & sickness compelled me to push on, cannot organise a party of practical men to return to test the country expense too great for private enterprise—

Phil: Saunders
Yam Creek
10.46 a.m. 18th

The Kimberley gold rush of 1885–1886

Phillip Playford

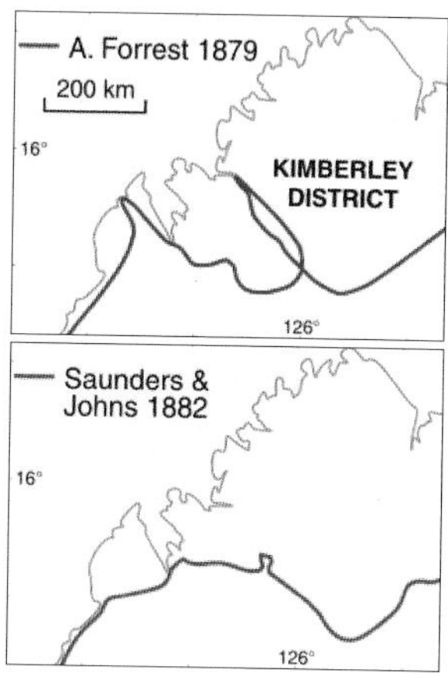

Opposite (top left) Figure 1. Public announcement by the Colonial Secretary, Western Australia, dated 2 September 1872, stating that a reward of £5,000 would be paid for the discovery of a 'workable' goldfield in the colony.

This page (top) Figure 2. Route followed by Alexander Forrest in 1879, when exploring the Kimberley District of Western Australia.

This page (above) Figure 3. Route followed by Philip Saunders and Adam Johns on their prospecting expedition to the Kimberley District in 1882.

Opposite (top right) Figure 4. Telegram sent by Philip Saunders to the Colonial Secretary in Perth from Yam Creek (in the northern territory of South Australia), announcing the discovery of gold in the 'head watershed of the Ord River'.

Opposite (bottom) Painting by Edward T. Hardman showing the cavalcade of the 1884 expedition passing Grant Range.

Western Australia (WA) in the mid 1800s was regarded as the 'poor relation' of the other Australian colonies. The citizens of WA envied the wealth that had been generated by major gold discoveries in the eastern colonies. As a result, the WA Government decided in 1872 to offer a reward of £5,000 for the discovery of the colony's first payable goldfield. Conditions for payment of the reward were that the field was within 300 miles (480 kilometres) of a declared port, had produced at least 10,000 ounces of gold within two years of registration of the discovery, and the gold had been shipped to Great Britain after being cleared at a Customs House of the colony (Fig. 1).

The Kimberley gold story began in 1879 with the exploring expedition of Alexander Forrest (Fig. 2). He crossed the Kimberley from west to east and continued across the border into the then northern territory of South Australia.[1] On reaching the Pine Creek gold-mining settlement he mentioned to the manager of the mine, Adam Johns, that he had observed similarities between the rocks at Pine Creek and those that his party had seen in the Kimberley. This inspired Johns to sponsor an expedition to look for gold in the Kimberley, with his mate Philip Saunders as party leader, together with James Quinn and Crawford (an Aborigine).

In July 1881 the party sailed from Port Darwin to Cossack, and after prospecting in the Ashburton River and Whim Creek areas, moved on to the Kimberley District in April 1882 (Fig. 3). In that district they found traces of gold at several places during August-September 1882, especially in the headwaters of the Ord River, probably near the present town of Halls Creek. Saunders reported this discovery in a telegram to the WA Colonial Secretary, indicating his belief that payable gold could probably be found in the area (Fig. 4).

In September 1882 there was spirited debate in the WA Legislative Council as to the best way of following up this exciting report. Some held the view that it would be desirable to send a geologist to examine the area, but others were scathing in expressing their

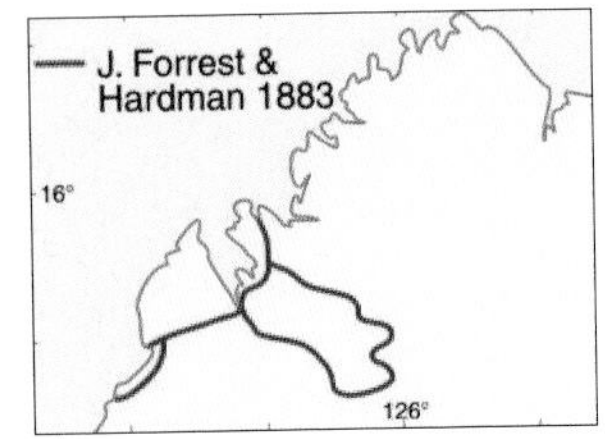

opinions about geology and geologists. One prominent member, Mr Septimus Burt, stated that 'people didn't want to know whether it is Eocene, Miocene, Pliocene or any technical rubbish like that… this "competent geologist" would only run about the Kimberley District in a trap or on horseback, and eat bacon and eggs'. Another prominent member, Mr McKenzie Grant, said that: 'Geologists never discover anything of practical advantage … why should we go to the expense of sending a geologist to accompany this survey party to Kimberley … it would only be money thrown away'.

The Legislative Council decided to invite Philip Saunders to prospect the area, and he responded with a detailed prospecting proposal. However, a request was also sent to the British Geological Survey inviting the nomination of a geologist to assess the gold and other mineral prospects of the colony. It was decided that Edward T. Hardman of the Irish Geological Survey would be appointed as a temporary Government Geologist to examine the Kimberley, and Saunders' proposal was rejected.

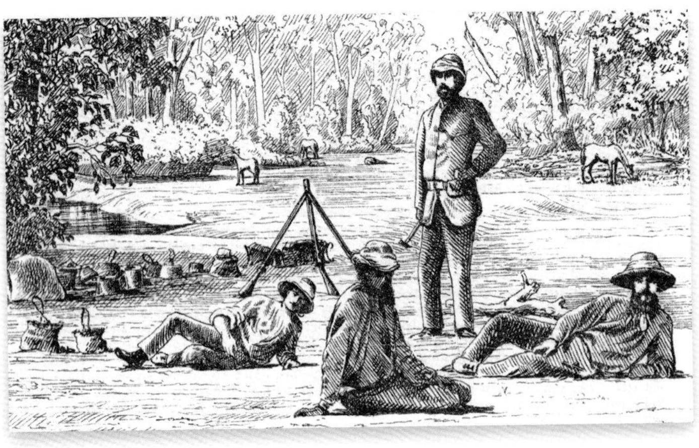

Above Figure 5. Route followed by John Forrest and Edward Hardman in 1883 while exploring the west Kimberley District.

Right Figure 6. Sketch taken from a photograph by John Forrest of members of his party exploring the west Kimberley in 1883. Edward Hardman is shown standing and holding his geological hammer.

Hardman's first task was to join John Forrest's survey expedition to the West Kimberley in 1883 (Figs 5–10). However, he found no positive signs of gold on that expedition.[2]

In the following year, 1884, Hardman accompanied a second surveying expedition, led by H. F. Johnston, this time to the East Kimberley (Figs 11–14). Hardman panned gold in several watercourses in that area, especially in the headwaters of the Elvire River, where the Halls Creek gold discovery would be made in 1885 by Charles Hall and his party. On Hardman's map showing the headwaters of the Elvire River (Fig. 14) he noted that 'The country colored thus (pink) is probably all more or less auriferous. It shows multitudes of quartz reefs, and gold colors have been obtained in the alluvium wherever examined'.[3]

Above Figure 7. Watercolour painting of Port Usborne on the west Kimberley coast, by Edward T. Hardman, 1883.

Above left Figure 8. Watercolour painting by Edward T. Hardman of a dead Brolga (Native Companion) held by a member of the 1883 expedition.

Left Figure 9. Drawing from a sketch by Edward T. Hardman of the west entrance to Windjana Gorge ('Devil's Pass'), showing members of the 1883 expedition, including Hardman himself again holding his geological hammer.

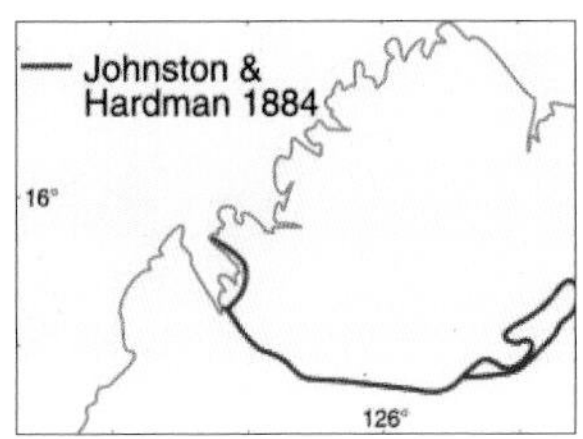

Top Figure 10. Drawing from a sketch by Edward T. Hardman of the south entrance to Geikie Gorge, showing an Aborigine crossing the Fitzroy River on a small raft.

Above Figure 11. Route followed by Harry F. Johnston and Edward T. Hardman when exploring the Kimberley District in 1884.

Hardman's published reports on his two expeditions included impressive coloured geological maps. I found during preparation of a talk on the discovery of gold in the Kimberley, delivered to the Kimberley Society in March 2005, that the only copies of Hardman's two maps held by the Geological Survey of WA had deteriorated badly; indeed they were falling apart. Consequently it was arranged for them to be scanned and repaired electronically, so that near-perfect copies are now available.

Hardman's notebooks and field illustrations were long thought to have been lost. However, that belief proved to be incorrect, at least in part. In 1988 Mr and Mrs A. B. (Tony) Wood of Perth were touring England, and while visiting a small village in the Lake District they sat down in a tea-shop beside an English couple, Mr and Mrs W. Konieczny of Thirsk, Yorkshire. In conversation with them, which soon turned to Australia, the Woods learned that the couple had found five old notebooks dealing with expeditions to the Kimberley District in 1883 and 1884. They included geological information, watercolour paintings, and pencil sketches. It seemed that when the couple had purchased their home in Thirsk in 1954, they had found an old tea-chest in the coal-shed that contained numerous old books and periodicals, left there by a previous occupant. They discarded most of this material as rubbish but decided that the notebooks and sketchbooks were sufficiently interesting to be worth keeping. As a result, they were stored for some 25 years in the old stables attached to the house, surviving several 'purges' when they could easily have been discarded.

The notebooks and sketches came to light again when the Konieczny's decided to renovate their home, by which time they had become more interested in 'things antique' and realized that the material was of historic importance. They noted the initials E.T.H. and the name Kimberley in the books, and initially thought that they related to the Kimberley District of South Africa. However, in 1986 a visitor who had worked with the Australian Archives suggested that the name 'Kimberley' referred to the Kimberley District in Western Australia, and enquiries showed that the initials E.T.H. stood for Edward Townley Hardman. The Koniecznys obtained documentary material on Hardman from the Australian High Commission, including my entry on Hardman in the *Australian Dictionary of Biography*.[4] They mentioned this to Tony Wood, who told them with some amazement that he had known me since childhood (we lived nearby in South Perth) and said that he and his wife would like to see the material. Consequently they visited the Koniecznys at their home in Thirsk, and arranged to purchase the notebooks and sketches. After consulting with me on returning to WA, the Woods generously donated the material to the J. S. Battye Library of West Australian History, and kindly allowed me to take photos and photocopies of the paintings.

The saga of Hardman's notebooks did not end there. In 1991 an Englishman named Neville Peat came into my office at the Geological Survey, having been directed there by staff of the Battye Library. He told me that he had found several old notebooks in the loft of his home in Thirsk, which turned out to be next door to the house of Mr and Mrs Konieczny. From his description it was clear that these were further Hardman notebooks. The Konieczny property had originally constituted a cottage, barn, and stables in a property that included the Peat house, and it appears that the Hardman documents must have been taken there from Dublin at some time during the 20-odd years between Hardman's death in 1887 and the early 1900s, when Neville Peat's father, as a small child, wrote in one of the notebooks. How this transfer from Ireland to Yorkshire took place is unknown, as neither Hardman's widow nor his daughter (who lived together and eventually died in Glasgow) nor his son (whose movements after his father's death are unknown) are known to have lived in Thirsk. However, it is possible that careful historical research on these three persons will eventually unravel the mystery.

The notebooks in question were at that time (1991) held by Neville Peat's brother Noel, who lived elsewhere in England, so I wrote to him and it was arranged for the notebooks to be sent to Neville in Perth. He then allowed me to take photos and photocopies of pages in the notebooks before arranging for them to be auctioned. I am not aware, nor is Mr Peat, of the name of the purchaser.

Scanned images of several of Hardman's paintings and sketches from the 1883 and 1884 expeditions (Figs 7–10, 12 & 13) were first shown during the 2005 Kimberley Society presentation, along with others by Arthur Forbes (Figs 15 & 16), who in 1886-1890 was a police constable, Clerk of Courts, and clerk to the Mining Registrar at Halls Creek.[5] Forbes was an accomplished artist, and his paintings and sketches vividly portray life on the goldfield and its environs as well as the conflicts that occurred with the Aboriginal inhabitants of the area.[6]

In early 1885, as soon as Hardman's report and map were released, several prospecting parties set off for the East Kimberley. One of these, consisting of Charles Hall (leader), John Slattery, Alexander Nicholson, Joseph McCague, John Campbell, and Augustus Pontt, travelled from Derby to the Elvire River area, where Hardman had reported his best gold showings (Fig. 14). They succeeded in finding payable gold in the headwaters of the Elvire River on 14 July 1885, at what they named 'Halls Creek',[7] formally reporting their discovery at Derby on 8 August 1885.[8]

As soon as the find became known, the Kimberley gold rush began, building up from relatively small numbers in 1885 to an avalanche in 1886. Thousands of men made their way to the Kimberley, from other parts of WA, the eastern colonies, and New Zealand. Most arrived by ship at Derby or (later) Wyndham, and then walked to Halls Creek, covering distances of about 600 kilometres from Derby and 400 kilometres from Wyndham. Others came overland from the

Right Figure 12. Members of the 1884 expedition at Point Torment. Said to have been 'a pleasant nightmare' while 'enjoying our privileges'.

northern territory of South Australia. They were from all walks of life, and most had no previous experience in gold prospecting or of life in the remote bush. Illness and disease were rife at the diggings, and when the first warden, C. D. Price, arrived on 3 September 1886, he wrote that 'great numbers were stricken down, in a dying condition, helpless, destitute of either money, food, or covering, and without mates or friends simply lying down to die'.

The Perth *Inquirer and Commercial News* reported in April 1887 that 'it was a pitiful sight to see men almost starving, selling all their possessions for a few shillings to get out of the country ... they had lost their all and many had wives and families to support ... poor deluded wretches, they will never forget Kimberley'. In November 1886 the same paper reported that 'not one in ten of the new arrivals give the place a day's trial; they sell their provisions and return ... but those without means have to remain'. Further, that 'these men, many of whom wheeled barrows and carried swags to the fields, embrace the traits most valued in national characters — pluck, endurance, and determination to overcome all obstacles ... but they may not enrich themselves until better country is discovered'. Similar articles appeared in newspapers in the eastern colonies and New Zealand.

Above Figure 13. Painting by Edward T. Hardman in 1884 of Caroline Pool in the east Kimberley. The town of Halls Creek was established nearby in 1886.

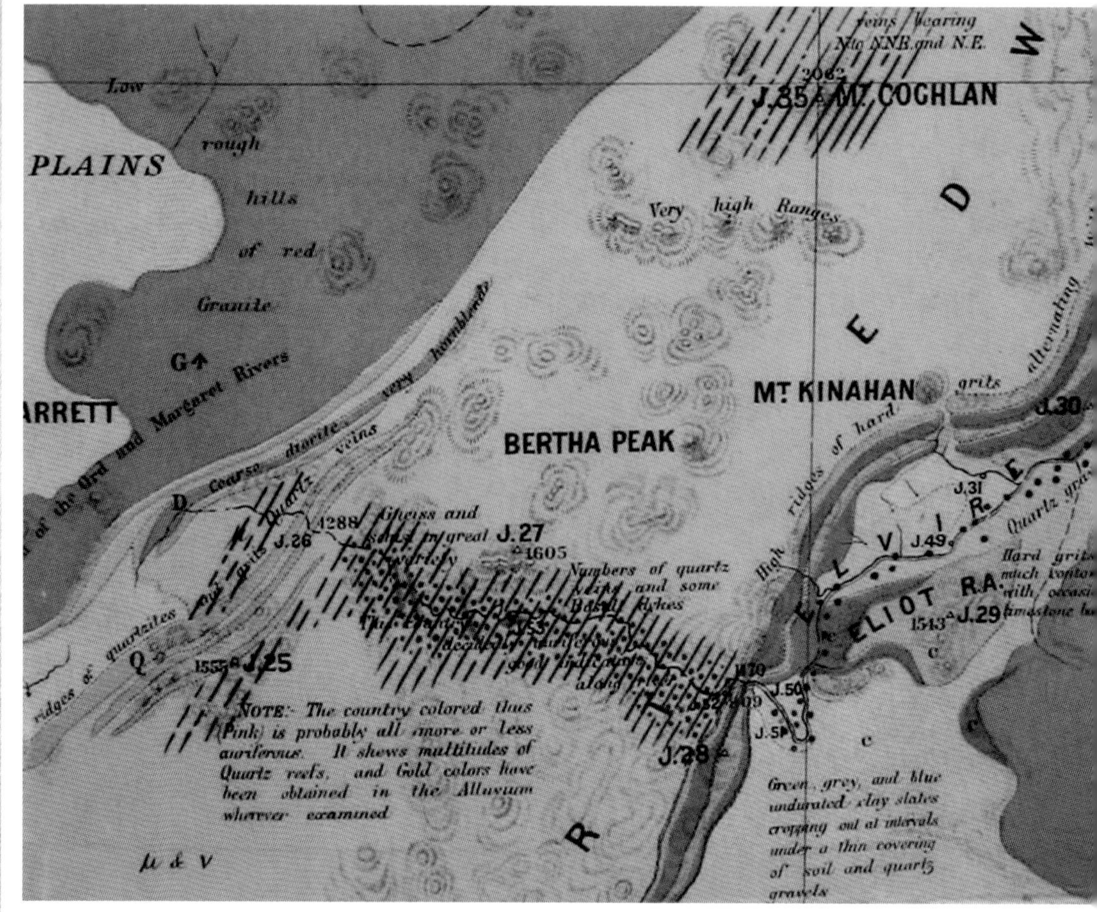

Most men found little or no gold and very few were lucky enough to locate rich alluvial or reef gold. Of those who arrived at the field with possessions, most sold or exchanged them for food within a day or two of arrival, and then made their way back to the ports, to escape the misery of life in Halls Creek. Those who had no possessions were compelled to remain, some finding enough gold to survive or move elsewhere in the colony.

Warden Price reported that there were about 2,000 men at the diggings when he arrived in September 1886, although it seems clear that the total number who had earlier joined the rush were four or five times that number. By the end of 1886 the rush had ceased, and in February 1887 only about 600 remained at the field.

Above Figure 14. Part of the geological map of the east Kimberley by Edward T. Hardman, illustrating localities where he found traces of gold.

In spite of the early promise of several underground mines, Halls Creek never prospered, as ore in those mines petered out at depth. The field was never more than a minor producer. However, the Kimberley gold rush drew world attention to the colony and its gold prospects, and some of the experienced prospectors who took

part in the rush moved on to make rich gold discoveries in the Pilbara and Southern Cross districts (1888), the Murchison (1891), Coolgardie (1892) and Kalgoorlie (1893). Those major discoveries captured the imagination of the world, resulting in a flood of immigrants and investment capital that transformed Western Australia from an impoverished colony in the late 1880s to one of Australia's wealthiest States at the time of Federation in 1901.

Applications for the £5,000 reward for the gold discovery were lodged by H. F. Johnston, E. T. Hardman, P. Saunders, C. Hall and party, and several others who had found gold in the Halls Creek area. Johnston based his claim on the fact that he was the leader of the survey party when gold was first found, while Hardman based his on being the person who had actually discovered traces of gold and reported that discovery. Hardman was scathing in his criticism of Johnston, saying that he had hindered, rather than facilitated, the discovery of gold.

Top Figure 15. Painting by Arthur Forbes: 'The Kimberley Rush – 1886', showing men and their belongings hauling a horse and cart along the track from Wyndham to Halls Creek. Painting from C. Clement and P. J. Bridge, *Kimberley Scenes*, Hesperian Press, Carlisle (WA), 1991.

Above Figure 16. Painting by Arthur Forbes: 'Warden and gold escort, Kimberley WA 1886'.

Both paintings courtesy of M. Barber.

Hall and party's claim rested on the fact that they were the first to report the discovery of payable gold at Halls Creek, in 1885. Saunders did not himself lodge a claim, but a submission received from a Justice of the Peace in South Australia was taken as an application on behalf of Saunders. That submission pointed out that Saunders had been the first to actually report signs of gold in the headwaters of the Ord River, near the site of what would become known as Halls Creek.

Hardman left Western Australia for Ireland in 1885, resuming his duties with the Geological Survey of Ireland. Sadly, he died of typhoid in Dublin on 6 April 1887 at the age of 42 years, leaving a wife and two small children. Prior to his death he had not been aware that his stated ambition to return to Western Australia would have soon been realized. An offer of appointment to the permanent position of Government Geologist (and founder of the Geological Survey of Western Australia) was approved by the Legislative Council on 13 June 1887, and an offer of appointment sent to him by mail. Soon afterwards members were shocked to learn of Hardman's death.

At the time of Hardman's death no decision had been made regarding payment of the reward. The Government eventually decided, on 31 May 1888, that the conditions for payment had not been met, and therefore the reward would not be paid to anyone. The main reason was that output from the field in the two years from 1885 had been less than the required 10,000 ounces. Total recorded production from 1886 to 1888 amounted to 8,668 ounces. However, the Government must have been aware, but did not wish to acknowledge, that the actual production had been much greater than this, perhaps amounting to more than 20,000 ounces, as claimed by Charles Hall. This was because Western Australia, alone among the colonies, put a duty of two shillings and sixpence an ounce on gold, and some miners consequently preferred to smuggle their gold out of the colony.

When the announcement withdrawing the reward was made, it was declared that a 'gift' of £500 would be made to Hardman's widow and an ex-gratia payment of £500 would go to Hall, Slattery, and party. None of the recipients were satisfied with this; indeed they objected strongly, but to no avail. Over the next four years Hall's party sued the Government three times and presented a formal petition to the Legislative Council, but those costly exercises were all unsuccessful. The last word from Hall came in a sad letter to John Forrest, written from Madagascar in 1896. There seems to have been no reply to this letter, and Hall presumably died in Madagascar as a broken man.

Opposite
Aerial view of Wyndham and The Bastion Range looking north, taken in 2006. The old town, seen in the left centre, was founded in 1886, to serve prospectors wishing to join the Kimberley gold rush to Halls Creek. It is now Wyndham's port. The modern town is situated at the foot of the Bastion in the right centre, with the main channel of Cambridge Gulf on the left. Note the wide tidal flats and channels lined with mangroves.
Photo – Phil Playford

The last appeal from one of Hardman's descendants was made in 1956, when his daughter, Bertha Hardman, wrote to the Prime Minister of Australia asking whether the Government could assist her, as she was then living under straightened circumstances in retirement in Glasgow. She said that her father had died at an early age because his health had suffered through trekking over the North West districts where he had to live on damper and poor food. Bertha Hardman's appeal was unsuccessful, but it did have the effect of reactivating the Mines Department file entitled 'Reward for discovery of the Kimberley Gold Field, applications for', which was otherwise due to be destroyed as it had not been accessed for many years. Today's policy of archiving such files did not apply at that time. Much of my information on the Kimberley gold discovery is derived from that file.

The other prominent applicant for the reward was Phil Saunders. He was a prospector who was held in the highest regard and affection by all who knew him, from diggers to politicians. Saunders never pressed his case for the reward, but many people who knew him felt that he deserved appropriate recognition as the first person to find gold in the Kimberley. In 1907 he was 70 years old and working a small gold show, with minimal returns, near Mt Ida (NNW of Kalgoorlie). The Mt Ida Progress Association wrote to the Minister for Mines asking that Saunders be granted an appropriate annuity by the Government in view of his many contributions to gold prospecting in WA. The Government reacted slowly to this request, until the Progress Association again wrote saying that 'the old gentleman is now rapidly declining and almost blind' and that he would appreciate receiving appropriate relief to assist him when 'his life is apparently very near its close'.

This moving appeal had the desired effect, and Saunders was immediately granted a Government pension of £70 per year. If he was really close to death in 1907, he recovered well after receiving the annuity. Indeed he lived on for another 24 years, dying in 1931 at the age of 93 years from the effects of rolling into his camp fire. Saunders received far more recompense than the other discoverers of gold in the Kimberley or their heirs — he received a total of £1800 compared with £500 to Hall and party and £500 to Hardman's widow. Saunders' grave in the Kalgoorlie cemetery is marked by an impressive monument, erected by the WA Historical Society and the State Government, recognizing that he had been the first to report the presence of gold in the Kimberley (Figs 17 & 18).

Left Figure 17. The grave of Philip Saunders in Kalgoorlie cemetery, funded by the WA Historical Society (through public subscription) and the WA Government.

Below left Figure 18. The headstone of the grave of Philip Saunders in Kalgoorlie cemetery. It is noted that the spelling of his first name is incorrect on the headstone.

There can be no doubt that the discovery of the Kimberley Goldfield and the dramatic rush that followed are among the most important events in the history of Western Australia. They marked the beginning of our gold-mining industry, and eventually led to the major mining developments that have placed Western Australia among the world's foremost mining provinces. Our huge and diverse mining industry, which had its true beginnings in Halls Creek, now dominates the Western Australian economy.

Notes

1 See Geoffrey Bolton, 'Alexander Forrest's expedition 1879 and early development of the cattle industry', this volume, for further discussion.

2 E. T. Hardman, 'Report on the geology of the Kimberley District, Western Australia', *Western Australia Parliamentary Papers*, no. 31 of 1884.

3 E. T. Hardman, 'Report on the geology of the Kimberley District, Western Australia', *Western Australia Parliamentary Papers*, no. 34 of 1885.

4 P. E. Playford, 'Hardman, Edward Townley (1845 – 1887)', *Australian Dictionary of Biography*, vol. 4, 1972, p. 342, accessible at http://adbonline.anu.edu.au/biogs/A040387b.htm.

5 C. Clement and P. J. Bridge, *Kimberley Scenes*, Hesperian Press, Carlisle (WA), 1991, p. 259.

6 P. E. Playford, 'The discovery of the East Kimberley Goldfield 1885', *Boab Bulletin*, vol. 70, 2005.

7 C. Clement, *Old Halls Creek: A town remembered*, National Heritage, Mt Lawley (WA), 2000.

8 P. E. Playford and I. Ruddock, 'Discovery of the Kimberley Goldfield', *Early Days*, Journal of the Royal Western Australian Historical Society, vol. 9, part 3, 1985, pp. 76–106. P. E. Playford, 'The Kimberley gold rush of 1885–1886', *Geological Survey of Western Australia Annual Review 2004–05*, pp. 33–7.

Joseph Bradshaw – Getting lost in the Kimberley and the art he found

Michael Cusack

Phillip Parker King had made four voyages to parts of the northern and western coasts of Australia.[1] The voyage in HMC *Mermaid* in 1820 was significant, where Joseph Bradshaw was concerned, as King had sighted and named features that Bradshaw was to become interested in. Those features were the Roe River, in Prince Frederick Harbour, the Prince Regent River in the St George Basin, and Mt Waterloo and Mt Trafalgar.

Above Joseph Bradshaw. Courtesy of John Bradshaw.

Opposite
Bradshaw's sketch of the art site, with a photo of the site taken by Michael Cusack.

Alexander Forrest had also contributed to Joseph Bradshaw's interest. Forrest was sent north by the WA government and traversed the Kimberley region in 1879. He sent reports to the government, settlers and speculators, telling of large areas of good pastoral land.[2]

Who was Joseph Bradshaw? One of seven children, born to a Melbourne landowner, he was young and ambitious and, in the 1890s downturn of the Victorian economy, Joseph Bradshaw read these glowing reports on the Kimberley and formed a small syndicate to look for opportunities in the region. He would have imagined prime pastoral land, either side of a large river, thinking of it as such because King had sailed up the Prince Regent River and said how good it was.

In June 1890, aged 35, Bradshaw sailed on a coastal steamer, via Adelaide and Fremantle, to Derby. On reaching Derby, and hearing of pastoral land available on the Prince Regent River, he was interested in inspecting this area. There was no vessel available to take him north to the Prince Regent, and going by land was also out of the question, as few Europeans knew of a way through the rugged King Leopold Ranges.

After he returned to Melbourne, the syndicate applied for pastoral leases. On 31 October 1890, Bradshaw received approval for 20 blocks, of 50,000 acres (20,250 hectares) each—one million acres of land all told—sight unseen, along both sides of the Prince Regent River. The tenure on the leases ran from 1 January 1890, to 31 December 1907.

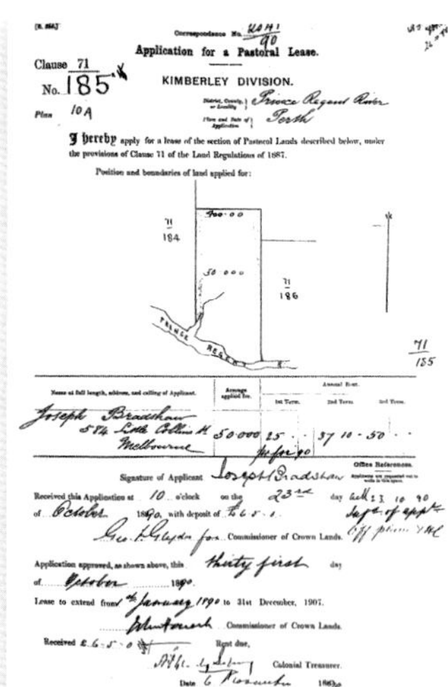

Correspondence No. 4041/90

Application for a Pastoral Lease.

Clause 71

No. 185

KIMBERLEY DIVISION.

District, County, or Locality: Prince Regent River

Plan 10A

Place and Date of Application: Perth

I hereby apply for a lease of the section of Pastoral Lands described below, under the provisions of Clause 71 of the Land Regulations of 1887.

Position and boundaries of land applied for:

Name at full length, address, and calling of Applicant.	Acreage applied for.	Annual Rent. 1st Term.	2nd Term.	3rd Term.
Joseph Bradshaw, 584 Little Collins St, Melbourne	50 000	25 . .	37 10 -	50 . .

Signature of Applicant Joseph Bradshaw

Office References.

Received this Application at 10 o'clock on the 23rd day of October 1890, with deposit of £6 5 -

Commissioner of Crown Lands.

Application approved, as shown above, this thirty first day of October 1890.

Lease to extend from 1st January 1890 to 31st December, 1907.

Commissioner of Crown Lands.

Received £ 6 - 5 - 0 Rent due,

Colonial Treasurer.

Date 6 November 1890

On 31 January 1891, Bradshaw left Melbourne for Wyndham, in anticipation of checking the Prince Regent River pastoral leases. Sailing by steamer, with his older brother Fred and a Victorian sheep farmer, William Allen, he spent three weeks in Palmerston (Darwin), waiting for a steamer to take them further. While there, Bradshaw added two of the local Larrakia Aborigines, Harry Pinadhy and Slocum, to his group. Another young man, Hugh Young, who had been a fellow passenger from Melbourne, joined the party in Wyndham.

On reaching Wyndham on 9 March, they found much of the town flattened by a cyclone. As there was no accommodation, they camped at the Six Mile (on water that distance out of town) while they got the last of the expedition together. They had brought most of the necessary pack saddles and equipment with them but they had to get horses and further essential supplies. The eleven horses they needed for the expedition were extremely expensive and hard to obtain, in such a remote locality. They used six horses for riding and five for their packs.

On 14 March, the party left the Six Mile, which had a small hotel dating from the Halls Creek gold rush of 1886.[3] Bradshaw had his own hand drawn map, which is now in the hands of John Bradshaw, a great nephew, from Sydney, and it looks to follow Charles Burrowes' survey map of 1886, drawn for the Victorian Squatting Company, another syndicate. The hand drawn map shows where Bradshaw's party rode, after leaving the Six Mile; south and west, to get around tidal flats and past Mt Cockburn; then north-west and west; very heavy going in the wet season.

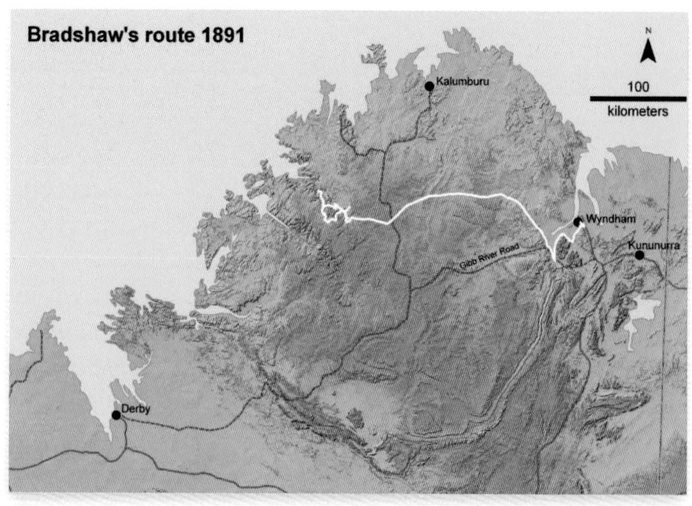

Above Copy of part of one of Bradshaw's applications for pastoral leases on the Prince Regent River. Courtesy of State Records Office of Western Australia.

Right Map of Bradshaw's 1891 expedition. Courtesy of Mike Donaldson.

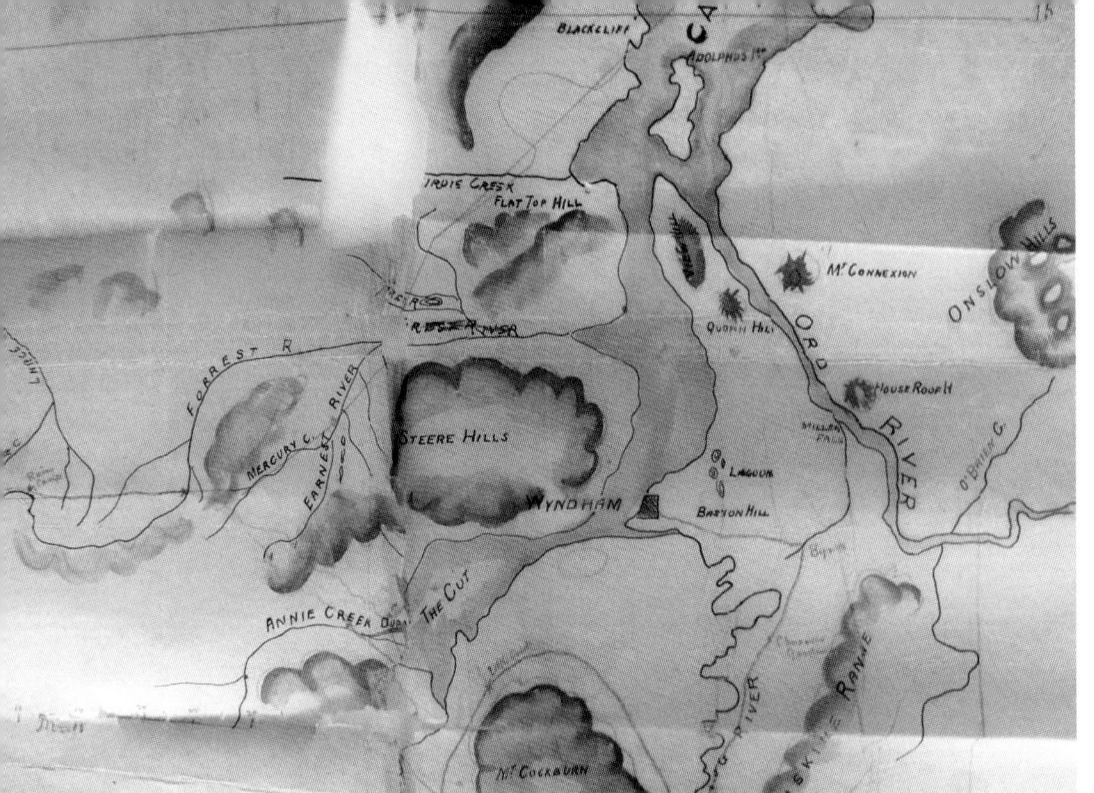

Other Europeans, including Harry Stockdale, Alexander Woodhouse and Bob Button, had already been into the area, looking for pastoral land and gold. Burrowes had shown the course of the Woodhouse River, on his map, entering the Drysdale River from the west, and he gave it that name because Woodhouse was in charge of the company's sheep. Woodhouse had camped between the Forrest and Durack Rivers in 1885, waiting for Burrowes to locate the company's leases.

On the map Bradshaw was following, he marked his expedition's camp sites, only until he reached Yellow Creek, near Mt Horace (north of where the Woodhouse joins the Drysdale). He noted, in his journal, that his next camp was on the Woodhouse River. An old Victorian Squatting Company camp there had been burnt out, but some watermelons remained. It is presumed that Bradshaw had lost his bearings by that stage and was really on Buffalo Flat Creek, a tributary of Meelarrie Creek, which runs parallel with the Woodhouse. From there Bradshaw went due west for three days and described the travel in his journal. If he had been on the Woodhouse, further south, his description of the land passed over would have been quite different. With Bradshaw having lost his bearings, it becomes important to note that, with the Prince Regent and the then unnamed Moran River following similar directions north-west, Bradshaw presumed, too soon, that he was near his blocks of land, on the Prince Regent.

Above Part of original hand drawn map, used by Bradshaw.
Courtesy of John Bradshaw.

Above Roaring cataract – camp 25 – Roe River.

Right Pinadhy Falls – camp 22 – Tributary to the Moran River.

Photos – Michael Cusack

In his journal, he started calling the river, the one we now know as the Moran, the Prince Regent, although he later called it the Eastern Regent and, later still, called the lower portion the Marigui.

After a difficult few days on the plateau, they eventually found a way down, travelling along Boa Creek, to the river (the Moran, but the one they thought of as the Prince Regent). Bradshaw and Allen rode out and climbed a small mountain, that he named Mt Allen. On riding back he found a ceremonial stone arrangement and vendetta site. He made a depot camp on the river and then, riding northward onto a tributary, he saw some lovely cascade falls, 95 feet (29 metres) high, which are now named Pinadhy Falls.

From where they were, after striking a sandstone barrier to the north, they went west and came onto another river. That discovery prompted Bradshaw to start using the names Western Regent (actually it was the Roe River, into which the Moran flows) and Eastern Regent (the Moran).

On Friday 10 April 1891, they camped at what he described as a roaring cataract, 80 yards (73 metres) wide. They then went north and saw mangroves growing on the tidal portion of the river (where the Moran enters the Roe). He described seeing many Aborigines there and he named the area Nigger Gorge. It has since been renamed Marigui Gorge, because Bradshaw heard the local Aborigines using the word Marigui, to describe the river and the locality.

Returning south along the east side of the Roe River, which is basalt country, compared to the sandstone on the west side, Bradshaw continued along the river until he was stopped by a sandstone gorge and was forced to retreat and traverse basalt country well to the east of the river. He re-joined the river but again was confronted by another sandstone gorge. From here he rode out, west of the river, and came across a site with exquisite art, in a great pile of immense rocks in a secluded chasm. The next day, he did four sketches of the art, which he described, "as being of great antiquity". This art style is now more commonly called "Gwion Gwion", but in 1938, the Frobenius Institute started calling it after Bradshaw.[4]

Bradshaw decided they could go no further south with their rations depleted, so they headed east, passing what they named Lalirimir Glen, where they planted some seeds, and then went over the watershed to their depot camp (on the Moran River). There they camped for two days, and Fred and Joseph rode out, went up a mountain, and blazed a tree B91.[5] From depot camp, Bradshaw and his party followed their outward tracks, back to Wyndham, as they had run out of supplies. They reached the Six Mile on 6 May 1891.

Back in Melbourne, Bradshaw's report recommended that all blocks on the west side of the Prince Regent River be abandoned and that land be taken up between that river and the Roe River. He was thinking that this was the good basalt land, seen in their travels. Bradshaw decided to settle on the new leases straight away. He purchased a schooner called *The Twins* (also known as the *Gemini*) and, in August 1891, Fred Bradshaw, his cousin Aeneas Gunn, and others sailed from Melbourne to Darwin with supplies and equipment for a station.[6]

In September, before following the others north, Joseph Bradshaw gave a paper to the Royal Geographical Society, Victorian Branch, called 'Notes on a Recent Trip to Prince Regent's River'. In it, he described the art and other features.

He also said he took observations, when he was in the vicinity of Cascade Falls, with a reading of latitude approximately 15° 50'. Also, by dead reckoning and triangulation, they estimated their longitude at 125° 40'. No readings appear in the journal. Bradshaw was carrying an aneroid barometer, which enabled him to record heights of hills and campsites, but he probably had no equipment to fix positions. He mentioned having made another map, on which he marked good country green, east of what he was calling the Prince Regent River, but that map has not been found.

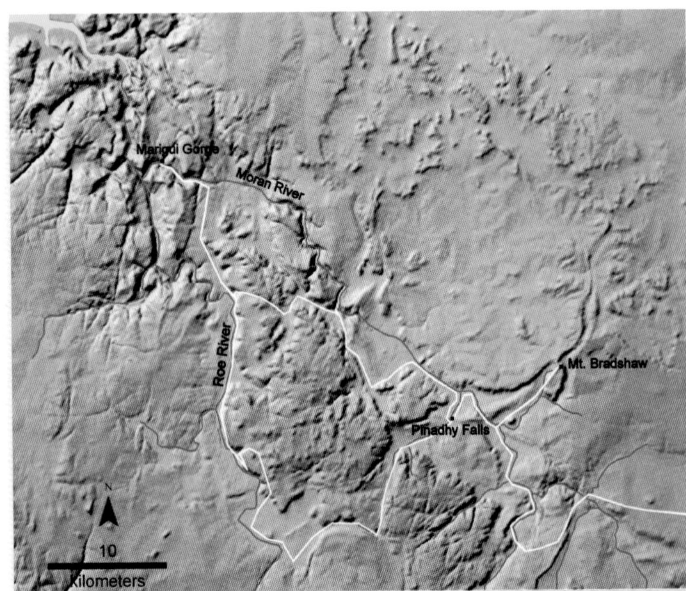

Right Detail of Bradshaw's 1891 expedition in the Roe and Moran River area. Courtesy of Mike Donaldson.

Above Tassel Bradshaw figures – Roe River. Photo – Michael Cusack

The position Bradshaw recorded is on the Prince Regent River, between Pitta Creek and Wulunge Chasm, well south of where the expedition actually travelled.

Notes

1 See Cathie Clement, 'Maritime exploration on the Kimberley coast', this volume, for further discussion.

2 See Geoffrey Bolton, 'Alexander Forrest's expedition 1879 and early development of the cattle industry', this volume, for further discussion.

3 See Phillip Playford, 'The Kimberley gold rush of 1885–1886', this volume, for further discussion.

4 A. S. Schulz, 'North-west Australian rock paintings' *Memoirs of the National Museum of Victoria*, 20, 1956.

5 F. S. Brockman, *Report on Exploration of North-West Kimberley*, 1901, Government Printer, Perth, 1902, records that Brockman found this tree in 1901 and named the peak Mt Bradshaw. His surveying work proved they were on the Moran River, and not the Prince Regent.

6 See Kevin F. Kenneally, 'Under a Regent Moon', two parts, this volume, for coverage of the settlement activities and conflict with the Indigenous people.

Sources and further reading

Bradshaw, J. Journal of Joseph Bradshaw from January 31st 1891 to June 6th 1891, Mitchell Library, B967, microfilm copy held by Battye Library, Acc 1271A.

Bradshaw, J. 'Notes on a Recent Trip to Prince Regent's River'. *Transactions of the Royal Geographical Society of Australasia (Victorian Branch)*, vol. 9(2), 1892, pp. 90–120.

Bradshaw, J. Original map, in the possession of John Bradshaw.

Parker, A. and Bradshaw, J. and Done, C. *A Kimberley Adventure: Rediscovering the Bradshaw Figures.* Gecko Books, Marleston (SA), 2007.

Willing, T. and Kenneally, K. (eds). *Under a Regent Moon: A historical account of pioneer pastoralists Joseph Bradshaw and Aeneas Gunn at Marigui Settlement, Prince Regent River, Kimberley, Western Australia, 1891–1892.* Department of Conservation and Land Management, Perth, 2002.

Under a Regent Moon. Part 1: Pioneer pastoralists, plant collecting and botanical patronage

Kevin F. Kenneally

For young men fond of adventure, who would seek profit on the deep sea, where in all the world is there to be found a virgin field to compare with coast of the Kimberley? – Joseph Panton (1883)[1]

In 2002 Tim Willing and I published *Under a Regent Moon: A historical account of pioneer pastoralists Joseph Bradshaw and Aeneas Gunn at Marigui Settlement, Prince Regent River, Kimberley, Western Australia, 1891–1892.*[2] The book included Gunn's memoir 'Pioneering in Northern Australia' originally published as 24 articles in the *Prahran Telegraph*, the *St Kilda Advertiser* and the *Malvern Argus* between May and November 1899.

In this paper, I will cover some of the material contained in *Under a Regent Moon* as well as providing additional information that has been discovered since the book was published. Reference will be made to the influence of some of Melbourne's establishment figures such as Ferdinand Mueller, Joseph Panton and William Osmand, and to the role of the Royal Geographical Society of Australasia in both promoting exploration and publishing accounts of explorers' journeys.

Joseph Bradshaw

Following Alexander Forrest's expedition in 1879 across the Kimberley, millions of hectares were allocated as pastoral leases and townships established. Much of the land acquisition was of a speculative nature, and focussed on the fertile floodplains of the Fitzroy and Ord Rivers.[3]

Ferdinand Mueller, the Government Botanist of Victoria, waxed lyrical about the potential of the region. He wrote:

> When we contemplate, that many millions of acres of open richly grassed and well watered pastoral country were discovered in addition to what was disclosed already by the expedition of 1855-1856, – when we consider, that the North-west of Australia is blessed by a salubrious clime, mitigated in its heat by the prevailing westerly and northerly sea breezes; when we recognise, that the tropical rains keep the pastures verdant also during the hot season

Opposite
The Bradshaw family taken in 1910 at their residence at what was then Nelson Street and is now 20 Trafalgar Street, Mont Albert, Victoria. Those in the photo are: Back row L-R Emily, Benjamin, Matilda (twin to Emily), Joseph, Charlotte and John; Middle row L-R Margaret, Helen (known as Ella), Margaret (the matriarch) and Mary; Front row L-R Guy, David and Dorothy Gibb (a ward of Charlotte). Photo courtesy of John Bradshaw.

> and that the cool season grasses and herbage remain also fresh; when we learn, that only a sparse and unresisting aboriginal population occupies this large territory; when we remember, that these fine tracts of country, on which the light of geography has so recently been shed, are adjacent to many safe and spacious harbours...[4]

Painful memories still lingered of the Camden Harbour fiasco of 1864–65, when Victorian families had attempted settlement and sheep-farming in the remote Kimberley.[5] The beckoning 'pastures' of green, described by Mueller and observed from sea-ward, proved an illusion. Closer inspection revealed prickly spinifex and cane grass, masking a harsh landscape of outcropping rock and stones, defended by hostile Aborigines. People and stock died and the settlement was abandoned in October 1865 after eleven months of heartbreak and misery.[6]

Against such a background, any pastoralist leasing a million acres (404,858 hectares), sight unseen, in the vicinity of Camden Harbour showed courageous commitment – or absurd optimism! Yet this was precisely what Joseph Bradshaw (Fig. 1) did in October 1890, when he leased from the Western Australian Government twenty blocks of 50,000 acres (20,250 hectares) each straddling the Prince Regent River, upstream from St George Basin (Fig. 2). Bradshaw described himself as an 'Investment Manager' of 584 Little Collin Street, Melbourne (Fig. 3). The address given was the office of his brother, John, who was listed, and acted on Joseph's behalf, as an 'Agent' (John Bradshaw – pers. comm.). His initial annual rent for Marigui was £500.

Above Figure 1. Portrait of Joseph Bradshaw. Courtesy of John Bradshaw.

Below Figure 2. Map showing the location of the Marigui Homestead at the mouth of the Prince Regent River.

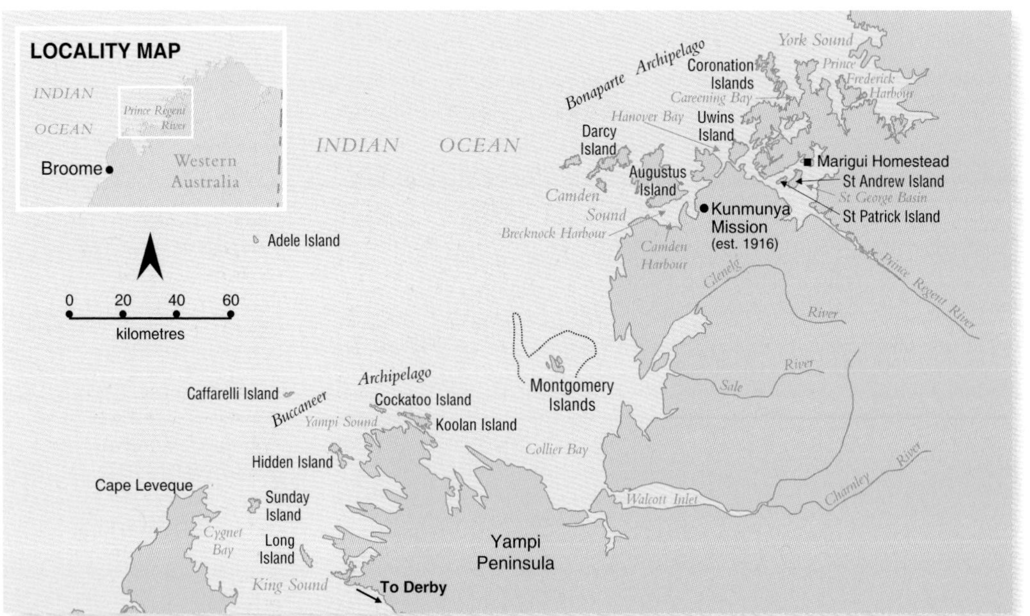

Bradshaw's 1891 overland expedition

On 31 January 1891, Joseph and his brother Frederick along with another Victorian, William Tucker Allen, left Melbourne aboard the *Aramac*. After arriving at Darwin, Bradshaw secured on 7 March the services of Harry Pinadhy and Slocum, both Larrakia Aborigines. The party sailed the following day by the *South Australian* for Wyndham. After purchasing eleven pack-horses and being joined by another Victorian, Hugh Young, the expedition set out from the Six Mile (out of Wyndham) on about 14 March to inspect the pastoral leases.[7]

On 21 April, Joseph Bradshaw ordered the expedition's return. By 6 May they were back at Wyndham, where Young was left in charge of the horses and equipment. The Bradshaw brothers embarked on the *Rob Roy* for Darwin, and, on 19 May, sailed for Sydney on the *Chingtu*. Joseph disembarked at Sydney and caught an express train to Melbourne where he was met by his 29-year-old cousin Aeneas Gunn. By his own account, Aeneas already regarded Joseph as a heroic figure.[8]

Above Figure 4. Views of the Bradshaw residence at 20 Trafalgar Street, Mont Albert, Victoria. The family photograph (Figure 3 on page 134) was taken on the front verandah shown to the right. Courtesy of John Bradshaw.

Left Old Wyndham Port (photographed in 1992), showing the extensive tidal mud flats and fringing mangroves of Cambridge Gulf with The Bastion Range towering behind the small coastal settlement.

Aeneas Gunn

In Greek and Roman mythology, Aeneas, meaning 'praiseworthy' was a Trojan hero, esteemed for his piety, prudence and valour. Aeneas features in Virgil's epic poem the *Aeneid*, escaping from Troy to establish a kingdom beyond the seas. Arguably, Gunn's own life had some parallels with this mythical hero (Fig. 5).

In August 1891, Gunn boarded Bradshaw's newly acquired 40-ton schooner *The Twins* (also referred to as the *Gemini*), sailing from Port Phillip Bay (Victoria) for the Kimberley (Fig. 6). It would be 33 days before the vessel reached Darwin, after sailing via Torres Strait. Shortly afterwards Joseph Bradshaw and Mary, his newly-wed wife proceeded to Darwin by the steamer *Catterthun*, arriving on 16 October to join *The Twins*.

Gunn writes:

> On a steaming day in October ... the ketch rigged schooner "Gemini" ... lay helplessly wallowing in the long lazy swell of the Timor Sea. Moving about her decks (hampered with hen-coops, dogs, dog-kennels, and a predacious nanny and billy goat), or reclining wherever the sails cast a scanty shade from the vertical rays of the sun, were twelve roasting human beings. The twelve represented the "ship's" company and the personnel of the party that was to form the white settlement at Marigui on the Prince Regent River.[9]

On 11 November the station log records that, 'Some tents were taken ashore today and pitched beneath some Baobab trees on a plateau between the base of Mount Waterloo and the seashore, and about 200 yards [183 metres] up the rise from Gunn's Spring' (Figs 7–12).[10] The next day the account continues, 'After tea to-night Mr. and Mrs. Bradshaw and Mr. Gunn were rowed ashore in the moonlight, and commenced the occupation of the territory by sleeping ashore, making the tents their temporary residence.' This was the start of the Marigui adventure that Gunn was to document, after his return to Melbourne, in his series of newspaper articles.

On 2 February 1894, the *Northern Territory Times and Gazette* reported that Joseph Bradshaw had arrived at Darwin aboard the steamship *Changsha*. It went on:

> From what we can hear it is doubtful if this gentleman will persevere with his station on the Prince Regent River (W.A.). He complains bitterly of the obstructive stock tax imposed by the western colony, and the upshot of his disaffection is going to be that he will establish himself on a run in the Victoria River District instead.

Above Figure 5. Portrait of Aeneas Gunn. Courtesy of Angela Berry.

Opposite
(Top) Figure 6. The ketch *The Twins*, typical of Bass Strait trading vessels in the 1880s. Courtesy of Colin Taylor, Williamstown, Victoria and the Port Albert Maritime Museum.
(Centre) Figure 7. Mount Trafalgar looking over mangrove embayments in St George Basin at the mouth of the Prince Regent River.
(Bottom) Figure 8. Mount Trafalgar in the Wet season (February) showing the lush growth of grass around the base.

In the latter part of 1893, Western Australia had expanded the scope of its stock tax to include animals brought from other colonies as stock for stations.[11] The economics of moving cattle and sheep to Marigui were changed overnight and this curtailed the development of the pastoral settlement.

In February 1894, Bradshaw's newly acquired steamer *Red Gauntlet* sailed from Darwin for the Prince Regent River. It is likely that the dismantling of the Marigui homestead began on this voyage and continued for some time, but the historical record is silent.

Bradshaw immediately took up a pastoral lease covering 4,800 square miles (12,432 km^2) on the estuary of the Victoria River in the Northern Territory. That station came to be known as 'Bradshaw's Run'.[12] With the assistance of Gunn and Hugh Young, it was stocked with sheep and later cattle. Bradshaw ran 'Bradshaw's Run' successfully for the remainder of his life. He died in Darwin Hospital on 23 July 1916 from complications associated with diabetes.[13]

By November 1895, owing to ill health, Gunn had severed his connection with Bradshaw's Victoria River venture and returned to Victoria. In June 1898 he was appointed Librarian with the City of Prahran.[14] It was during the Prahran episode of Gunn's life that he penned the newspaper articles.

On 31 December 1901, Gunn married school teacher Jeannie Taylor. The newly-wed couple proceeded to Darwin, as he had accepted a position as manager of Elsey Station, 480 kilometres south of Darwin on the Roper River. In 1887 the Elsey property had been purchased by Osmand and Panton, who were in the process of developing their holdings in Western Australia. The Gunns sailed from Port Phillip Bay, their vessel reaching Darwin on 16 January 1902, while the whole journey to the Elsey took one month.[15]

Barely a year later, in March 1903, tragedy struck with Aeneas' untimely death at 41, from malarial dysentery. Following his burial, a widowed Jeannie returned to Hawthorn, Victoria. It was here she commenced writing her memoirs of life at Elsey Station, under the name Mrs Aeneas Gunn. Her first work was *The Little Black Princess*, a comic account of an Aboriginal orphan girl and her puppy.[16] However, it was *We of the Never-Never* that catapulted her to national fame.[17] In this classic of Australian literature, Gunn was immortalised as 'The Maluka' a genial, kindly and thoughtful hero.[18] It is ironic that although immortalised through his wife's writings, Gunn's own writings had remained largely unread for close to a century.

Opposite
(Top) Figure 9. View from the Marigui settlement site over St George Basin. Note the rank cane grass (*Sorghum*) in the foreground.
(Centre left) Figure 10. The 'Target Tree', a boab (*Adansonia gregorii*) near the homestead site that bears the bullet scars resulting from target practice by the Bradshaw party.
(Centre right) Figure 11. A close-up of the 'GUNN' inscription on a boab tree, at the Marigui settlement site.
(Bottom) Figure 12. Gunn's Spring at the Marigui settlement site, fringed by the screwpine (*Pandanus spiralis*).
Photo – Tim Willing

The establishment and naming of Marigui

In Bradshaw's account of his 1891 overland expedition he describes an encounter with a large party of Aborigines, and goes on to state:

> They indicated themselves by the word "Woolyammi," and the locality where we were, the creek and the direction of their camp by the name "Marigui." The latter word may have a common origin with "marega," which, according to Dampier and King, was the name applied to the coast opposite this region by the Malayan cruisers for more than 200 years past.[19]

The "Malayan cruisers" he refers to are Indonesians (Macassans) who sailed across the Timor Sea in search of trepang, also known as *bêche-de-mer* or sea-cucumbers (Figs 13 & 14). This quest is believed to have commenced in about 1700.[20] Captain (later Rear Admiral) Phillip Parker King (Fig. 15) who had conducted three hydrographical surveys of the Kimberley coast between 1819 and 1822, anticipated encountering Indonesians during his visit.[21] King had gathered information on Indonesian voyages to the north Australian coast when he had visited Kupang (Timor) in 1818. He was advised by one of the fleet leaders that the Indonesians called the coast 'Marega'.[22] This term was later shown to be applied to Arnhem Land and the Gulf of Carpentaria and the term 'Kayu Jawa' or 'Kai Jawa' to the Kimberley coast.[23]

In a letter to the Commissioner of Lands, Perth, Bradshaw states 'I have named the promontory and seaport formed by the Regent and Roe Rivers "Marigui" (abor) (King voyages etc.)' [24] Another letter on the same file, dated 1 December 1893, indicates that Bradshaw also named his residence in Brinsley Road, Camberwell, Victoria 'Marigui' (Fig. 16).

Below Figure 13. An Indonesian fishing vessel photographed in June 1977 at Ashmore Reef in the Timor Sea.

Bradshaw's Marigui Correspondence

Three files of Bradshaw correspondence still survive in Western Australia.[25] The first file contains eight letters, written between October 1890 and January 1894, all to the Commissioner for Lands (Figs 17 &18A&B).[26] Examples of these letters are reproduced below.

> Sir, Referring to my pastoral leases for one million acres Prince Regent Riv., Kimberley. I beg, that you will permit me to alter the boundaries, so as to relinquish all the land on the West side of the Regent Riv and to take up in lieu thereof all the land between the PReg' Riv [Prince Regent River] and the Roe River, approximately to the boundaries colored blue in the accompanying sketch. I had a look at the country last month and find that very little of it comes up to my expectations, and it must be many years before a station there would pay even working expenses, but I do not like to abandon the country without giving it a fair trial, though I must say that the rents in Kimberley are excessively high and the terms of pastoral leases very stringent and limited as I understand the concession allowed under clause 73 terminates next year, instead of 5 years from the commencement of the lease as I was informed when I took up the country. On receipt of the sketch plan showing your approval of the alteration of the boundaries that I suggest I will forward you the amount of rent for the current year.[27]

Top Figure 14. Evidence of Indonesian fishermen visiting the Kimberley coast and processing trepang is the stone cooking hearths found along the Kimberley coast.

Above Figure 15. Phillip Parker King, c. 1816, 'oil on canvas by unknown artist'. Courtesy of Mitchell Library, State Library of New South Wales (Ref: ML 11, Digital: a2324001).

Above left Figure 16. The Bradshaw residence 'Marigui' in Brinsley Road, Camberwell, Melbourne, photographed by the author in 2009. Bradshaw purchased Brinsley Road in March 1893 and sold it in 1914.

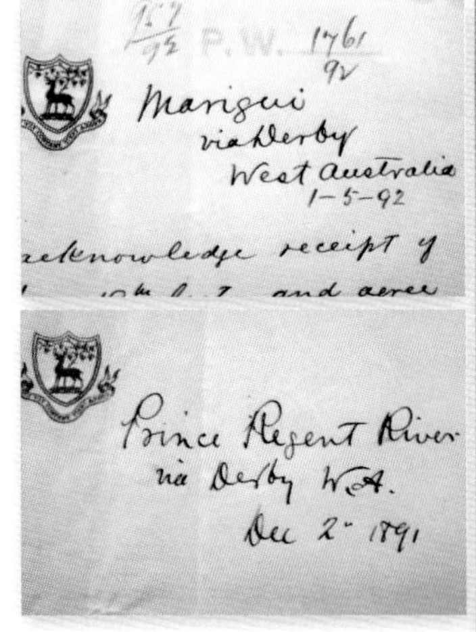

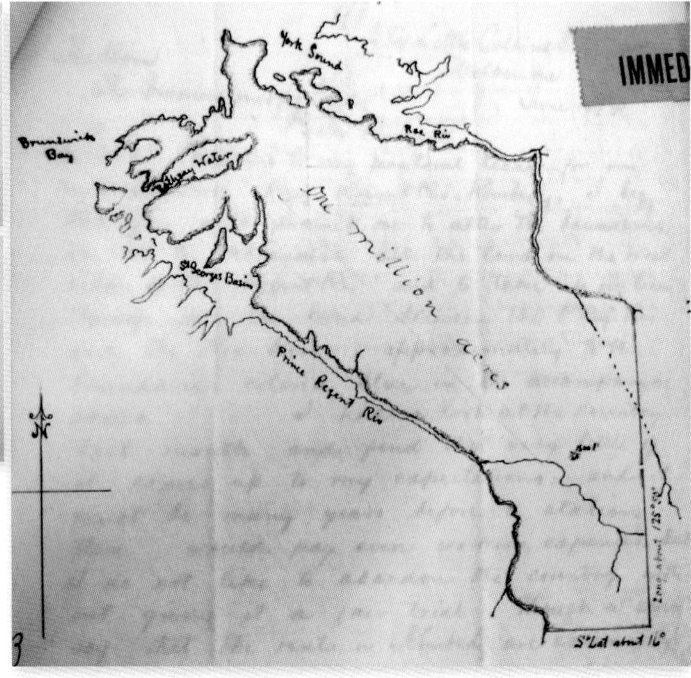

Above right Figure 17. A hand-drawn map by Bradshaw showing his desired lease adjustments outlined in blue wash. Courtesy of State Records Office of Western Australia.

Above Figures 18A&B. Bradshaw's letterheads showing heraldic crest. Courtesy of State Records Office of Western Australia.

Sir, Referring to my lease of pastoral lands in the Prince Regent River, Kimberley Division. I respectfully beg to intimate that I had no wish for all the blocks to be included in one lease as that would compel me to pay for two blocks of worthless, stony desert for each block of grazing land, it was therefor[e] my intention, as I noted the country to relinquish certain blocks and take up others by this process I propose, should your government offer sufficient inducement, to bring my acreage up to three millions during the next year or two, but I am compelled to say that the land laws relating to the Kimberley Division do not compare favourably with those of the Northern Territory.

I also beg you to note that the disastrous drought which has recently pervaded the whole of Australia will prevent me from stocking up, as soon, and to the extent, that I originally intended.

I have constructed buildings water tanks etc on the west side of Mts Trafalgar and Waterloo. I have up till the present confined myself to experimenting in a small way with horses, sheep, pigs, poultry, rice, maize, sugar, cane etc and many other tropical and semi tropical products, and so far as I can judge, with every prospect of success.

The Bingi Natives are very numerous, and daring they are of splendid phisique [sic], and of tawny or olive colored complexion; as their movements are daily becoming more aggressive I must apply to the Government for police protection or else for license or executive power to protect the lives & property on the settlement at my own discretion. I have named the promontory and seaport formed by the Regent and Roe Rivers "Marigui" (Abor) (King voyages etc). Mr Young our surveyor has named an abrupt mountain in lat 16.30S* long 125.30E (approx) "Mount Bradshaw".[28]

Stocking of Marigui

In September 1892 Bradshaw strongly endorsed the potential of the Kimberley as a cheap source of mutton supply for Darwin.[29] In the same month, his request to drastically reduce his Prince Regent holdings to a mere 100,000 acres (40,484 hectares), centred on Marigui, was granted with the approval of lease 71/234.[30] Items from the *Northern Territory Times and Gazette,* Darwin, give some indication of the stock being purchased and delivered to the Marigui settlement. Examples are reproduced below:

> Friday 27th May 1892
>
> WANTED TO PURCHASE
>
> From 500 to 600 Well-bred Heifers from one to three years old. Approved on station, but delivered at or near Hall's Creek, Kimberley. Terms Cash. Address without delay, stating lowest price, to JOSEPH BRADSHAW, Marigui, Derby, W. Australia.

> Palmerston: Fri 10 Nov 1893
> Notes of the Week
> A steamer called the "Moreton" has been chartered by Mr. Bradshaw to carry a cargo of sheep from Melbourne to the Prince Regent River, W.A. The flock will number about 3,000 head and the steamer should even now be on the way up north.
>
> Another stage towards removing the sheep from Victoria Downs has been reached by the arrival at Palmerston of Mr. Gunn, the manager of Mr Joseph Bradshaw's Marigui station, to where the sheep are to be transferred. The sheep, we understand, are to be sold on approval, and Mr. Gunn will most likely be starting for the Victoria River on Tuesday next to inspect and take delivery and set the flock out towards Western Australia. Assuming that the bargain suits the visitor, the sheep will be travelled over the border to Wyndham, from where they will be shipped per special boat to the Prince Regent River. The capacity of Marigui for the breeding of sheep has been tested in a very small way already, and it was the success of the experiments up to date that led Mr. Bradshaw to favour the notion of taking Goldsbrough, Mort & Co's. experimental flock off their hands. The number to be delivered runs to about 3,900.

The Bingi natives are very numerous, and daring
they are of splendid phisique, and of tawny
or olive colored complexion; as their movements are daily becoming more aggressive I must
apply to the Government for police protection
or else for licence or executive power to protect

Left Extract from Bradshaws's letter transcribed on opposite page.

Sir Ferdinand Mueller (Baron von Mueller), botanical collections and the Royal Geographical Society

Top Figure 19. Ferdinand Mueller, Government Botanist, Victoria 1852-96. Image reproduced with permission from Pictures Collection, State Library of Victoria.

Above Figure 20. A profile of Ferdinand Mueller (about 1893), sketched on a piece of blotting-paper by Joseph Panton who had studied art in Paris. Original sketch in possession of the Historical Society of Victoria.

Ferdinand Mueller was the Government Botanist of Victoria from 1852 to 1896. He was probably the greatest Australian botanist of his time and arguably the most famous scientist in the southern hemisphere (Figs 19 & 20). He was himself an intrepid explorer in his younger days of areas previously unvisited by Europeans.[31]

Mueller later became an authority on exploration and on Australian geography more generally. He was a leading advocate and generous promoter of expeditions by others into previously unexplored regions of inland Australia and New Guinea. Once established in his own field, Mueller was active in linking and promoting the work of other Australian naturalists. Mueller was well connected and influential. The public lectures that he offered from time to time, usually in support of some new geographical venture, were great social occasions, with the Governor of the colony inevitably in the chair and the cream of Melbourne society in the audience.[32]

His own journeys and the interest he took in others were chiefly influenced by his desire to obtain botanical knowledge, but still he took a deep interest in geographical matters, as shown by the fact that for many years in succession he was President of the Victorian Branch of the Royal Geographical Society of Australasia.[33]

The Geographical Society of London was founded in 1830 under the name 'Geographical Society of London' as an institution to promote the 'advancement of geographical science'. The Geographical Society of Australasia was inaugurated at a Sydney meeting on 22 June 1883. Later that year branches were formed in Victoria and Queensland. In July 1886 the society became the Royal Geographical Society of Australasia. Its principal objective was to encourage exploration in Australia and surrounding islands, especially New Guinea.[34]

Throughout his working life Mueller kept up an enormous correspondence.[35] In November 1890, Bradshaw had written to him asking about the occurrence of plants poisonous to stock in the Kimberley. This may have been prompted by the 1860s experience at Camden Harbour where it was said that:

> Some 5,000 sheep were landed, but at the end of three months only 1,400 had survived, the remainder having died apparently from eating a poisonous weed, which, however, could not be discovered.[36]

Mueller was very familiar with such plants having experienced first-hand the poisoning of horses on the A.C. Gregory exploration to Northern Australia in 1855–56. It was on this expedition he collected and named the iconic Kimberley Boab (*Adansonia gregorii*) after the expedition's leader (Fig. 21). He replied to Bradshaw and invited him to collect plant specimens on his expedition to the Prince Regent River. Mueller's letter is reproduced below:

> The various kinds of poison-bushes in W.A., dear Mr Bradshaw, are well known to me since the last 40 years, so also those mentioned by you; they are nearly all species of Gastrolobium, few only belong to the genus Oxylobium.
>
> When your party proceeds to Prince Regent's River, I should like to see one of the members, to arrange, that specimens of plants be gathered, and I would gladly provide paper and envelopes for the purpose. You would obtain full public credit for this. It will not take up much time, nor will it give particular trouble.[37]

Left Figure 21. The original (Type) collection of the boab (*Adansonia gregorii*) collected and described by Mueller. Reproduced courtesy of the National Herbarium of Victoria, Royal Botanic Gardens, Melbourne.

Bradshaw appointed William Tucker Allen as his botanical collector and superintendent of the company's projected settlement. Before they left Melbourne, Mueller presented Allen with:

> ... a quantity of the seed of the Grand Fodder Plant *Euchlaeana Luxurians*, commonly known as the *teosinthe*, a native of Guatemala, South America, for him to sow in the Kimberley District.[38] This Mr. Allen scattered freely about the various camping places of his party and along the rich river flats, together with the seeds of other useful tropical fruits and trees.[39]

On the expedition's return to Melbourne the plant specimens were passed to Mueller for cataloguing and identification. Mueller was very excited by the plant collections and wrote to Bradshaw congratulating him on several new discoveries and invited him to attend a meeting of the Victorian Branch of the Royal Geographical Society of Australasia.

> I would have answered earlier your last kind letter, dear Mr Bradshaw, had I not been eager, to look over your very creditable collection of dried plants first, so as to report to you theron preliminarily, I can congratulate you now to the discovery of several new species, which I will soon describe, and one of the best shall be named in honour of yourself, another be dedicated to Mr Allen. Let me hope, that you will be able, to attend the postponed geographic meeting next Friday. I shall probably be able to arrange for an adjourned meeting, to be held in the week following, when antarctic subjects will be discussed. On that occasion we would however have also time, to hear an account of you Expedition to Prince Regent's River. As this paper need not be a long one in first instance, may I ask, whether you could favour us with an extract from your diary by that time? The exact date of the adjourned meeting will be announced at the close of the meeting on Friday evening. Do you wish any of the botanic specimens back? I shall bring the rare and new sorts to the meeting when your paper will be read.[40]

Bradshaw's paper was read to the Society on 10 September 1891 and published in its journal.[41] The paper also contained descriptions of Aboriginal rock art that became known as 'Bradshaw Figures' but are more commonly referred to today as Gwion-Gwion or Girrigirro. This art form has, in recent years, attracted increasing international attention.[42] At the conclusion of the talk Mueller (as President) commented that: "Mr Bradshaw had found several new species of plants during his expedition to Prince Regent's River, and these he (the President) had classified and named."

What was never publicly acknowledged by Bradshaw was that due to an error in navigation his actual course was well north of the Prince Regent River. In 1901, the surveyor F. S. Brockman rediscovered the Bradshaw expedition's blazed tree "B91" on the Moran River.[43] Bradshaw apparently mistook the Roe River for the Prince Regent River.

On 19 September 1891 Bradshaw presented another paper entitled 'The Future of North Australia'. Mueller mentions informing Mr Panton, a member of the Society and Police Magistrate for Melbourne. Joseph Panton (Fig. 22) and William Osmand (Fig. 23) were still partners in Ord River Station (WA) and Elsey Station (NT). Panton had given a paper to the Society some years earlier.[44]

> I mentioned, dear Mr Bradshaw, at the meeting last evening that you would read your important treatise at the next meeting; and now am glad to learn, that you will favour us with a second essay then also.
>
> I have forwarded to Mr Macdonald your kind letter, and asked him, to inform Mr Panton also of your further friendly intention, and to place that Gentleman in communication with you.[45]
>
> It occurred to me in thought, dear Mr Bradshaw, that you might like me to give footnotes on the pages of the print of your treatise in reference to such plants, as you specially mention. In that case, the slips, from which you were reading, should not be paged, until the notes have been added. I could make Tuesday-afternoon free for you, if you like then to come to my place, so that you could look with me over your botanic specimens, to settle about what notes should be furnished for your memoir.[46]

Botanical discoveries

In 1891, Mueller published a paper on the plants collected during Bradshaw's expedition.[47] Altogether 161 different species were collected. Among them were a few novelties which Mueller went on to name and describe in detail: a handsome wattle, *Acacia kelleri* (Fig. 24);[48] a white flowered herb which he intended naming *Bradshawia* but placed in *Ramphicarpa* [now *Lindernia*] *macrosiphonia* (Fig. 25); and a curious shrub he named *Triumfetta bradshawii* (Fig. 26). W. T. Allen was honoured with *Corchorus allenii*, a name now regarded as synonymous with *Helicteres cana* (Fig. 27).

The majority of plant specimens collected by Bradshaw and Allen and now in the National Herbarium, Melbourne are labelled 'Prince Regent River' and therefore must be considered suspect as to their true collecting locality. Given that Bradshaw in his 1891 unpublished journal listed names for each campsite,[49] it is surprising that I have so far only found two specimens with 'precise' localities. They are a specimen of Swamp Bloodwood (*Eucalyptus ptychocarpa*) labelled 'Welcome Creek' (Fig. 28) and an insectivorous plant (*Drosera derbyensis*) labelled 'Paradise Creek' (Fig. 29).

Top Figure 22. Joseph Panton (1831-1913), Melbourne police magistrate and vice-president of the Royal Geographical Society of Australasia, Victorian Branch. Image reproduced with permission from Pictures Collection, State Library of Victoria.

Above Figure 23. William Osmand (1824-1901), President of Stawell School of Mines (1890), and member Victorian Parliament, (MLC for Nelson 1888-1901). Courtesy of The Library of the Parliament of Victoria.

Top Figure 24. The Kimberley wattle *Acacia kelleri*, another undescribed species collected by Bradshaw and Allen. Courtesy of Bruce Maslin/DEC.

Above Figure 25. Flowers of *Lindernia macrosiphonia*, a plant restricted to the Kimberley and first collected by Bradshaw.

Right Figure 26. Fruiting branches of the shrub *Triumfetta bradshawii*, one of the undescribed species collected on the expedition and named by Mueller.

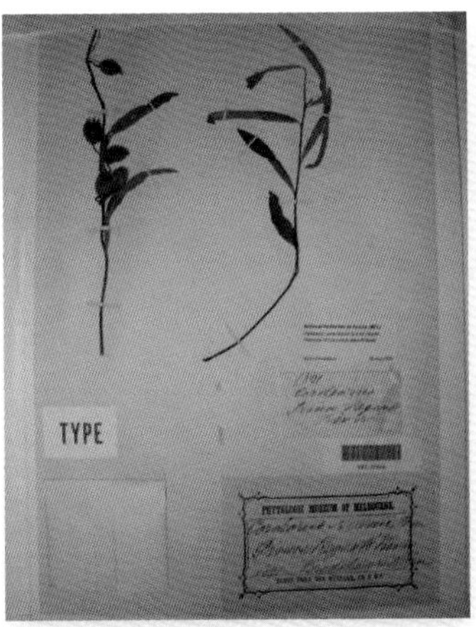

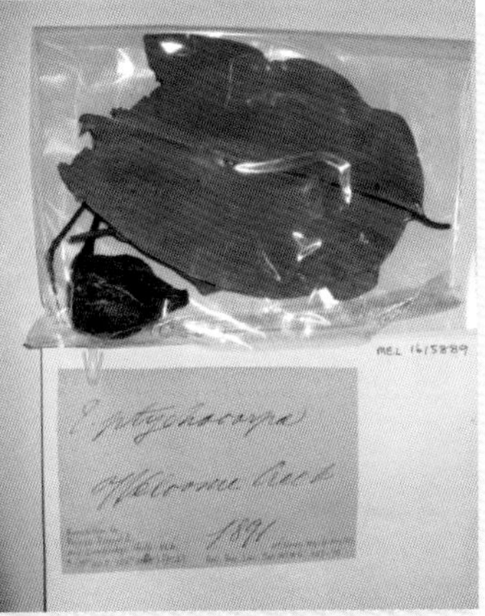

DIED. 16.3.1903.
RESIGNED.........
REMOVED..........

CERTIFICATE OF CANDIDATE FOR ELECTION.

Name Aeneas Gunn Esqr

Description Pastoralist in Arnhem Land (Kimberley District)

Residence Victoria River, via Port Darwin. much engaged in North Western Australian Exploration

being desirous of admission into the Royal Geographical Society, We, the undersigned, recommend him as likely to become a useful and valuable Fellow.

Dated this 13th day of August 1895

Ferd. von Mueller F.R.G.S. (From personal knowledge.)

F.R.G.S.

F.R.G.S.

Proposed 11th Nov 1895

Elected 25th — 1895.

NOTE.—State for information of the Council the Geographical work or qualifications, if any, of the Candidate.

Top from left
Figure 27. Mueller acknowledged W.T. Allen's contribution to the expedition's plant collecting and named *Corchorus allenii* in his honour. However, further studies revealed it was a later name for the already described *Helicteres cana*.

Figure 28. A specimen of the swamp bloodwood (*Eucalyptus ptychocarpa*), a tree always associated with creeks or damp places, labelled 'Welcome Creek'.

Figure 29. The insectivorous plant *Drosera derbyensis* labelled 'Paradise Creek'.
All herbarium specimens courtesy of the National Herbarium of Victoria, Royal Botanic Gardens, Melbourne.

Above left Figure 30. Aeneas Gunn's certificate of election (in Mueller's handwriting) as a Fellow of the Royal Geographical Society.
Courtesy of John Bradshaw.

As a result of their exploration and botanical discoveries Mueller nominated Bradshaw and Gunn for election as Fellows of the Royal Geographical Society entitling them to use the post-nominal FRGS after their names (Fig. 30). Such was the distinction at this time, that when Gunn applied for the position of Librarian, the Prahran Council was very impressed that he was a Fellow of the Royal Geographical Society![50]

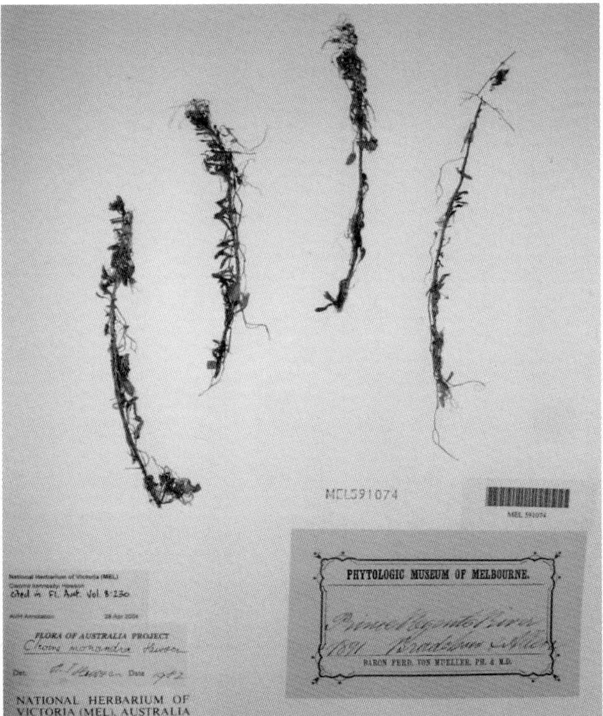

Postscript

The author has a link to the Marigui story, albeit a tenuous one! Included amongst the Bradshaw and Allen plant collections at Melbourne is a specimen of *Cleome* not identified by Mueller. In 1982 it was recognized by botanist Helen Hewson as a new species and named *Cleome kenneallyi* (Figs 31–32).[51]

Acknowledgements

I would particularly like to acknowledge and thank the following people and institutions for their assistance and advice in the preparation of this paper.

Dr Cathie Clement, for her invaluable advice on Kimberley historical events and for her helpful and constructive editing of this paper — not to mention her incredible patience, great fortitude and amazingly good humour throughout!

Tim Willing of Broome, my friend, colleague and fellow Kimberley researcher, for his ongoing collaboration and for permission to use his photographs of Marigui.

John Bradshaw, Parramatta, New South Wales, for permission to reproduce photographs and for information and valuable insights regarding the Bradshaw family history.

The staff of the State Records Office of Western Australia, for advice and access to records relating to Bradshaw's leases at Marigui.

The Director and staff, National Herbarium of Victoria and Royal Botanic Garden, South Yarra, Melbourne, for access to historical botanical specimens collected by Joseph Bradshaw and named by Ferdinand Mueller. For access and guidance to early botanical publications held in the Herbarium Library I am grateful to librarians Helen Cohn, Jill Thurlow and Nekane Kandina. Dr Monika Wells kindly provided information on Mueller correspondence and related documents.

Above Figure 31. An herbarium specimen of *Cleome* collected by Bradshaw and Allen and not identified by Mueller. Reproduced courtesy of the National Herbarium of Victoria, Royal Botanic Gardens, Melbourne.

Opposite Figure 32. **(Top)** Showing sandstone habitat of *Cleome kenneallyi* in the Wet season. **(Below)** The plant in full flower. Courtesy of Greg Keighery/DEC.

Notes

1 J. A. Panton, 'The Discovery, Physical Geography, and Resources of Kimberley District, Western Australia', *Proceedings of the Royal Geographical Society of Australasia*, vol. 1, 1883, pp. 119–32, with the quote taken from the last page.

2 T. Willing and K. Kenneally, *Under a Regent Moon*, Department of Conservation and Land Management, Perth, 2002.

3 See Geoffrey Bolton, 'Alexander Forrest's expedition 1879 and early development of the cattle industry', this volume.

4 Baron von Mueller, A catalogue of plants collected during Mr Alexander Forrest's geographical exploration of north-west Australia in 1879, *Journ. & Proc. Royal Society New South Wales*, vol. 14, 1880, pp. 81–95.

5 K. Coate,'The 1990 expedition to Camden Harbour, northwest Kimberley: Part 1 - Background and Narrative', *The West. Aust. Naturalist*, vol. 27(4), 2011, pp. 193–229. See also Tony Quinlan,'1865 – Camden Harbour – The Quinlan Connection', this volume.

6 C. Richards, *There were three ships: The story of the Camden Harbour expedition 1864–65*, University of Western Australia Press, Nedlands, 1990.

7 See Michael Cusack, 'Joseph Bradshaw – Getting lost in the Kimberley and the art he found', this volume. Part of the original hand-drawn map used by Bradshaw is included in this paper.

8 Willing and Kenneally, *Under a Regent Moon*, p. 49.

9 ibid., p. 24.

10 ibid., p. 25.

11 *West Australian*, 14 August 1893, p. 4.

12 P. Ogden, *Bradshaw via Coolibah: the history of Bradshaw's Run and Coolibah Station*, Historical Society of the Northern Territory, Darwin, 1989, pp. 1 & 4.

13 M. Cartwright, *The Never Never country: a history of the Roper River & Urapunga*, Max Cartwright, 1999, p. 115.

14 S. M. Barber, *The Pride of Prahran. A history of the Prahran library 1860-2010*, City of Stonnington, Victoria, 2010, p. 26.

15 I. Nesdale, *The little Missus: Mrs Aeneas Gunn*, Lynton Publications Pty Ltd, Blackwood, South Australia, 1977, pp. 31, 74 & 75.

16 Mrs Aeneas Gunn, *The Little Black Princess*, Alexander Moring Ltd, London, 1905.

17 Mrs Aeneas Gunn, *We of the Never-Never*, Hutchinson & Co., London, 1908.

18 Maluka derives from 'Marluga' or 'old man' in the local Yangman language at Elsey. See F. Merlan (compiler), *Big River Country: stories from Elsey Station*, IAD Press, Alice Springs, 1996, p. xv.

19 J. Bradshaw, 'Notes on a Recent Trip to Prince Regent's River', *Transactions of the Royal Geographical Society of Australasia (Victorian Branch)*, vol. 9(2), 1892, p. 99.

20 C. C. Macknight, *The voyage to Marege*', Melbourne University Press, Carlton, 1976, p. 1; and 'Macassans and the Aboriginal past', *Archaeology in Oceania*, vol. 21(1), 1986, pp. 69–75. See also Cathie Clement, 'Maritime Exploration on the Kimberley Coast', this volume.

21 P. P. King was the first Australian to reach the rank of Rear Admiral, hydrographer and naturalist, he sailed with Allan Cunningham and J. S. Roe to map the north-west coast.

22 P. P. King, *Narrative of a survey of the intertropical and western coasts of Australia. Performed between the years 1818 and 1822*, London, 1827, facsimile, Libraries Board of South Australia, Adelaide, 1969, vol. 1, p. 135.

23 Ian Crawford, *We won the victory: Aborigines and outsiders on the north-west coast of the Kimberley*, Fremantle Arts Centre Press, Fremantle, 2001, pp. 75–7.

24 State Records Office of Western Australia (SROWA), Cons 514, Department of Lands & Surveys (L & S), item 1890/2041, *Bradshaw, Joseph, Pastoral leases - re applications for*, letter, Bradshaw to the Commissioner, 20 April 1892.

25 All three files are held at the SROWA. In addition to the file mentioned above, there are letters in items 1892/0819 & 1892/0957 of the Colonial Secretary's Office (CSO) Inward Correspondence, Cons 527.

26 Only the first Bradshaw letter of October 1890 is on plain paper. Thereafter all the letters, on good quality paper, display an embossed heraldic crest, featuring a stag under a fruiting grapevine with a French inscription "Qui vit content tient assez" which means "Who lives content holds enough". The letter of 15 June 1891 is unique in that it features an uncoloured embossed crest. Thereafter, three 1891 and one 1892 letters display a blue crest, while all subsequent correspondence has a red crest.

27 SROWA, Cons 514, L & S, item 1890/2041, Bradshaw to the Commissioner, 15 June 1891. Bradshaw's address on this letter was 584 Little Collins Street, Melbourne.

28 SROWA, Cons 514, L & S, item 1890/2041, Bradshaw to the Commissioner, 20 April, 1892. *Note in red ink on letter reads "evidently 15°30'S". Bradshaw's address on this letter was Marigui via Derby.

29 *Northern Territory Times and Gazette*, 30 September 1892 and *West Australian*, 27 October, 1892.

30 C. Clement, *Kimberley District Pastoral Leasing Directory, 1881–1900*, National Heritage, Mount Lawley (WA), 1993.

31 C. Daley, 'Baron Sir Ferdinand Mueller: botanist, explorer, and geographer', *The Victorian Historical Magazine*: vol. 10(1&2), 1924, pp. 1–55; J. H. Maiden, 'Ferdinand von Mueller' *Agricultural gazette of New South Wales*, 7, 1896, pp. 742–5.

32 R.W. Home, A. M. Lucas, S. Maroske, D. M. Sinkora, and J. H.Voigt, *Regardfully yours: selected correspondence of Ferdinand Mueller.* Volumes 1–3: 1840–1896, European Academic Publishers, Berne, 1998, 2002 & 2006.

33 J. S. Battye, 'Memoirs of the late Baron von Mueller', *Journal of proceedings of the Mueller Botanic Society of Western Australia*, vol. 1(5), 1900, pp. 5–12.

34 http://acms.sl.nsw.gov.au/item/itemDetailPaged.aspx?itemID=422826 (accessed 31 July 2010).

35 Home, et al., *Regardfully yours.*

36 *West Australian*, 1 November 1900, p. 4.

37 Ferdinand Mueller to Joseph Bradshaw, 29 November 1890.

38 *Euchlaena* is a genus of grasses in the family Poaceae that includes both annual and perennial species. Commonly known as teosintes they are native to Mexico, Guatemala, and Nicaragua. *Euchlaena luxurians* is now placed in the genus *Zea* that includes the domesticated maize, or corn. There is no evidence that any of these plants survived.

39 *Inquirer and Commercial News*, Perth, 19 August 1891, p. 6.

40 Ferdinand Mueller to Joseph Bradshaw, 21 June 1891. All the Mueller letters to Joseph Bradshaw cited in this paper are in the possession of John Bradshaw and are used with his permission.

41 Bradshaw, 'Notes on a Recent Trip to Prince Regent's River'.

42 M. Donaldson and K. Kenneally (eds), *Rock art of the Kimberley*, Kimberley Society, Perth, 2007. K. Kenneally, M. Lewis, M. Donaldson, and C. Clement (eds), *Aboriginal rock art of the Kimberley*, Occasional Paper No. 1, Kimberley Society, Perth, 1997.

43 F. S. Brockman, *Report on Exploration of North-West Kimberley, 1901*, Government Printer, Perth 1902. See also Mike Donaldson and Ian Elliot, 'Brockman's North-West Kimberley Expedition, 1901', this volume.

44 See footnote 1 for details.

45 Ferdinand Mueller to Joseph Bradshaw, 4 July 1891.

46 Ferdinand Mueller to Joseph Bradshaw, 12 September 1891.

47 Baron von Mueller, 'Observations on plants, collected during Mr Joseph Bradshaw's expedition to the Prince Regent's River', *Proceedings of the Linnean Society of New South Wales*, vol. 2(6), 1891, pp. 457–78. Bradshaw, 'Notes on a Recent Trip to Prince Regent's River'.

48 Named by Mueller to honour 'Heinrich Keller of Darmstadt [Germany], one of the leading promoters of rural culture during the latter half of this century through many parts of the world'.

49 J. Bradshaw, Journal of an expedition from Wyndham to Prince Regent River District. January 13-6 June 6 1891, [121 page manuscript], Mitchell Library, Sydney, NSW, B967, pp. 25–7.

50 Barber, *The Pride of Prahran*, p. 26; and see Willing and Kenneally, *Under a Regent Moon*, p. 9.

51 H. J. Hewson, Brassicaceae (Cruciferae), in *Flora of Australia*, Volume 8, Lecythidales to Batales, Australian Government Publishing Service, Canberra, 1982, pp. 230 & 389.

All photographs by the author unless otherwise indicated.

Under A Regent Moon. Part 2: Frontier conflict at Marigui

Kevin F. Kenneally

There are many humorous things in the world; among them the white man's notion that he is less savage than the other savages – Mark Twain, *Travels Around the Equator*, 1897.

One cannot discuss the Marigui settlement – the subject of the previous paper – without reference to the impact Bradshaw's party was to have on the Indigenous people who occupied the area. The question of 'Frontier Conflict' has been discussed at length by other authors.[1] This paper relates primarily to the Marigui exploration and settlement.

Aeneas Gunn in his 'Pioneering in Northern Australia' reports on Aboriginal contact and conflict during their time at Marigui.[2] Today, people of very different beliefs can take the same events and interpret them as a precise vindication of their own worldview. There is no disguising that what Gunn has to say comes across as surprisingly frank, hostile, offensively racist and downright patronising but it must be understood that his views reflect the then social attitudes and milieu of a long-dead, colonial Australia. His writing also highlights the ignorance and frustration of settlers who had no understanding of Indigenous culture or Aboriginal dispossession via land appropriation.[3] Bradshaw and Gunn were not "rednecks" but had good personal reputations and regarded themselves as 'chivalrous bushmen'.[4] However, they quickly discovered how difficult, complicated and often contradictory life could be on the Australian frontier.[5] They could not understand why Aboriginal people opposed 'the inevitable and invincible march of progress'.[6]

In colonial Australia, European notions of property and possession sanctioned the Crown's assertion of perfect sovereignty over the continent.[7] Cathie Clement has pointed out that: 'In making provision for land tenure in Western Australia, early legislation did not confront the issue of Aboriginal access after allocation.' On 22 March 1850, an Order in Council (issued in Britain) laid down fresh terminology for pastoral tenure. The Order reserved the usual rights to the government and, for the first time in Western Australia,

Opposite
Mickey Bungani, one of Howard Coate's most trusted informants.
Image – Howard Coate, courtesy of Kevin Coate.

it reserved rights to Aborigines. The Order stated that:

> Nothing contained in any pastoral lease shall prevent the aboriginal natives of this colony from entering upon the lands comprised therein, and seeking the subsistence therefrom in their accustomed manner.[8]

819/92

Mărigui
via Derby W.A.
25-4-92

COLONIAL SECRETARY'S OFFICE
23 MAY.92
PERTH, W.A.

The Government Resident
Derby—

Sir. I respectfully request that you will take steps to afford me adequate police protection at Marigui between the Prince Regent and Roe Rivers. Kimberly; where I am forming a pastoral settlement; The recent murders of pearlers and others on the coast of my country indicate the attitude and daring of the Natives; and only the care and vigilance of the party at my settlement has hitherto held them in check; as the Hon the Premier in his letter to me of Jan 19th last, refuses me the necessary executive power to deal with the Aborigines. I trust you will be able to comply with the request of this letter. I can place my schooner at your service for transit of men & horses

I have etc.

Yours most obediently
Joseph Bradshaw

As early as 1865, the Western Australian colonial Governor John Hampton had warned Robert Sholl, the Resident Magistrate appointed to oversee the ill-fated Camden Harbour settlement, that the Aborigines were supposedly 'troublesome and treacherous'. The guidelines given to Sholl repeated advice given to Colonel B. T. Finniss for the new Adam Bay settlement in the Northern Territory. The South Australian government had told Finniss that:

> ...while it may be well to encourage communication with them, by showing them you are prepared to trust them, you will take every precaution against them taking you by surprise, by always being prepared to act upon the defensive, by keeping regular watch in your camp, and by ordering your party not to move about the country in small parties, or unarmed. Above all you must warn your party to abstain from anything like hostility towards them, and to avoid the extremities of a conflict, which must be only had in recourse to self-defence, and only then from absolute necessity.[9]

Bradshaw, writing about his 1891 overland expedition, recorded that he 'had four white men and two Palmerston blacks, from the Larigea tribe, who proved as useful and reliable as any European'. He gave the Aboriginal men 'some instruction and practice in rifle and revolver shooting and they appeared to be efficient marksmen'.[10] He also stated:

> I had given strict orders that, except in cases of emergency, no shot was to be fired at natives without my permission or instructions. Fortunately no such emergency occurred during the whole of our journey, unless, perhaps one night when we were camped near Nigger Gorge...[11]

Bradshaw recounted how at this location a sentry on early morning watch had seen 'a dark object' crawling towards the camp. Then:

> The discharge of a rifle caused the intruding object to disappear as if by magic, and an inspection of the ground round the camp in the morning proved that a considerable number of blackfellows had left their tracks there, but whether their object was curiosity or hostility it was hard to determine.[12]

In his unpublished journal Bradshaw noted that:

> A place at the tidal water was called Nigger Gorge on account of the number of nigger encampments there. But I do not think there would be any serious trouble with the Blacks, nor do I consider them to be as numerous or vicious as the pearlers and others represent them.[13]

Yet, only a year later, he wrote:

> The Bingi Natives are very numerous, and daring they are of splendid phisique [sic], and of tawny or olive colored complexion; as their movements are daily becoming more aggressive I must

Opposite
Bradshaw's letter requesting police protection at Marigui. Courtesy of State Records Office of Western Australia.

apply to the Government for police protection or else for license or executive power to protect the lives & property on the settlement at my own discretion.[14]

Another man who had been in the locality in 1886 described it as 'a hunter's paradise, and stocked with game of all kinds of game'. His account continued:

> These delights, however, were counterbalanced by dingoes (very plentiful), hostile natives, March flies, mosquitoes and spear grass. With the exercise of care and caution the niggers could be kept off but they used to run the horses into bogs, kill them, cut off their manes and tails, which they plaited into fringe ornaments, and tear the shoes off to make weapons and chopping implements...
>
> The ranges about the Prince Regent are the favourite haunts of aboriginals. They are a powerfully built race, the men average 6ft., and are both cunning and fierce, and although many overtures of friendship were made to them they were always very hostile.[15]

In a later newspaper feature on Joseph Bradshaw reference was made to his contact with Aboriginal people during his many expeditions:

> Mr. Bradshaw has had numerous interviews of a risky nature with the blacks, to whom he was the first presentment they had ever seen of a being with pale complexion and dressed, or, as it often happened, partially dressed. On one occasion, when fording the Roe River, he and his blackboy dismounted to lead their horses up through the jungle of the opposite bank, when the boy gave a sudden scream, and fell doubled up between his horse's legs, with a shattered spear and spurting blood. As Mr. Bradshaw stooped to pick up his boy's Winchester another spear swished through the collar of his tunic, taking the skin off the left side of his neck. The men following with the packs commenced firing overhead, and drove off the horde of assailants. Mr. Bradshaw carried his devoted blackboy to a clear space a quarter of a mile away, where he died in a quarter of an hour. He has always treated both Binghais and Malays with consideration and justice; but he says that there occur times when quick and stern measures are necessary to meet emergencies.[16]

Four letters, written in 1891–92, have been found relating to Bradshaw's interest in gaining 'security, and ability to control the settlement, the aborigines, the pearlers, and others if I were appointed to the commission of the peace and protector of aborigines'.[17] One was sent to Derby,[18] and the other three directly to the Premier Sir John Forrest. There is also a letter of support from Joseph Panton, Police Magistrate, Melbourne, to the Premier.[19] Bradshaw's appointment as a Justice of the Peace was eventually announced in the *Government Gazette* of 16 June 1892 and in the final letter in that file, he promises to visit Derby to be sworn in. His swearing in is confirmed in a report from the Resident Magistrate in Derby.[20]

Frontier conflict - The European View

Gunn wrote:

> The natives on the Prince Regent River were reputed to be the most truculent savages on the Australian mainland, and we were informed that if our party were allowed to affect a landing at all, it would certainly be massacred and eaten the very first night it camped ashore.[21]
>
> We were not a large party to repel an attack should they have displayed any hostility. Two of us were passable shots, and one of the two never levelled a rifle at anything more formidable than kangaroos. The cook was a more dangerous enemy to his friends than to the enemy, and Francisco Blanca had a wild, enthusiastic way of shooting that was costly in the item of cartridges, but likely to be inexpensive to life in the ranks of the enemy.[22]

In early 1892 Kolumboi, a young Aboriginal man originating from an area south of Halls Creek, reported the presence of 'lots, plenty wild blackfellow' at a waterhole near the Prince Regent River. Bradshaw despatched Gunn and Hugh Young 'to interview the dusky warriors' and, as Gunn later recalled, 'if there should be any necessity for shooting, gave us instructions not to waste a shot'.[23]

Within the next few weeks, a pearler, Captain Frank Biddles, asked the Marigui men 'to cooperate with him in wreaking vengeance on the natives for their foul and unprovoked murder of Martin Liljroth'.[24] Gunn recalled that he led a party 'on an ostensible exploring expedition to the region beyond Trafalgar, but my private instructions were to "disperse" any blackfellow's camp we might meet.' Gunn's party attempted to surprise a group of Aborigines in their camp but all of those people fled into the adjacent mangroves. On meeting back at the Aboriginal camp after splitting up during the pursuit in the mangroves, Gunn noticed that the other members of the party 'were all strangely silent'." He later wrote: "I asked no questions. It is considered a breach of northern etiquette to ask a man whether he has shot a blackfellow or not."[25]

Comparatively little conflict appears to have occurred during the next two years. In late 1893 the *Northern Territory Times and Gazette* reported that:

> The blacks in the Prince Regent district have not given much trouble up to date, and no annoyance is feared on that head. It has been a principle of the station folk to keep them at a respectable distance morning noon and night, and the system has so far worked very well.[26]

Gunn wrote:

> There are few, if any, of the Northern pioneers who would not prefer to live at peace with the natives. But the hostilities are, in the majority of instances, forced upon them. The truth of the matter is that the blackfellow is almost everywhere a refractory ore in the crucible of civilisation and does not submit readily to its processes. He almost invariably opposes the inevitable and invincible march of progress... Practically he contributes less than nothing to the development of the country. He kills the squatters' cattle, horses and sheep in wanton lust of blood, and he often spears the squatter's men for the sake of seeing them wriggle and writhe in mortal agony. Hardly a station has been settled or a goldfield opened without the sacrifice of one or more valuable lives. The roads to the Kimberley goldfields are lined by graves of men killed in cold blood by the blacks. And many a station has a little fenced mound that tells the same pathetic tale. Southern people and Exeter Hall [London] philanthropists, to whom the black fellow is either a name or a bogie to scare children with, have got the impression that whites are often murdered because they interfere with the blackfellows' women. In ninety-nine cases out of a hundred the accusation is a contemptible slander...[27]
>
> But the most interesting facts about the blackfellow are that he exists, that he defies identification with other living types, that he has existed without considerable modifications of type or custom longer than any other human being, and that his inevitable destiny is to be, in a few years, trampled down by the march of Progress, or to become a pariah, a reproach, a scarecrow in the cast off garbs of civilization.[28]

Frontier Conflict - An attack at Marigui

Gunn wrote with regard to a night that seems to have been in 1892:

> A very wheezy mopoke call came down the slope of Mount Waterloo... I thought "well, now, that mopoke up the slope has asthma, and ... they are all around the house. It's niggers." I reached for my Martini, prodded Young with it... Kolumboi came, rubbing his eyes... We slipped out into the dark... We each selected a spot from which the nearest sounds came, and levelled our rifles... For an instant my finger quivered on the hair trigger, and then a sharp bark rang out, followed, almost simultaneously, by two others. There was a solitary groan, a stampede of rushing feet ... The mopoke calls ceased... It was a well organised attack, and had our vigilance and knowledge of natural history not been equal to the blacks' craft, we would in all probability have been massacred, and added another case to the long list of Aboriginal atrocities. The mopoke attack was the last assault the blacks made on our Marigui homestead, but it was not by any means the last occasion on which we had a brush with them.[29]

Frontier Conflict - Aboriginal View

It is clear from Gunn's writing that members of the local Aboriginal groups kept close watch on the Marigui settlement from the time of their arrival. This resulted in an uneasy truce. Gunn wrote: 'The blackfellows came within 200 yards [182 metres] of our camp without our being appraised by some means or other...' and 'Although we often came on the tracks of the disturbing element in the morning, we never succeeded in sighting our quarry when in pursuit of it at night.'

The following is a story connected to the Bradshaw and Gunn settlement at Marigui as told to Howard Coate by Bungani, an old Aboriginal man who was a boy there at the time.[30] His story is reproduced in full below to provide the meaning of what happened (as well as the relationship between present and past).[31]

> The ship came in from the belly of the ocean. It came across the ocean to the country looking for a place with the intention of building (a station). The boat was full up with animals. These were the first whites to come here to the mainland. They found a passage between some basalt islands here and were weaving in and out everywhere around the Mowari Islands over there. Oh yes, this is the mouth of it they said. This place was the Prince Regent River where it opens out, this the place, we'll go in they said. Anguleluna entrance they went thro' over there only. Those Yam islands are over there. Let it stay here.
>
> The whites camped at Banargud – the yam place. There were two boats here belly side up – flat decks – and over this way in the bottom side the horses were standing up in the aft looking about the place. They (men) looked out in different places and tried this way in the dinghy (small craft). Let's paddle along and look at the place, they said. 'Where shall we build? They said. Therefore they paddled along looking at the places. "Oh yes, here's water here, we'll put our things down here in the high open country (open camping place) they said. At Nubanari they built. What natives are here? They said. They didn't expect any trouble with the natives. "We'll build, they said. Then the whites already unloaded their gear and were carting it. They landed all the horses and the cattle they put in the flat bottom barge. Altogether they towed it in. The horses and cattle were standing in the belly part and at the shore they landed them then they jumped, the horses (did) and they led the cattle. These cows were milking cows. They used to squeeze their udders. The cows had understanding "come on they called to her". They fed about on the water side they were on good green grass on the side of the hill where many lady apples grow. That's how they did.
>
> Then the whites began building. While they didn't firmly establish it they built three houses. This boat that brought them the whites in, the natives had seen from the top of the hill. "Must be something what's moving about. It looked as if it was the

backside of Mount Trafalgar moving away, they said. Oh they are different sort and belong to the deep wide open sea, they are these" they said to themselves. (Hither to they had seen steamers far out to sea and never knew what they were and considered they just belonged to the deep). Astonishing it was at that time; the boat had smoke going out of it.[32] Amazement got hold of them at the smoke (because of the smoke) and faeces started to fall out of the men, women and children. (They got such a shock that they nearly lost control of their bowels.) They shouted. Then they gathered together. "What are these? Which they said to each other, are these things we have seen. Several of them were edging along and they said to each other "What are these things, what, they said. Then they hold a war council, men and women altogether. (What) are we sitting here masturbating ourselves (for) they were saying? "What shall we do?" We want to try and let a spy go, they said amongst themselves. Still they were discussing the place. So three or four spies went out. The mob stayed. In the hide out, that rock, the scrubby place they were watching (from).

These whites were unloading, they told them. They were watching them moving about. "Oh yes, these are devils. These are devils" they said. Already all of them the Landadnari-ites (Hunter-river-ites) Bregural-ites (cockroach-ites) Ganeri-ites (grape-vine-ites of Scotts Straight) and many people they went. Already the spies had returned (saying) "many devils they are, they took over our country for us". So they took council. The important man said "we'll wax-up". They emptied their pouches of spear heads in making many spears. The womeras 'threw it for them' (probably means quivered the spears for them). They waxed them up for them at Imalala (the nice place). Already they made them new with yellow ochre, both the spears and the womeras and the fighting sticks they dressed up in white paint and they donned white headbands. The crowd was bright with feathers and they string lined along. You could see their foreheads (they were near) strung out to the shore, from end to end the mob was strung out. They made themselves like a range altogether from end to end.

On top they shouted and charged. "What's that" they said, the whites did. Only natives they said. They were firing out and landed spears on them. "Wait, wait" the whites said. They had good sense, these devils. They didn't fire at that time what-you-ma-call-it, with this they always fire - the fire arms when they did. This head man of the whites. No, already we'll get after them he told his team. 'Yes' they said then they fired after them. She Djarun, got shot in the knee the skin was cut off with the edge of a bullet (probably from a shot gun). That's the only one they shot, they cleaned them up. They shot the spears and womeras down and splintered them. They took the spears, that's how they did to them they beat them. They, the natives went back to their place and came out to their store place over there, where they left them at Imalala. All the wounded ones went there for their sickness and held them there. Even the horses they speared down already they killed them, the horses and cattle and after a while they turned back and were camping about from place to place.

What-its-name, roundabout they burnt the country Nalnbu (Roe River) place Worewad that side. Then after a good while they came back after some months they came out to the place. A good while had passed, we'll try and visit them so they string-lined. They swam across the Hunter River and across the Roe River and they came out to Banamba (the crocodile place). There was nothing at the place it was lonely they said. 'Oh, they have shifted themselves; they said one to another over there in the camping place where they speared them, where they had built. They checked over the place (they tramped it down) many people. "What are these they said it was shining bottles and iron, ah yes try and made tomahawks, iron tomahawks. They got the ones left behind by the devil fellows. Black wire, spears they joined with these and they speared the animals with the wire. We spear animals so this is strong, they said. They were picking up the wire. They cut honey in the trees and altogether they were chopping up the trees. The best tomahawk, 'ah, these have taken my eye she was saying (they, the people said). The women had faith in what they were getting. The mob was sharpening them and the mob went to cut sugar-bag (honey comb out). The devils have gone bush to their own place, the ones the natives were firing on. They didn't spear them tho' they just went by themselves. The whites shot the natives and they (the natives) retreated and all the wounded. Some of them had flesh wounds. The devils had stayed two years at this place where they had built. They scattered the natives. They could have stayed and it might have been a big place, if they hadn't had any trouble. These white devils got annoyed and so the devils returned (to their own place). They killed all the horses and that's how they did to the cattle. The story is finished and told. This man was a little boy. They saw Bungani with them. This is him putting the story he is now old and grey headed and that is what he said.

Left Gunn's pursuit of Aborigines into the mangroves was made almost impossible by the mud and tangled nature of the root systems. Photo – Kevin Kenneally

Acknowledgements

Dr Cathie Clement, for her invaluable advice on Kimberley historical events and for her helpful and constructive editing of this paper.

Kevin Coate for allowing access to the Howard Coate archives.

Notes

1 See for example H. Reynolds, *The Other Side of the Frontier: Aboriginal resistance to the European invasion of Australia*, 1981, UNSW Press, Sydney, 2006, and *Frontier: Aborigines, Settlers and Land*, Allen & Unwin, St Leonards (NSW), 1987; and B. Attwood & S. G. Foster (eds), *Frontier Conflict: The Australian Experience*, National Museum of Australia, Canberra, 2003.

2 T. Willing and K. Kenneally, *Under a Regent Moon: A historical account of pioneer pastoralists Joseph Bradshaw and Aeneas Gunn at Marigui Settlement, Prince Regent River, Kimberley, Western Australia, 1891–1892*, Department of Conservation and Land Management, Perth, 1992, pp. 21–64.

3 F. Merlan, '"Making people quiet" in the pastoral north: reminiscences of Elsey Station', *Aboriginal History*, vol. 2(1), 1978, pp. 71–106.

4 On his death the *Prahran Telegraph* (28 March 1903, p. 3) described Gunn as 'a gentleman who by his genial nature endeared himself to all he came in contact with...'

5 R. Murray, 'Three of the Never Never', *Quadrant*, March 2004.

6 Willing and Kenneally, *Under a Regent Moon*, p. 28.

7 P. Cochrane, 'Was Batman robbing?', *Australian Literary Review*, 7 September 2011, p. 15.

8 C. Clement, Australia's North-west: A study of exploration, land policy and land acquisition, 1644-1884, PhD Thesis, Murdoch University, 1991, pp. 70, 85 and 87.

9 ibid., pp. 249–50.

10 J. Bradshaw, Journal of an expedition from Wyndham to Prince Regent River District, W.A. Jan 13-June 6 1891, [121 page manuscript], Mitchell Library, Sydney, B967, pp. 12 and 90; J. Bradshaw, Notes on a Recent Trip to Prince Regent's River, *Transactions of the Royal Geographical Society of Australasia (Victorian Branch)*, vol. 9(2), 1892, p. 91.

11 Bradshaw, 'Notes on a Recent Trip to Prince Regent's River', p. 97.

12 ibid., pp. 97–8.

13 Bradshaw, Journal, p. 99. See Michael Cusack, 'Joseph Bradshaw', this volume, for the renaming of the gorge.

14 State Records Office of Western Australia (SROWA), Cons 514, Department of Lands & Surveys, 1890/2041, *Bradshaw, Joseph. Pastoral leases – re applications for*, letter, Bradshaw to the Commissioner, 20 April 1892.

15 'Our Unexplored Territory. The Prince Regent River Country' by "B", *Sunday Times*, 5 May 1901, p. 6.

16 *Northern Territory Times and Gazette*, 19 March 1914, p. 5, reprinted from the *Farmer and Grazier* of 20 January 1914. The spearing incident occurred not at the Roe River but at the junction of the Gregory and Victoria Rivers (NT), and was reported in newspapers that include *The Sydney Morning Herald*, 7 July 1894.

17 SROWA, Cons 527, Colonial Secretary's Office (CSO), Inward Correspondence, 1892/0957, letter, Joseph Bradshaw to Sir John Forrest, 2 December 1891.

18 SROWA, Cons 527, CSO, 1892/0819, letter, Joseph Bradshaw to the Government Resident, Derby, 25 April 1892.

19 SROWA, Cons 527, CSO, 1892/0819, letter, Joseph Panton to Sir John Forrest, 21 May 1892.

20 SROWA, Cons 527, CSO, 1892/0957, letter, Joseph Bradshaw to Sir John Forrest, 30 June 1892; letter, Ernest Black, Resident Magistrate, Derby to the Under Secretary, Perth, 21 July 1892.

21 Willing and Kenneally, *Under a Regent Moon*, p. 26.

22 ibid., p. 28.

23 ibid., p. 42.

24 ibid., p. 44. The murder of Martin Liljroth took place on 22 December 1891 in a bay near Anderdon Islands at the mouth of Prince Frederick Harbour.

25 ibid., pp. 43–7.

26 *Northern Territory Times and Gazette*, 10 November 1893. Notes of the Week.

27 Willing and Kenneally, *Under a Regent Moon*, p. 28.

28 ibid., p. 31.

29 ibid., pp. 54–5.

30 Transcription by Howard Coate from a taped interview (Tape 12) with Mickey Bungani, one of Howard's most trusted informants. He and Howard spent time together in the Prince Regent River and Roe River region and the interview was most likely recorded in the early 1950s. The notes in brackets were inserted by Howard when he was transcribing the tape. Howard Coate was a lay missionary, who moved to the Kimberley in 1934 to work with Aboriginal people. His interest in linguistics and Aboriginal mythology brought him to the notice of Professor A. P. Elkin and Dr Arthur Capell in what was to become a long association. For an overview of Howard's life and work in the Kimberley see W. McGregor, 'Introduction' in *Studies in Kimberley languages in honour of Howard Coate*, Lincon Europa, Munchen & Newcastle, 1996, pp. 1–12. Before his death in 2002, Howard gave his papers and photos to his nephew Kevin Coate who kindly made the transcription available to me.

31 For comment on the role and value of Aboriginal oral history see D. B. Rose, 'Oral histories and knowledge' in Attwood & Foster (eds), *Frontier Conflict*, pp. 120–31.

32 It is possible that the smoke from the *Moreton* chartered by Bradshaw to transport stock to the settlement caused fear and trepidation and this may have been a trigger for the attack on Marigui. According to J. R. B. Love (*Stone-Age Bushmen of To-day: Life and Adventure among a Tribe of Savages in North-Western Australia*, Blackie and Son Ltd, London, 1936) fire accompanies every important rite of the Worora and is regarded as a giver of energy and strength. Love also noted that, at every important ceremony held on the men's meeting ground, the men conclude by piling green leaves on the fire and smoking themselves. Kim Akerman (pers. comm., 2010) has suggested that smoke 'was regarded as mist – which is said to be produced by both wandjinas and rainbow serpents (wungguurr snake)'.

Below Summit of Mount Trafalgar showing the wattle, *Acacia tumida* var. *extenta*.
Photo – Kevin Kenneally

Mt Agnes
Pearson R
James R
ISDELL R
BARNETT R
Mt Barnett
PHILLIPS R
Harriss Ck
Edkins Ck

The Kimberley exploration expeditions of Frank Hann in 1898

Mike Donaldson and Ian Elliot

By the 1890s the Kimberley coast had been mapped by the detailed surveys of Phillip Parker King in 1819–22,[1] and John Clements Wickham and John Lort Stokes on the *Beagle* in 1837–38.[2] Inland exploration, however, remained minimal despite the efforts of people who included George Grey in 1837–38,[3] Trevarton Sholl in 1865,[4] Alexander Forrest in 1879,[5] Chas. Burrowes in 1886,[6] and Joseph Bradshaw in 1891,[7] as shown in Figure 2.

Grey had unfortunately chosen a particularly rugged part of the Kimberley to attempt penetration with horses, goats and sheep, and succeeded in progressing only about 80 kilometres inland in three months. Sholl, who followed an earlier exploratory trip of his father's, located some potential grazing country he called Panter Downs on the Sale River, but did not determine its extent. Forrest was unable to find a way across the King Leopold Ranges, but did find large tracts of fine grazing country along the Fitzroy River. Bradshaw encountered mostly rugged sandstone country on his route from Wyndham to the Roe River (which he mistakenly took to be the Prince Regent River), and prospectors who rushed to Halls Creek following the discovery of gold in 1885 did little to explore the area over the ranges. A few prospectors and explorers did, however, find passes through the King Leopold Ranges in 1886, 1887 and the early 1890s and were thus able to examine country north of those ranges and west of the Durack Range.[8]

In 1898, near the junction of the Hann and Fitzroy Rivers, Frank Hann came across a tree marked 'R.B. 44' which he identified as Mr Robert Button's 44th camp. He comments that Button 'has been a great traveller and explorer, and it is a pity he has not published any account of his explorations in these regions'.[9] So, as late as the mid 1890s, the extensive areas of the central inland Kimberley suitable for cattle remained almost totally unknown to pastoralists.

Opposite
Part of Hann's tracing of his route (red line) and the country around the upper Isdell and Phillips (Hann) Rivers, Mount Barnett, and Mount Elizabeth.
Original held by State Records Office of Western Australia.
(Inset) Figure 1. Frank Hann (seated) and Talbot, ca. 1910.
Courtesy of State Library of Western Australia (025949PD) and Royal Western Australian Historical Society (Inc.).

Frank Hann

Frank Hugh Hann was born in Wiltshire, England, in 1845 but came to Australia with his parents Joseph and Mary in 1851. After growing up on cattle stations pioneered by his father near Charters Towers in Queensland, he set up his own pioneer station at Lawn Hill in north-west Queensland in 1875 and became the quintessential Australian bushman: he discovered rich silver-lead deposits near Lawn Hill in 1887, was shot in the chest by 'bushranger' Joe Flick in 1889,[10] and in 1895, after 20 years developing Lawn Hill as a cattle station, he was forced to walk off it when the banks foreclosed during a period of severe rural depression. His departure was only delayed by a broken thigh received when his mount fell while mustering horses.

Hann's exploration diaries, with explanatory footnotes and generalized route maps, were published by Donaldson and Elliot,[11] and the diary extracts below are from that publication. One of the few photographs of Hann, thought to date from about 1885, is shown in Figure 1.

Leaving Lawn Hill in April 1896 with not much more than a mob of 67 horses and associated plant, he travelled overland to Halls Creek with one white and six Aboriginal companions to begin a new life.

Below Figure 2. Major exploration expeditions in the Kimberley prior to Hann's 1898 trips across the King Leopold Ranges. Background topography is SRTM digital elevation image courtesy of NASA.

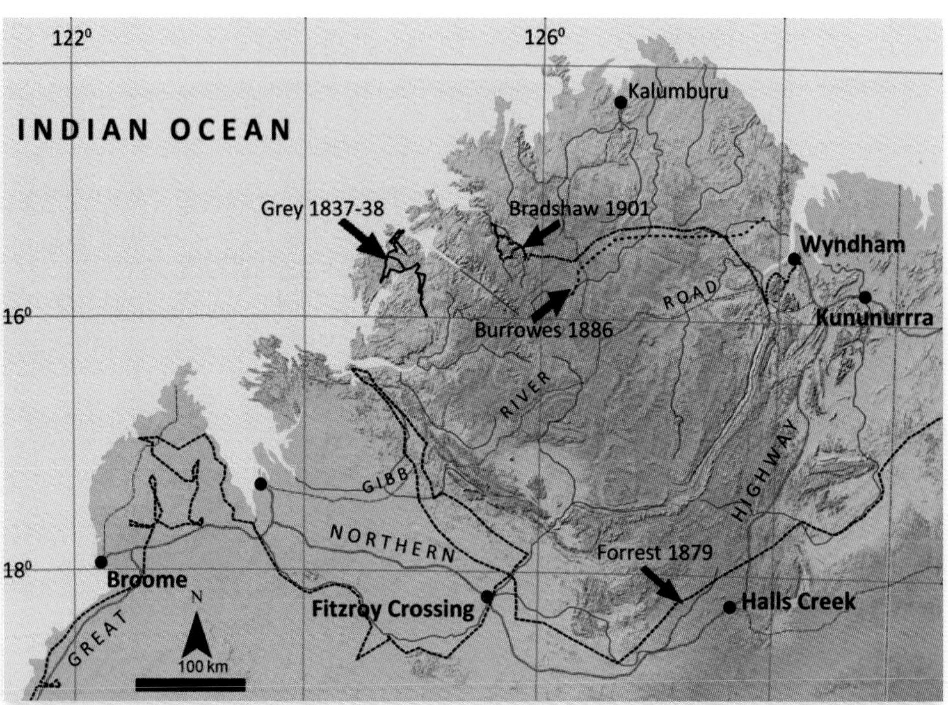

Finding things pretty quiet in the 'gold rush' town of Halls Creek, he continued on to the Pilbara and for about 18 months he travelled through the eastern Pilbara in search of pastoral country and also prospecting for gold. Based in a camp near Nullagine, his travels took him as far into the desert as Lake Disappointment, which he named along with many other topographic features in the area. He was within 40 kilometres of the huge Telfer gold deposit, but its discovery had to wait another 75 years.

Hann applied for a pastoral lease on the Davis River near Nullagine in June 1897, but apparently had difficulty raising money to stock it. Finding no opportunities in Western Australia, and having run out of money, he became increasingly depressed, as the following diary extracts reveal:

> Christmas day. Wet morning and very windy ... This is the worst Xmas I ever had. Oh I wish I had not left Lawn Hill. This life is most wretched. Kill any one ... I feel heartbroken now. Everything appear to be gone now. All up. (25 December 1897)

> This is the last day of 1897. Every year is worse and worse for me ... I made a fearful mistake in coming to W.A. as I am sure now there is nothing I will be able to do over here ... Oh how happy some people are tonight, and me so miserable. (31 December 1897)

> Flies bad today ... I am very much downhearted at everything. Oh, will I ever be happy again? I feel death would be a happy relief ... If I could only make a rise at something, what a good thing it would be to be sure. (23 January 1898)

After months of agonizing, Hann decided to return to Queensland:

> Gins Talbot and I went into Nullagine and got what rations I wanted and came back to camp ... My eyes are very bad ... I am going back to Queensland but what to do I do not know. (4 February 1898)

His party was just himself and his six Queensland Aboriginal companions: Talbot, Spider, Thorlow, Minnie, Mina, and Dora. He travelled from Nullagine to Bamboo Creek and across a patch of sandy desert to Wallal on Eighty Mile Beach, along the coast road to Lagrange and Broome, and then east to Derby.

Hann picked up in spirits in Derby and was advised by 'Inspector Ord of the police' to go to the Mount Broome area at the foot of the King Leopold Ranges, about 200 kilometres east of Derby, where prospectors had recently found some gold.[12] After spending ten days in the area prospecting and finding just a few specks of gold, Hann decided to find a way over the ranges, presumably to prospect for gold, but also undoubtedly always with a view to finding some new pastoral country he could take up and make a new start.

The King Leopold Ranges were still a formidable barrier to exploration at this time but Hann found a way up the range, albeit very rough, just west of Mount Broome, and saw there was abundant water on the other side. So a few days later, on 30 May 1898, he took his party and horses over the range, which is 500 metres above sea level at this point, and about 300 metres above the gullies he was prospecting. Two of the horses rolled down the range on the way up, smashing everything, but apparently not doing much damage to themselves. Having made it over this first obstacle of the King Leopolds, and finding no gold in a few gullies on the other side, he pressed on and struck a large creek which he correctly took to be the headwaters of the Lennard River. From there he followed the next ridge of the King Leopolds around to the north-west and with some difficulty went through what is now called Satans Pass, past Bold Bluff, and ran down what is now known as Honeysuckle Creek to a large stream that he subsequently named Bell Creek.[13]

Hann then followed the creek down keeping a big precipice range to his right, before turning east around what is now called Rifle Point, which is a few hundred metres south of the present Gibb River Road near the Silent Grove turnoff. For the first time north of the King Leopold Ranges he comments that this was good cattle country. Travelling through open grassy country for a few days the party continued to prospect for gold without success although one of the women found a little silver. Hann records having a shot at a brolga, but missing it, and that they caught five possums 'and they

Right Figure 3. Flat-topped Mount House is an isolated high point in an extensive grassy plain that Hann immediately recognized as excellent cattle country.
Photo – Mike Donaldson

were very good'. He named a prominent flat-topped hill Mount House after Dr House of Derby (Fig. 3), and a 'creek' at its base the Adcock 'after the Adcocks of Derby' (diary 4 June 1898). The 'creek' was shown on his plans as Adcock River and that is how it is known today (Fig. 4).

A few more days were spent in the Mount House area covering considerable distance on horseback while most of the party stayed at camp. The diary entries record many comments as to the 'splendid cattle country', 'fine cattle country' and 'splendid creeks, fine banks'. On 5 June 1898 he wrote:

> Saw good place for a station. I must try and take this country up. The gins had caught a lot of splendid black brim.

After inspecting the country as far north as the Isdell River he was even more impressed with the cattle potential of this area, and on 8 June he wrote:

> I will go right back to Derby if all go well and take this country up as it is too big a thing to lose but at the same time I doubt if anybody will be out here. I had no idea the country was so good. I never saw a better watered creek in my life. Marked a Boab tree at gorge on the left bank going down F.H.V111/VI/98 and Box tree here FH
> IX

Above Figure 4. The Adcock River is a permanent stream that runs through the grassy plains on the northern side of the King Leopold Ranges. Hann was impressed by the accessibility of the water courses in the area for cattle.
Photo – Mike Donaldson

Hann essentially back-tracked to the King Leopold Ranges but found a better pass through the first ridge south of Bold Bluff, naming it Brownrigg Pass after Dr Brownrigg of Broome. He came across some Aborigines in this area who he described as 'very cheeky': 'They thought they had us. I put a few shots over to them which blocked them for a time' (diary, 12 June 1898).

This was not the only encounter with Aborigines on this trip, but there does not appear to have been any direct conflict. He was always concerned that if the Aborigines knew how small his party was, they might be tempted to attack, so he tried his best to keep them at a distance.

Arriving back in Derby on 19 June, Hann made up his maps and tracings over the next few days and wrote to the Under Secretary for Lands in Perth reporting his trip. On 25 June he 'Went in to Derby and took up 793,000 acres. Gave a cheque on the Union Bank, Perth for £197/10/-' (diary, 25 June 1898).

Over the next few days Hann met with many of the West Kimberley's finest, including Dr and Mrs House, and others whose names are well known from rivers and ranges that Hann named subsequently, including Messrs Adcock, Ashton, Barnett, Bell, Blythe, Edgar, Manning, and Ord. He then picked up more stores and on 27 June he headed back to the country he had just discovered in order to more formally mark out the area he wanted to take up as a pastoral lease, and also to test a likely gold prospect he found on the way back from the earlier trip. Travelling to the gold diggings near Mount Broome, he again met the prospectors working there and readied his horses and packs for another trip across the King Leopold Ranges.

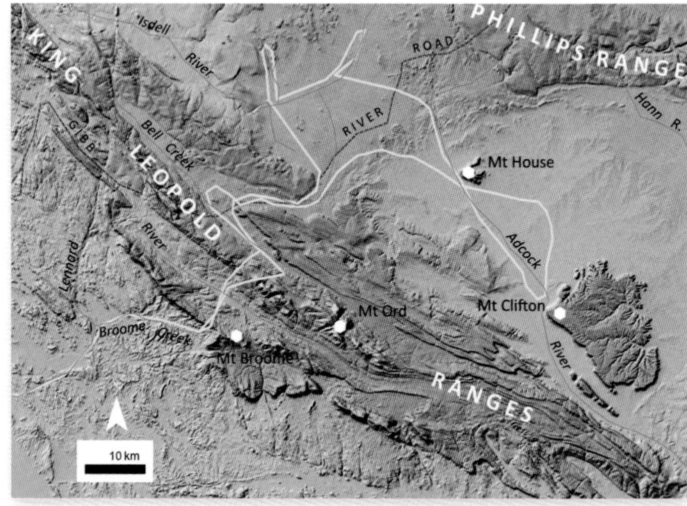

Right Figure 5. Map showing the route of Hann's first exploration trip across the King Leopold Ranges, May–June 1898. The position of the present Gibb River Road is shown for location purposes only. Background topography is SRTM digital elevation image courtesy of NASA.

On 9 July 1898 he crossed the range at the same place as previously, this time in the company of Messrs Ashton, Blythe, and Inspector Ord, in addition to his six Aboriginal companions. They did not find any gold in the reef Hann thought looked promising, and continued on to the Isdell River. Ashton and Blythe left Hann's group here and went on to the north-west to find some pastoral country of their own. Mr Ord went with Hann to Mount House, the Adcock River, and Mount Clifton, where they saw 'a big lot of blacks'. Ord then returned to Derby and Hann continued on to the south-east, climbing Mount Brennan and taking lots of sights before striking the Fitzroy River at a spectacular gorge he named Sir John Gorge (Fig. 6):

> Struck the Fitzroy. I never saw such a gorge before, cut right through the rocks, about 100 feet deep, could ride right up to the side (diary, 19 July 1898).

Skirting around the rocky ranges, Hann came across a large river coming from the north which he named the Phillips after the Commissioner of Police. He followed it down to its junction with the Fitzroy at the northern end of Sir John Gorge and also ran up the Fitzroy to the western end of another gorge that starts near the prominent hill he named Mount Warton, 'after Mr Warton of Broome'. On a tributary of his newly named Phillips River: 'The boys saw a marked tree. I saw it, it was one of Button's R.B. so shall call the creek Button's Creek.' (diary, 20 July 1898).[44]

Above Figure 6. The Fitzroy River cuts through the Sir John Range in the spectacular Sir John Gorge, named by Hann after Sir John Forrest, Premier of Western Australia at that time.
Photo – Mike Donaldson

Hann then followed the Phillips River (which was subsequently renamed the Hann River as there was already a Phillips River in the Ravensthorpe area in the south-west of the state) up to its headwaters, naming numerous tributaries along the way: Traine River, Dora, Ashton, Urquhart, and Macnamara Creeks, and a 'fine little lake I have called Lake Gladstone' (diary, 22 July 1898).[14] Where the Hann River comes out of Moll Gorge in the Phillips Range, he wrote: 'went on nice hill on right bank which I called Mount Caroline after my dear sister, and the Creek Caroline Creek' (diary, 25 July 1898).

All the time Hann comments on the quality of the country for cattle:

> I never saw better watered country in my life ... the best country I have seen ... splendid cattle country ... fine place for a station ... I never saw such a splendid country for water, and really good country ... good breeding country.

Above Figure 7. Boab tree on Barnett River marked 'F H' by Hann in July 1898 (photographed in August 1989). Photo – Mike Donaldson

Following the southern side of the Phillips Range, Hann went as far as the Isdell River before cutting back to the flat-topped range he named Mount Barnett ('after Barnett of the Lennard') and the 'creek' at its base he named the Barnett River. This is where the present Mount Barnett Roadhouse and Kupungarri community is situated on the Gibb River Road. During this expedition Hann marked many trees, both boabs and box (eucalypts), with a distinctive 'F H', which he used to describe the boundaries of his subsequent applications for pastoral lease blocks. Many of the boabs survive, such as that shown in Figure 7 which is near the present Mount Barnett station homestead.

He then followed the Barnett River almost to its headwaters before rejoining his 'Phillips' (Hann) River and following that up to its source in the Caroline Ranges. On the way he named Mount Elizabeth ('a big mountain') after his 'dear mother'.

Wanting to head more west than the water courses were heading, he went across the Caroline Ranges, finding it pretty rough going, until he came on the Charnley River, which he named after one of his Nullagine supporters. Continuing west and away from the river, he named Mount Blythe (he had earlier found Blythe's tracks near the river and 'was sorry to see them'), and continued south-west naming Synnot Creek and the Edkins Range before coming on the major gorge of the Isdell River (Fig. 8) after a five mile (8 kilometre) walk over rough rocky country. He saw it was impossible to get down

Above Figure 8. Isdell River gorge close to where Hann came on to it while looking for a route to the coast on 15 August 1898. Photo – Mike Donaldson

to the river as it was all a gorge with 'thousands of palms on it', so he went south east, naming the Sprigg River which joins the Isdell at Junction Hill on the northern side of the King Leopold Ranges.

On 19 August Hann and his party crossed the Isdell near Junction Hill and found a relatively easy route up what he called Gorge Creek over the top of the King Leopold Ranges to a tributary of the Barker River. His track down the range he described as 'a wonderful track... A dray track can be made over the range this way' (diary, 20 August 1898). This is shown on modern maps as Hann Pass at the headwaters of Talbot Creek, near Mount Hart station homestead. Although it has probably never been used as such since, this must have been a surprising find to Hann given the difficulty Alexander Forest had in trying to cross this range in 1879.

Once over the King Leopold Ranges, Hann followed the Barker River down through Barker Gorge in the Napier Range to the station that Blythe managed near the junction with the Lennard River, arriving there on 23 August. He went on to Derby arriving on 27 August, having been away for two months.

Although Hann does not mention it in his diaries, in his later paper to the Royal Society of Queensland, and in correspondence to the Under Secretary for Lands and Premier Sir John Forrest, he indicates that on his second Kimberley expedition, having confirmed the extensive excellent pastoral country, he tried to find a route to the coast. He recognized that access to a port in the area would be necessary to allow the country to reach its potential, particularly as the only routes he found across the King Leopold Ranges would require extensive work to make a road. However, the rugged impassable gorge of the Isdell River made it clear that there was no easy route to the coast in that vicinity.

Hann spent the next few years trying to raise money and interest in taking up and stocking this new country. He travelled to Perth, Sydney, Brisbane, and Melbourne but could not find any backers for this new project. There are no surviving diaries of this period, the last entry for this expedition being 5 September 1898, near Derby. The next known diary starts on 3 July 1901 at Menzies, Western Australia, and details a trip to Ravensthorpe. However, some further details of Hann's Kimberley expeditions are provided in the paper read to the Royal Society of Queensland on 7 April 1900 by Major A. J. Boyd, and published the following year.[15] Surviving correspondence relating to Hann's applications for pastoral leases

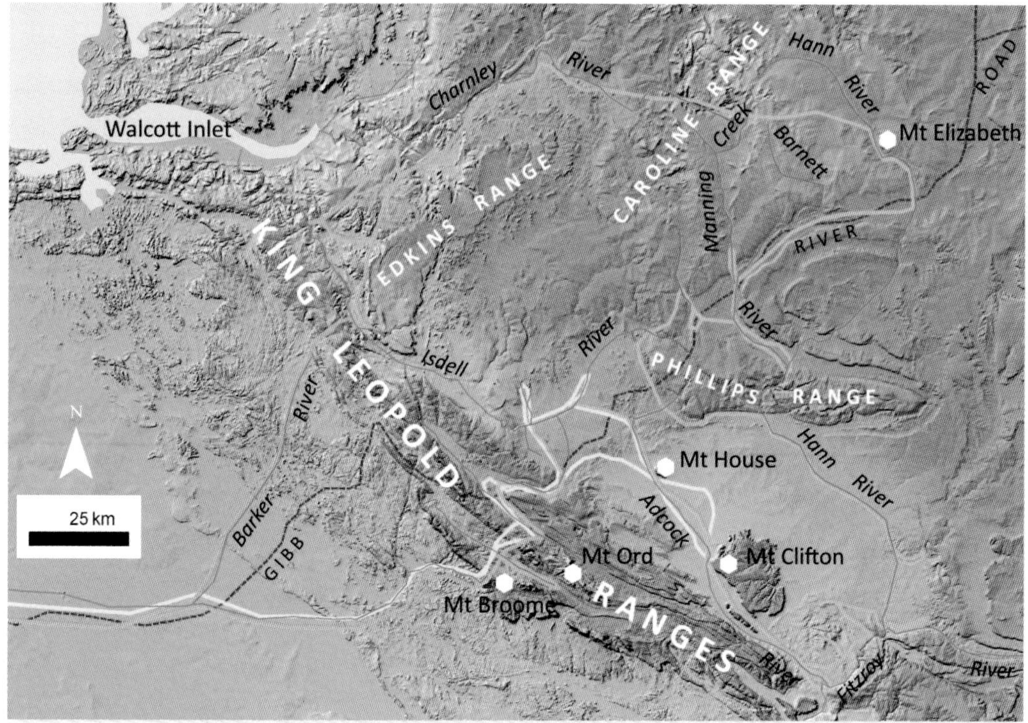

in the Kimberley is archived in the State Records Office, Perth: he applied for 12 blocks totalling about 740,000 acres, in the area that is now part of Mornington, Mount House, Glenroy, and Mount Barnett pastoral stations.

In February 1903 Hann again wrote to the Lands Department advising that he was confident of forming a company to stock the land he had applied for in the Nullagine area, but it also never eventuated.

He continued exploring in the desert regions of Western Australia and South Australia until 1908 when camels on loan to him from the Western Australian government were taken back. Hann stayed at his camp site near Laverton until he was invalided to a Cottesloe nursing home after being thrown from a horse in 1918. He died in 1921 and is buried in Karrakatta cemetery. Hann named more geographical features in Western Australia than any other person; features named by him in the Kimberley include 14 mountains, 33 hills and ranges, 9 rivers, 17 creeks, and 2 lakes or lagoons (Appendix 1).

Although he didn't manage to take up the country he discovered and applied for, it was recognized that the discoveries were important for the State, and in 1901 the government organized an expedition led by surveyor Fred Brockman to follow up and accurately locate the features Hann had found and named.

Above Figure 9. Map showing the routes of Hann's two exploration trips over the King Leopold Ranges in 1898: yellow, first trip May–June 1898; orange, second trip July–August 1898.
Background topography is SRTM digital elevation image courtesy of NASA.

Appendix 1. Kimberley topographic features named by Hann, 1898

Mountains

Mt Agnes	Mt Barnett	Mt Bell
Mt Blythe	Mt Brennan	Mt Caroline
Mt Clifton	Mt Elizabeth	Mt Hamilton
Mt House	Mt Ord	Mt Shadforth
Mt Smith	Mt Warton	

Hills and Ranges

J D Hill	Lady Forrest Range	Margaret Hill
Miss Glass Hill	Packhorse Range	Phillips Range
Plovers Hill	Pollys Hill	Precipice Range
Quartz Hill	Rocky Mountain	Artesian Range
Bluebell Hill	Bold Bluff	Brownrigg Gorge
Caroline Ranges	Edkins Range	Fork Hill
Graces Point	Harris Range	Isdell Range
Junction Hill	Scented Knob	Sir John Gorge
Sir John Range	Spider Hill	Surprise Hill
Synnot Range	Table Top Mountain	Talbot Range
The Dromedaries	The Estaughs	Warton Range

Rivers

Adcock River	Barnett River	Charnley River
Isdell River	James River	Pearson River
Sprigg River	Traine River	Throssell River

Creeks and Lakes

Annie Creek	Ashton Creek	Bell Creek
Blythe Creek	Button Creek	Dora Creek
Edkins Creek	Harris Creek	Honeysuckle Creek
Macnamara Creek	Manning Creek	Maudie Creek
Mina Creek	Minnie Creek	Station Creek
Synnot Creek	Urquhart Creek	Gladstone Lake
Spider Lagoon		

Notes

1 P. P. King, *Narrative of a survey of the intertropical and western coasts of Australia. Performed between the years 1818 and 1822*, Vol. 1 and 2, John Murray, London, 1827; and M. Hordern, *King of the Australian Coast*, Melbourne University Press, Melbourne, 1997, 2nd ed., 1998.

2 J. L. Stokes, *Discoveries in Australia ... during the voyage of H.M.S. Beagle in the years 1837-38-39-40-41-42-43*, 2 vols, London, 1846, facsimile edition, Libraries Board of South Australia, Adelaide, 1969.

3 G. Grey, *Journals of two expeditions of discovery in North-West and Western Australia during the years 1837, 38, and 39*, 2 vols, London, 1841, facsimile edition, Hesperian Press, Victoria Park (WA), 1983.

4 T. C. Sholl, Journals of Trevarton C. Sholl 1865-1866, typescript manuscript, J. S. Battye Library of West Australian History, Perth.

5 A. Forrest, *Journal of expedition from DeGrey to Port Darwin, 1879*, Government Printer, Perth, 1880.

6 C. A. Burrowes, Sketch of exploration in the east Kimberley, September 8th 1886, [Exploration plan 72], 1886, State Records Office of Western Australia, Cons 3423, item 72.

7 J. Bradshaw, 'Notes on a Recent Trip to Prince Regent's River', *Transactions of the Royal Geographical Society of Australasia (Victorian Branch)*, vol. 9(2), 1892, pp. 90–103.

8 Information provided by Cathie Clement, Kimberley Historical Sources Project.

9 F. H. Hann, 'Exploration in Western Australia', *Proceedings of the Royal Society of Queensland*, vol. xvi, 1901, pp. 9–34.

10 N.W. Bauer, 'Tragedy at Lawn Hill', *Sphere*, October, 1979, pp. 21–4.

11 M. Donaldson and I. Elliot (compilers & eds), *Do not yield to despair: Frank Hugh Hann's Exploration Diaries in the Arid Interior of Australia 1895-1908*, Hesperian Press, Carlisle (WA), 1998.

12 Hann, 'Exploration in Western Australia'.

13 Hann recorded Honeysuckle and Pandanus in this creek on his way down it on 1 June, and subsequently named it Honeysuckle Creek on his return up the creek on 11 June.

14 Spelt Urquart and McNamara in Hann's diary, but shown as Urquhart and Macnamara on modern maps.

15 Hann, 'Exploration in Western Australia'.

Left Charnley River cliffs.
Photo – Mike Donaldson

Brockman's North-West Kimberley Expedition, 1901

Mike Donaldson and Ian Elliot

Although several parties of Europeans had found passages through the King Leopold Ranges before Frank Hann found two more in 1898, it was the Hann reports that revealed the extent of fine grazing country in the central Kimberley. Hann also discovered and named many new major rivers, although he did not map their full course, and did not find a route to the coast in that area.[1]

The Western Australian Government acted promptly to further assess these promising discoveries and in March 1901 approved a north Kimberley exploration expedition to be led by Chief Inspecting Surveyor Fred S. Brockman. Apart from successfully mapping unexplored parts of the Kimberley, and collecting important natural history samples, the expedition's wonderful collection of glass plate photographs taken by Dr F. M. House remains a valuable record of the country and the Aboriginal paintings discovered.

Frederick Slade Brockman

Brockman was born on 9 July 1857, near Northam in Western Australia. After receiving his early education at Hale school in Perth, he worked as an apprentice surveyor with J. S. Brooking.[2] In 1882 he married Grace Bussell, the heroine of the *Georgette* disaster in 1876. Grace, the daughter of the pioneer Busselton farming family, helped to save some fifty lives following the beaching of the ship on Redgate Beach near Margaret River.

Fred Brockman joined the Lands and Surveys Department as a surveyor in September 1886 and transferred to the Department of Public Works and Railways 12 months later. During the years 1887 to 1890 he was surveyor-in-charge of the road and telegraph routes put in from Wyndham to Halls Creek following the gold discovery at Halls Creek. He transferred back to Lands and Surveys in 1891 and became Chief Inspecting Surveyor in 1894. His previous Kimberley experience was obviously a great advantage to him in leading the 1901 expedition.

Above Figure 1. Fred Brockman.
Courtesy of State Library of Western Australia (52120P).

Opposite
Brockman party under boab tree at Camp FB 11 in the Chamberlain Valley.
Courtesy of Western Australian Museum.

The 1901 Expedition

Brockman's party comprised himself as leader, surveyor Chas. Crossland as second in command, Dr F. M. House as naturalist and botanist, Government Geologist Andrew Gibb Maitland, Assistant Geologist C. G. Gibson, assistants T. Hickey, T. Wade, J. F. Connelly, T. McCrann, J. H. Brooking, two Aboriginal men, and 70 horses. The group arrived in Wyndham by steamers from Fremantle over a period of several weeks in April and May in order to procure the necessary horses, equipment and stores sufficient for seven months. The routes followed by Brockman, and the separate trips led by Crossland, are shown in Figure 2.

Brockman left his depot camp at Parry Creek near Wyndham on 9 May 1901, travelled around the southern side of the Cockburn Range to the Pentecost River, then along that watercourse's western branch, which he named Chamberlain River. One of the Aboriginal members of the expedition, a prisoner from Rottnest Island, absconded on the second day, and reported himself to the police in Wyndham a few days later. He was replaced by a prisoner from Wyndham. Once the party was all together on the Chamberlain, they proceeded up that river in a south-south-westerly direction until they could get the horses and stores across the river and head towards the west. Dr House's excellent photograph of the expedition in the Chamberlain River valley is shown on page 182.

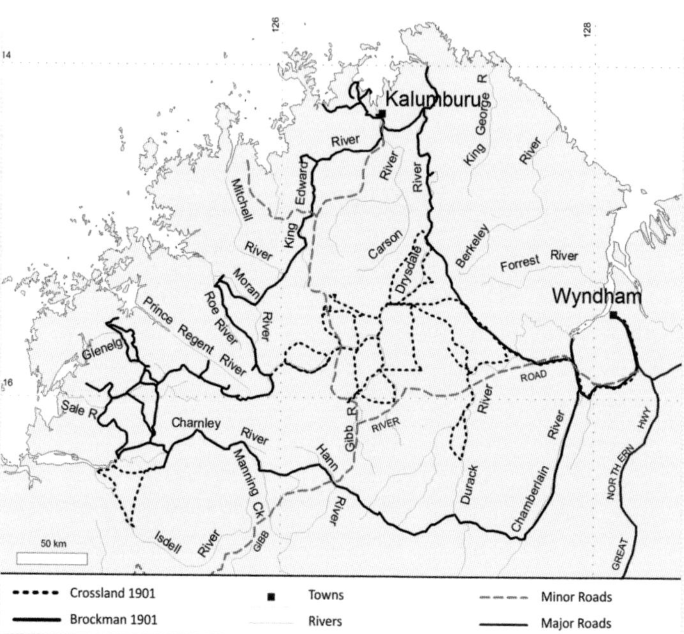

Right Figure 2. Routes of the Brockman expedition, 1901.

Once the party left the Chamberlain River, it travelled west-north-west for some 130 kilometres until the Hann River was struck just south of Mount Elizabeth, named by Hann three years earlier. After following the Hann River upstream for 11 kilometres, Brockman then turned again to the west-north-west and travelled over rough sandstone country for about 40 kilometres to his camp FB 25 on what he thought was the Isdell River. This was in fact the upper reaches of Manning Creek, also named by Hann, but as neither Hann nor Brockman had followed this stream down to its junction with the Barnett River, it was incorrectly shown on the expedition map. An Aboriginal art site just east of this camp was photographed by Dr House (Fig. 3).

The expedition travelled up Manning Creek to its headwaters and proceeded north-west to the Charnley River, following Hann's route of 1898. After following the Charnley downstream to the south-west for about 50 kilometres, at Hann's marked tree FH XXXIII (Fig. 4), it became too difficult to continue following the river, as Hann had also found. Being unable to find a route through the rough sandstone country of the Edkins Range to the west of the river, Brockman established a depot camp, FB 32, on Synott Creek, about 10 kilometres from the Charnley. From here he despatched Crossland, Gibb Maitland, and two of the men, with eight horses and supplies for 20 days, to explore the country south to the King Leopold Ranges, and to determine the course of the Isdell River.

Above Figure 3. One of House's glass plate photographs of the Wandjina art site near Manning Creek. This wonderful art site is still rarely visited and despite considerable natural deterioration due to weathering it remains in reasonable condition. Courtesy of Western Australian Museum.

Brockman went with three men towards the north-west, crossing the Charnley River and the rough Edkins Range and naming the Calder River before continuing to the north-west where he came to a large creek he subsequently identified as the Sale River. This river was named by T. C. Sholl, son of the Resident Magistrate of the Camden Harbour settlement, when he led an exploration trip through here in 1865.[3] Brockman followed the Sale down for some 20 kilometres and noted the extensive expanses of 'fine basaltic country'[4] in the area between the Calder and Sale rivers which Sholl had called the Panter Downs. Prevented from travelling further north by 'very rugged sandstone ranges, seamed by deep gorges', Brockman was determined to reach the coast near here, so he left Gibson and the Aboriginal 'Dicky' at the camp and continued north-west on foot with Constable Hickey. They travelled about 20 kilometres down a stream he named Gibson Creek after his Assistant Geologist, reaching a high point he called Mount Methuen close to a tidal estuary of Doubtful Bay.

After returning on foot to his camp, Brockman's party spent some days mapping the course of the Sale, Calder and Charnley rivers. Near the mouth of the Calder he encountered a prospecting party led by John Calder, who had been out from Derby for over two months. Calder provided Brockman with useful information about the country to the north, including the advice that the ranges immediately south of the Prince Regent River were impassable. Brockman returned to his depot camp FB 32, following his earlier track, having been away three weeks. He found that Crossland's party had returned a few days previously.

Crossland's separate trip covered the area to the south and south-west of the depot camp FB 32. He travelled over mainly well-grassed, undulating basaltic country, essentially following Hann's route to the junction of the Isdell and Sprigg rivers, where Hann's blazed tree, FH XLI was found. The party then followed the Isdell downstream for almost 30 kilometres to the dramatic twin hills of the Dromedaries, where the river enters a narrow and precipitous gorge before entering Walcott Inlet (Fig. 6). Crossland's party was hemmed in by mudflats at the mouth of the Isdell and an impassable gorge at the mouth of the Charnley River, and he commented that 'Alligators were plentiful in the muddy waters'. He therefore had to return to the depot camp through the Artesian Range on routes 'too rough for stock'.[5]

The full party then retraced Brockman's tracks back across the Charnley to the Calder River, and followed that river up for some 55 kilometres to its source at the watershed with the Prince Regent River. Finding the way north blocked by rugged sandstone ranges,

Opposite
(Above) Figure 4. Brockman's party at camp FB 33 on the Charnley River. The blazed tree is also Hann's tree FH XXXIII, although the FH is partly obscured in this image due to a crack in the glass plate. Courtesy of Western Australian Museum.
(Below) Figure 5. This sandstone gorge on the Charnley River was too rough for Brockman's horses, and the party skirted around it to the south on more accessible basaltic country. Photo – Mike Donaldson

Brockman left most of the party in camp and travelled east with Crossland 'and a light party' for almost 20 kilometres to a creek running north into the Prince Regent. They followed this creek to the Prince Regent gorge and obtained views down the valley to Mount Waterloo, distant about 75 kilometres. Brockman also noted extensive cave paintings in this area, although they were 'all of crude design and poor execution'.[6]

Having determined the way ahead to the south-east was practicable, the light party returned to camp from where Brockman directed Crossland to take the main party towards the south-east, then head north-easterly and establish a depot camp on the first large creek. Brockman, accompanied by Gibson and Dr House and a light party, retraced their tracks to the Calder with the intention of heading north-west to locate some of George Grey's points on the Glenelg River. Before heading off in that direction, Brockman 'made a short excursion' south and named Bachsten Creek, where he found 'some excellent specimens of cave paintings'.[7]

Brockman's party then proceeded west to the Sale River, then north to the headwaters of the Glenelg, and then followed that stream north-west for 40 kilometres, almost to the tidal waters. From there Brockman went north-west, passing just south of Mount Lyell, a prominent hill named by Grey in March 1838, 'after C. Lyell, Esq.', the distinguished English geologist of the time.[8] Brockman continued on to a high hill that he named Mount Trevor, as a

Right Figure 6. Isdell River gorge and the twin hills of the Dromedaries. Crossland's party kept back from the gorge and the rough sandstone country around it on their way downstream to Walcott Inlet.
Photo – Mike Donaldson

cairn was found on the summit that he identified as having been placed there by T. C. Sholl in 1865. Sholl had incorrectly taken this peak to be Grey's Mount Lyell. Brockman's party travelled back to the Calder River by a more direct south-easterly course. He took the opportunity while there of having Dr House photograph the Aboriginal paintings discovered previously on the banks of Bachsten Creek (Fig. 7), and then followed Crossland's tracks to the east, climbing Mount Agnes en route. He met up with Crossland at his depot camp C 9 on the headwaters of the Drysdale River near Mount Hann on 1 September, having been away from the rest of the group for two weeks. Brockman, Crossland, and Maitland climbed Mount Hann, the highest point in the area (originally named Mount William by Hann in 1898), to take sights and survey the country (Fig. 8).

At the depot camp C 9 on the Drysdale River, on 5 September Brockman again split the party, directing Crossland to explore the country to the east and proceed back to Wyndham no later than the end of November. Brockman, with four men and 20 horses, headed north-west, travelling for about 40 kilometres to where he struck the head of the Roe River.[9] Following the course of the river for a further 40 kilometres, he discovered and named the Moran River where it joins the Roe in its tidal estuary. He then followed the Moran upstream for 40 kilometres where he found a tree marked B 91 on the summit of a high basalt hill, which he realised must be Mount Bradshaw. Joseph Bradshaw led an expedition through here in 1891, but thought he was on an arm of the Prince Regent

Above Figure 7. One of several photographs Dr House took at the art site on Bachsten Creek. Courtesy of Western Australian Museum.

Above left Figure 8. Pack horses near Mount Hann. Courtesy of Western Australian Museum.

River.[10] Brockman then headed north-east for almost 40 kilometres until he struck a large river which he named the King Edward (Fig. 9). On this path he would have crossed the headwaters of the Mitchell River. Although not mentioned in Brockman's report, the accompanying map shows small creeks in the area wrongly interpreted as being the headwaters of the Lawley River, which enters Port Warrender. The discovery and naming of the Mitchell River had to wait for William Easton's expedition in 1921.[11]

Brockman struck the King Edward about 20 kilometres upstream from the present Mitchell Plateau road crossing, and followed it downstream for some 70 kilometres to a point about 15 kilometres east of Admiralty Gulf. Finding access to the coast there blocked by precipitous sandstone cliffs, he continued down the river in a north-easterly direction to its mouth in Napier Broome Bay, where he established a base camp (FB 79) on a 'well-watered creek' (Monger Creek, just west of the present Kalumburu community). From here he spent 10 days exploring the country around Napier Broome and Vansittart Bays.

Having rested his horses, Brockman then headed east to the Drysdale River which he followed downstream for some 30 kilometres to tidal waters. On the way he named the Barton River, a large creek entering the Drysdale at the northern end of well-grassed basaltic country. He then followed the Drysdale upstream for 60 kilometres over grassy basaltic plains (Fig. 10), to the point where the river emerges from a steep sandstone gorge. After spending several days negotiating a route through this rugged country, he continued upstream for another 65 kilometres where, on 4 November, he found Crossland's marked tree C 41. Brockman commented that 'This was the first point marked by Mr. Crossland with which I connected since 5th September.'

Above Figure 9. The King Edward River flows through flat, generally well-grassed country for much of its length. Photo – Mike Donaldson

Brockman's party then left the Drysdale and headed south-east for 120 kilometres, crossing the Durack River and 'several less important creeks' before reaching the Pentecost River on 20 November and his camp FB 4 a few kilometres further down the river, commenting 'here completing my circuit and the exploration of the district'. The party continued on to Wyndham, passing again to the south of Mount Cockburn, arriving on 26 November. They had been away for six and a half months.

When Crossland left Brockman at the depot camp C 9 on the headwaters of the Drysdale on 6 September, he travelled down the Drysdale for about 100 kilometres with Dr House and two others, while Maitland went north-west towards the Prince Regent River with his three men. These two parties arranged to meet up from time to time at pre-arranged locations. The combined parties then went south along a prominent stream that Crossland named Gibb River after the Government Geologist. The adjacent 'bluff-face table-top range' was named Maitland Range. They then proceeded east and south-east some 80 kilometres to the Durack River near its junction with the Chapman River, then along the Durack, ultimately mapping the country around Mount Lawley and almost to the tidal limits of the river. Crossland, mindful of his arrangement to meet Brockman around 20 October at a point some 100 kilometres to the north-west, then headed in that direction while Maitland and his party turned south. Crossland arrived in the area of the agreed meeting place on 19 October, but was blocked from going further west by the sheer cliffs of the Carson Escarpment. He saw no signs of horses or camps in the valley of the Carson River at the foot of the escarpment, so as per the arrangement with his leader, he headed back towards Wyndham, marking the tree C 41 at his camp of 21 October on the Drysdale that Brockman was to find 13 days later.

Above Figure 10. The upper reaches of the Drysdale River flow through undulating, well-grassed basaltic country. Photo – Mike Donaldson

Crossland continued travelling south-east to the head of the Forrest River, then on to the Durack near Mount Lawley. After completing his survey observations and triangulations the party travelled to the south of Mount Cockburn and arrived in Wyndham on 18 November.

Brockman summarised the results of the six month expedition:

- 2,300 miles (3,680 kilometres) travelled by the combined parties on the main routes
- All prominent points approached were ascended
- Course was checked by rough triangulations between prominent points
- Latitudes were obtained by astronomical observations at frequent intervals
- Accuracy of locations was checked by connection to Admiralty survey points on the coast
- Well-grassed basaltic areas comprise one quarter of the district surveyed with perhaps 7 to 8 million acres of valuable pastoral country
- The area could be serviced by a port established at Napier Broome Bay or Vansittart Bay, both areas having easy access from inland
- 8 new streams were discovered, mapped, and named by the expedition: Chamberlain, Calder, King Edward, Barton, Moran, and Gibb rivers, and Gibson and Bachsten creeks
- 6 mountains or ranges named and locations fixed: Mounts Methuen, Trevor, Beatrice, Dorothy, and Hickey, and Maitland Range.

Brockman also praised the accuracy of Frank Hann's locations from his 1898 expeditions across the King Leopold Ranges, and fixed key locations of George Grey, Joseph Bradshaw, and Trevarton Sholl.

Dr House, in a separate appendix to Brockman's report, listed the natural history samples collected on the expedition, but also complained that he was not given sufficient time or resources to carry out these collecting tasks. He also managed to acquire a valuable collection of glass plate photographs of the country, and in particular the Aboriginal rock art encountered, and made useful comments on the Aboriginal inhabitants and their material culture. Despite Dr House's complaints, the Director of the Western Australian Museum and Art Gallery, Mr B.H. Woodward, praised House's collections:

> The native implements, weapons, etc., number 37, and include many specimens of great ethnological value. The Natural History specimens were all in excellent condition, and reflect the greatest credit on Dr. House, as it is not an easy matter to preserve the skins of small birds in a tropical climate.[12]

The museum's Honorary Consulting Ornithologist, Mr A.W. Milligan, also praised the collection of birds, although the total of 43 specimens was less than might have been expected. There was one bird, the Black Grass Wren, totally new to science, and Mr Milligan 'with due and

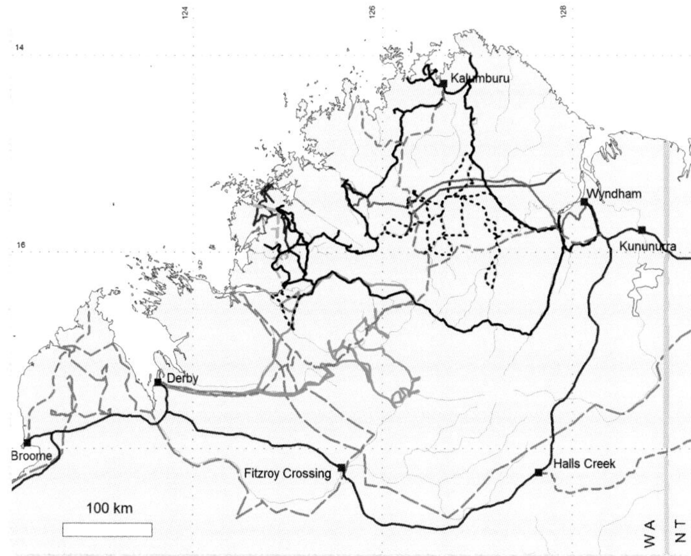

Left Figure 11. Routes of European Expeditions 1838–1901.

proper appreciation of Dr. House's labours and travail' took the liberty of naming it after the doctor with the scientific name *Amytis housei*.[13]

The Government Geologist, Andrew Gibb Maitland, did not submit a report on his findings and activities.

The Brockman expedition filled in much of the Kimberley map in the parts poorly known to Europeans (Fig. 11), but the discovery of some of the remaining major rivers still had to wait for others: the Berkeley and King George Rivers were named by C. P. Conigrave in 1911, the Mitchell in 1921 by William Easton, and the Morgan mapped by John Morgan in 1954, but named in his honour in 1958.

Notes

1 See Mike Donaldson and Ian Elliot, 'The Kimberley exploration expeditions of Frank Hann in 1898', this volume.

2 *Australian Dictionary of Biography* (online version), accessed December 2010.

3 T. C. Sholl, Journals of Trevarton C. Sholl 1865-1866, typescript, Battye Library, QB/SHO.

4 F. S. Brockman, *Report on Exploration of North-West Kimberley, 1901*, Government Printer, Perth, 1902, p. 5.

5 C. Crossland, Appendix A in Brockman, *Report on Exploration of North-West Kimberley, 1901*, p. 13.

6 Brockman, *Report on Exploration of North-West Kimberley, 1901*, p. 6.

7 ibid.

8 G. Grey, *Journals of two expeditions of discovery in North-West and Western Australia During the Years 1837, 38, and 39*, T. and W. Boone, London, 1841, Facsimile edition, Hesperian Press, Victoria Park, 1983, p. 178.

9 The Roe River was named by P. P. King in 1820 following its discovery by his second-in-command, midshipman John Septimus Roe; however, as Roe declined the offer of having it named after him, saying that 'it deserved a name of greater distinction than could be attached to any friend of mine', King named it 'after the rector of Newbury, the reverend father of my zealous and diligent assistant Mr Roe'. M. Hordern, *King of the Australian Coast*, Melbourne University Press, Melbourne, 1997, 2nd ed., 1998, p. 244.

10 J. Bradshaw, 'Notes on a Recent Trip to Prince Regent's River', *Transactions of the Royal Geographical Society of Australasia (Victorian Branch)*, vol. 9(2), 1892, pp. 90–103. See also Michael Cusack, 'Joseph Bradshaw', this volume.

11 K. Epton, *Rivers of the Kimberley*, Hesperian Press, Carlisle (WA), 2003.

12 Appendix E in Brockman, *Report on Exploration of North-West Kimberley, 1901.*

13 Appendix F in Brockman, *Report on Exploration of North-West Kimberley, 1901.*

Mixed Blessings: Establishment of Christian missions in the Kimberley

Christine Choo

First came the immigrant farmers, pastoralists and other adventurers to seek their fortunes in the new country. They asserted White[1] authority over Indigenous inhabitants as the frontier spread from the initial settlements in the Swan River Colony. Then came the Christian missionaries who were frontier pioneers and colonisers in their own right.[2] The role of the Christian missions can be summarised as evangelisation, protection from abuse, procreation, education and training.

The presence of missionaries in the Kimberley was a mixed blessing for Indigenous inhabitants who, in most early contact situations, at first rejected them. The points at which State and Church met in their attempts to provide corporal and spiritual service to Aboriginal people become points of friction, juxtaposed with the potential for reconciliation and mutual support.

Catholic Missions

Earliest Catholic missions

From its infancy the Western Australian Catholic Church was in the vanguard of mission work with Aboriginal people. The Benedictines established the first Catholic mission to Aboriginal people at New Norcia in 1846 – it became a model for Catholic missions in the Kimberley.

The first Christian mission to the Kimberley at Goodenough Bay, near Derby, was established by Irish priest Father Duncan McNab, who had previously worked among Aboriginal prisoners on Rottnest Island.[3] Father McNab set sail for the Kimberley in February 1884 with six months' supplies all paid for with private funds.[4] He was sent north by Bishop Griver because that was where Aboriginal people 'were said to be more numerous than in any other position thereof'.[5] In 1885 the Australian Plenary Synod in Sydney, a meeting of Bishops and Catholic hierarchy of the Australasian region, voted to

Opposite
(Top) Forrest River Mission, c. 1922.
E. R. Gribble (seated in centre), James Noble (in white seated to his left), Angelina Noble (seated to right of Gribble), Ruth Noble (standing on her mother's right), Yelma (in front of her mother), John and Mark Noble (standing between their parents and Gribble), and some mission residents.
Neville Green Forrest River Collection. Reproduced with permission of Neville Green.
(Bottom) Port George IV Mission (Kunmunya), c. 1913–23. Residents of Mission.
Courtesy of State Library of Western Australia (341356PD).

constitute Derby as the centre of a New Vicariate Apostolic 'for the black Aboriginal people of Western Australia' and in July that year Bishop Griver asked Rome for the assistance of a Religious Order for the evangelisation of the north-west.[6] By the end of 1887 Father McNab's mission was abandoned; he moved to Melbourne under the impression that there were soon to be successors.

Beagle Bay (1890-1976), Lombadina (1892-1985) and Broome (1895-)

It was not until 1890 that the first permanent Catholic mission in the Kimberley was established at Beagle Bay by Trappist (Reformed Cistercians of the Strict Observance) monks from Sept Fons in France. Beagle Bay has been called the 'birthplace and cradle of Catholic presence in the Kimberleys'.[7] The missions in Beagle Bay, Lombadina and Broome are inextricably linked through their common foundation – established by the Trappists and encouraged by Bishop Matthew Gibney.[8] Aware of their gross oppression and ill-treatment in the north-west and convinced of the need to treat Aboriginal people with compassion, in 1888 Bishop Gibney wrote to the Colonial Secretary requesting a lease for a mission.[9] The government agreed to grant a lease of 100,000 acres (40,500 hectares) on King's Sound Native Reserve for the use of a native mission of 10,000 acres as soon as the mission had spent £5,000 on improvements. Governor Broome indicated that this lease for the Church was granted at a time when 'concessions to Religious Bodies [were] watched with jealousy', referring to the strong sectarian tensions between Protestants and Catholics. The terms of the lease agreement reflect the close connection between 'evangelisation' and 'civilisation' – the missionaries explicitly indicated they would attempt to civilise the Aboriginal people of the district.

The Trappists arrived in Beagle Bay in 1890; more recruits followed in 1892. Father Alphonse Tachon, one of the first Trappists there, attempted to learn the language, customs and practices of the local people and, despite ill health, cooked for all at the mission (which in two years reached around 30 people). Although many of the local Aboriginal people attended services, singing in French, Latin and their own languages, they maintained their own religious beliefs and customs. As early as 1892 the monks recognised the need for the presence of an order of nuns to assist in the education of the young women and children.[10]

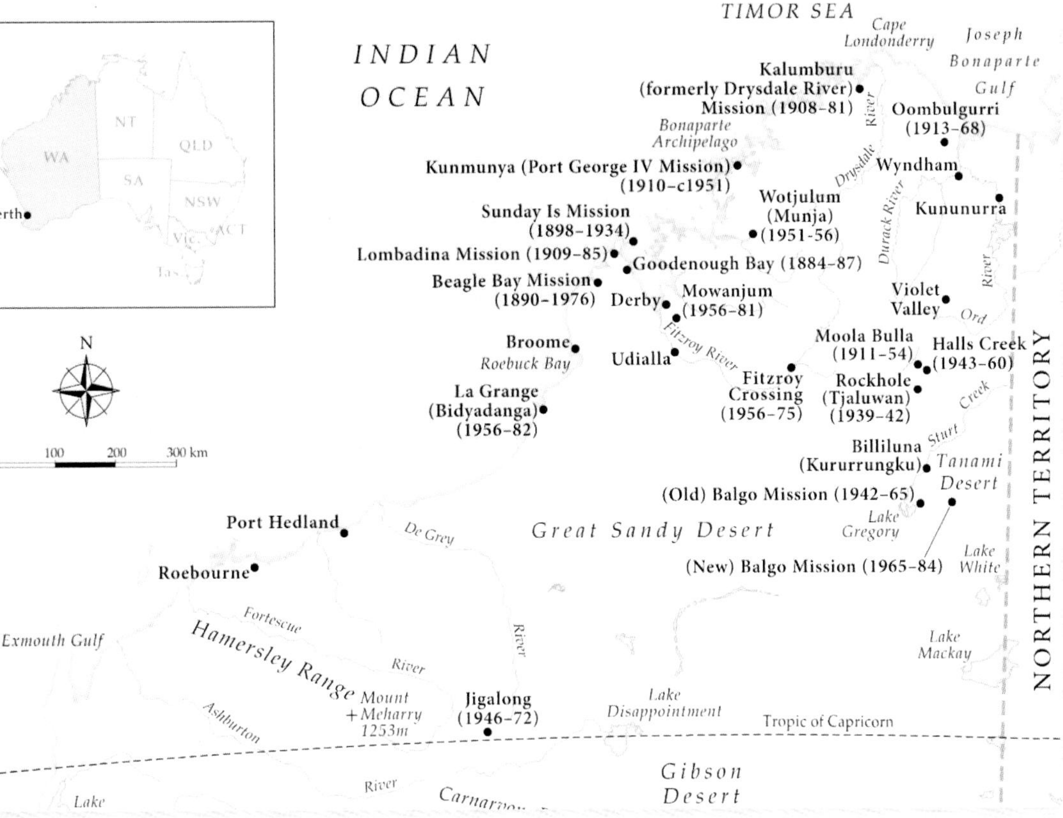

In February 1892 the station 'Lombadina' about 50 miles (80 kilometres) north of Beagle Bay, a pastoral lease and pearling plant previously held by Harry Hunter and Sydney Hadley, was purchased by Bishop Gibney. It was operated by the mission between 1902 and 1905. In 1906 Thomas Puertollano, a Filipino (Manilaman) and Agnes, his Aboriginal wife, took it over; Thomas and his family were staunch supporters of the Catholic missionaries.[11] Lombadina became a base for Father Nicholas Emo, a pioneer missionary in Broome, from 1910 until his death in March 1915. Throughout this time there were tensions between Lombadina and the non-denominational Sunday Island Mission established by Hadley as both involved Bardi and Jawi people.

1898 marked the beginning of a period of insecurity for the Catholic missions as the new Aborigines Department tightened the availability and administration of funds. The grant to Beagle Bay for the care and rationing of its vulnerable residents stopped but in July 1899 the government granted a £150 subsidy to the mission.[12] By this time the Trappists had left the mission.

Above Location of Christian missions in the Kimberley.
Map created by Demap. 2010.

On 12 January 1901, Beagle Bay Mission was transferred to the Pious Society of Missions (later known as the Society of the Catholic Apostolate or Pallottines), beginning their long relationship with the people of the Kimberley. Father George Walter led a group of German Pallottine priests and lay brothers to Beagle Bay in April 1901. The Pallottine method of evangelisation was for clergy and lay people to work in partnership to revive, uphold and spread the Catholic faith.[13] In July 1904 they obtained permission to 'collect and train the fatherless half-castes and other aboriginal children who were destitute in Broome'.[14] In September 1904 the eleven lay brothers at Beagle Bay included a carpenter, a blacksmith, a bricklayer, a shoemaker, three farmers and other tradesmen. The school teacher taught 21 boys and ten girls from Broome, Beagle Bay and Disaster Bay 'reading, writing, arithmetic, music, object-lessons, religious and Bible history'. On Sundays about 100 people came to the mission to attend to their religious duties and obtain food. The missionaries fed only those who could not work, including the crippled and blind.[15]

Father Walter was very concerned about the negative impact of pearling on the local people and believed 'Asiatics' especially should be kept away from Aboriginal women. He stressed that it was 'important for the future of the State of Western Australia, and for the future of the black race, that the children, both half-caste and black, should be removed from those centres of vice, such as Broome and other places, and brought to this or any other institution which [was] working in the interests of the blacks'.[16] In October 1906, Father Walter pressed Chief Protector Prinsep to send the neglected native children in the north-west to his mission 'at once', estimating that there were about 200 'most obvious cases'.[17]

Besides the care, protection and training of half-caste children, the mission's agenda for evangelisation included marriage between mission 'boys' and 'girls' to establish good Catholic families. Married couples were offered homes in the mission compound, the 'Colony', just as Father Emo had encouraged couples to build homes on land in Broome obtained by the Church on their behalf. Children from the Colony entered the segregated dormitories for boys and girls as soon as they were of school age. The arrival of St John of God sisters in 1907 facilitated the establishment of dormitories for girls.

The war years were difficult for Beagle Bay Mission as the German Pallottines, unfairly suspected of espionage, were severely restricted. Church authorities brought in members of other orders, including the Redemptorists and for a short time the Salesians, to assist in

the Kimberley.[18] In 1917 Father Thomas Bachmair commenced the construction of the Sacred Heart Church with the assistance of mission residents. A.O. Neville, who became Chief Protector of Aborigines in 1915, was hostile to missions; he preferred to develop the government-run Native Settlements at Carrolup and Moore River in the south, and Moola Bulla and Violet Valley in the Kimberley. The reduction of government assistance to missions in the inter-war years severely affected their work.

World War II brought a crisis of another kind to missionaries at Beagle Bay and Broome. First, the German Pallottine missionaries were interned as enemy aliens, to be released only after Archbishop Mannix interceded on their behalf. Second, evacuation of the coloured population from Broome to Beagle Bay placed enormous pressure on the resources of the mission where evacuees were forced to remain, often against their will. Third, the war itself, and granting of social security payments to eligible Aboriginal families and institutions, including the missions and orphanage, brought a new level of financial security. After World War II the education needs of Aboriginal children and the role of the missions in their education also changed.[19]

Above Beagle Bay Church, 1974, interior showing mother of pearl decoration.
Courtesy of National Library of Australia (vn3550863, Michael Jensen Collection).

St John of God sisters in Beagle Bay and Broome (1907-)

When nine St John of God sisters arrived in the Kimberley from Ireland via Kalgoorlie on 6 June 1907, they were the first women missionaries there. Consequently Beagle Bay Mission was able to take in more young people, including girls, who were removed from their families throughout the Kimberley.[20] The sisters ran the Beagle Bay school and girls' dormitory and, with the older girls, provided the domestic services at the mission. Mother Superior Antonio O'Brien transferred the sisters to Broome in 1908 to establish a new convent and St Mary's school. The sisters also cared for so called 'abandoned children', the work that Father Nicholas Emo had started. The school and orphanage provided a home for young women trained for employment in and around Broome.

In 1940 Bishop Raible and the sisters built a home for girls near the convent where young mission women could live when they left Beagle Bay. Not long afterwards, the sisters evacuated to Beagle Bay but returned after the war to operate the home for generations of young women.[21]

Daughters of Our Lady, Queen of the Apostles

One of the dreams of the Catholic missionaries was for the Aboriginal people of the Kimberley to be evangelised by locally trained Aboriginal Catholics. The story of the short-lived Daughters of Our Lady, Queen of the Apostles (*Regina Apostolorum*), the first and only order of Aboriginal nuns in Australia, is central to the Catholic evangelisation in the Kimberley. By the time Bishop Raible established the order in Beagle Bay in 1938 there were at least three generations of Catholics. Six young girls who had been raised at the mission commenced training for the sisterhood. On 22 June 1940, as part of the jubilee celebrations marking the 50th Anniversary of Beagle Bay, four of the original six took on 'habits' and new names as Daughters of Our Lady, Queen of the Apostles. The 'native sisters' assisted the St John of God sisters at Beagle Bay during World War II. After the war, native sisters were sent to help the Pallottines establish Balgo Mission. The dream of evangelisation of fellow Aboriginal people was an enormous challenge which contributed to the demise of the order as the young women from the coast were unprepared for their new roles as missionaries. The order finally closed in the early 1950s when there was only one native sister left.[22]

Above Drysdale River Mission (Pago), c. 1930s. Abbot Catalan addresses the congregation. Reproduced with permission of the Archives of the Benedictine Community of New Norcia (65256P).

Above left Kalumburu Mission, May 1937. Fr Thomas Gil (blessing the new building site) with Sisters, mission girls and boys and Marcello Bianchini, stonemason (3rd from R). Reproduced with permission of the Archives of the Benedictine Community of New Norcia (65992P).

Kalumburu (1908-1975)

Drysdale River Mission, established by Benedictine monks at Pago, Napier Broome Bay, was officially opened on 15 August 1908 by the Abbott of New Norcia, Fulgentius Torres with a special mass at the site, two years after he had personally chosen it.[23] A party comprising Abbott Torres and three Benedictine monks, Father Nicholas Emo, three Manilamen and the family of one of them, and three Aboriginal young men from Beagle Bay, were the pioneers of the permanent monastery at Pago.[24] After struggles against the weather, isolation and hostility from local Aboriginal people for eleven years, the mission eventually baptised the first local residents. Benedictine Oblate sisters arrived in Drysdale River Mission in 1928 enabling the mission to reach the women and children more effectively. Between 1931 and 1940 the mission was gradually transferred from Pago and to the better-watered site at Kalumburu which officially became its headquarters in November 1936. On 27 September 1943 the mission was destroyed by Japanese bombs but was immediately rebuilt.[25]

At Kalumburu, the missionaries lived in a monastery segregated from local Kuini and Kulari communities, who were divided into 'mission natives' living in tiny one-roomed western-style houses, and 'myals' or 'bush natives', who lived in humpies a little further away. Until the 1980s, the missionaries ran a paternalistic system which provided for all the community's needs including daily cooked meals. In exchange community members undertook all the work in and around the mission, supervised by nuns, priests and volunteer lay workers.[26]

Because of its isolation, Kalumburu remained relatively independent of government involvement for a long time. Attempts by the missionaries to improve Aboriginal peoples' situation inadvertently led to changes in the balance of power within communities. Young people with a little education, and a mastery of introduced technologies, gained more status in the eyes of missionaries than older men who held traditional knowledge. Many Aboriginal people on the mission reminisce on 'mission time' with fondness.[27] Kalumburu has produced artists and storytellers renowned far outside the isolated community. Ambrose Mungala Chalarimeri who was raised in Kalumburu Mission before he left as a young man, writes:

> It was only when I left Kalumburu and work on the stations that I find out more about Aboriginal way of living... We mission children were separated from our people or family, and from our own Aboriginal ways. Nobody tell us about 'em in the mission, and I think our old people didn't teach us about our culture because we were in the mission.[28]

Right New Balgo Mission, c. Nov 1965. Procession from Church on Feast of Christ the King.
Reproduced with permission of Brian McCoy.

Rockhole (1934-1939) and Balgo (1939-1980)

As Catholic missions in the Kimberley were concentrated on the coast, the Pallottines decided to establish a mission inland to reach desert people. From the early 1930s, Bishop Raible travelled around the East Kimberley on horseback undertaking pastoral work while searching for a suitable location. In 1934 the Pallottines acquired Rockhole Station, 800 kilometres east of Broome and 23 kilometres west of Halls Creek. In October that year a group led by Father Francis Huegel moved there. The Pallottines' plan to establish a hospital with the help of a German husband and wife team, the Doctors Betz, and the St John of God sisters was opposed by Chief Protector Neville. Rockhole was sold in 1939, to the great disappointment of Bishop Raible.[29]

In 1939 Bishop Raible was granted a lease of about five million acres (two million hectares) of land adjacent to the Canning Stock Route where the Pallottines established a new mission and pastoral station. At the mission in Balgo Hills the school and dormitories were run by Aboriginal sisters and St John of God sisters, and Aboriginal lay people from Broome and Beagle Bay were involved in the evangelisation of desert people. A Native Welfare Department patrol report of 1955 states: 'in its present position at the edge of the desert [Balgo] serves a useful purpose, acting as a staging camp for the primitive desert native before he contacts more Northern civilised parts'.[30] Balgo Mission was noted to be where numbers of desert people first came into contact with *gadia*.[31] Although the mission encouraged the maintenance of traditional hunting and gathering, these activities waned as rations became a more reliable food source.

Above The Pound, Balgo Hills, Tanami Desert, 2003. Courtesy of National Library of Australia (vn3294966). Reproduced with permission of Francis Reiss.

A major setback occurred in 1955 when, to their great embarrassment, the Pallottines discovered that their mission buildings were ten miles (16 kilometres) within the boundary of neighbouring Billiluna Station. The mission had to shift from Old Balgo Hills to a new well-watered location twenty miles away at Wirrimanu, a move that took ten years to complete.[32] Here they remained until the dormitories were dismantled and the local community, with the support of the missionaries, gained management of their land in 1980.

La Grange Mission (1955-1982)

The country around La Grange[33] (Bidyadanga) was an important location where desert people met salt-water people on Karadjarri land. A government telegraph station was used as a rationing depot before it was taken over by the Catholics. In the pearling boom, Asian lugger crews would come ashore to exchange cloth, rice and other provisions for wood, water and sexual favours, extending the traditional exchange that had occurred in the vicinity from time immemorial. When the short-lived Udialla reserve near Derby was closed in 1950 its few residents were transferred to La Grange Ration Depot. After repeated requests Pallottine missionaries were granted control of La Grange on 1 January 1955. The Western Australian government preferred not to hand over the place to the German Pallottines during World War II. La Grange Mission depended on the assistance of lay missionaries, including Aboriginal families and individuals originally from Beagle Bay. Non-Aboriginal lay workers were teachers, builders and gardeners.

Attempts to integrate Aboriginal with Christian ways had begun with the work of anthropologist-priest Father Ernst Worms, who, as parish priest of Broome since 1930, had undertaken serious study of Aboriginal languages and cultures of the Kimberley. Linguistic work continued with Father Kevin McKelson particularly in Bidyadanga.[34] The integration of Christianity with traditional ways was successfully applied in Bidyadanga, Turkey Creek, Halls Creek and Wyndham. It also found expression in integrated liturgical ceremonies and art throughout the Kimberley.[35]

Protestant Missions

Forrest River (1896-1968)

After unsuccessful attempts to establish a mission in the Gascoyne district, the Church of England exchanged that mission for a 100,000-acre (40,500-hectare) lease in the Marndoc Aboriginal Reserve, 50 miles (80 kilometres) up the Forrest River from Wyndham, and gazetted a mission reserve on 2 April 1897. Financed by the Anglican Board of Missions and the Aborigines Protection Board, the Anglican venture comprised Harold Hale, ex-pearler Sydney Hadley, Thomas Omerod and Alex Gathercole. The mission, on the Dadaway Lagoon site abandoned by the Victoria Squatting Company in 1889, was abandoned in 1899. In 1910 the Presbyterian Board of Missions declined an offer to take it up for its new mission to the Kimberley.[36]

In April 1913 Bishop Gerald Trower, the new Anglican Bishop of the North-West, travelled to Cambridge Gulf with five lay missionaries. At Dadaway Lagoon the well-fortified new Mission of Saint Michael of All Angels was placed under Reverend Robins. By July about 30 local Aboriginal people, including children, worked on the construction in exchange for flour and other provisions. The missionaries were constantly at risk of attack and by September they had all resigned.[37] The hostility towards Europeans at Dadaway Lagoon has been attributed to the traditional owners needing to protect several important sacred sites in the vicinity.[38]

Above Forrest River Mission, c. 1930s. Work Parade (All able-bodied men, women and children attended a daily muster when they were allocated their duties for the day). Neville Green Forrest River Collection. Reproduced with permission of Neville Green.

Reverend Ernest Gribble, son of Reverend J. B. Gribble who had been hounded out of Carnarvon in 1886,[39] came to Forrest River in December 1913, having worked in Aboriginal missions at Yarrabah, Mitchell and Roper River. He immediately invited Aboriginal converts James and Angelina Noble, his close associates from Queensland, to assist him. The Nobles' presence facilitated the development of enough trust to cease the attacks on the mission.[40] Gribble was highly unorthodox in his approach and an authoritarian. The principles on which he structured the mission were:– segregation; training in discipline, cleanliness and work; evangelisation; improved living conditions. The highly regimented mission welcomed mixed race children who, it was hoped, would raise Christian families. It housed children in segregated dormitories, provided food for all residents and taught allegiance to the British monarch.[41]

Ernest Gribble, like his father, strove against injustices suffered by Aboriginal people. In 1922 ex-servicemen Leopold Overheu and Frederick Hay were granted a pastoral lease, Nulla Nulla, near the Pentecost River. There was antagonism between them and the mission. In June1926 Gotegotemerrie and other places on the Marndoc reserve became the sites of a massacre of Aboriginal people who also frequented Forrest River. Gribble persistently worked to bring the matter to the attention of the authorities. Following the report of Royal Commissioner Wood, Constables St Jack and Regan were charged with the murder of one man, Boondung, but there was insufficient evidence to go to a jury trial.[42] In December 1927, charred remains salvaged from the killing sites were interred at the mission in a ceremony attended by over 200 people.[43] Ernest Gribble left in November 1928, deeply troubled and exhausted, dogged by controversy to the end.[44] The mission at Forrest River, the only self-supporting one in Western Australia, relied totally on the inmates' work.[45]

When Reverend John Best arrived in 1942 he brought a more relaxed and respectful attitude towards the residents which was deeply appreciated. As Connie McDonald recalled, Best 'spoke our English… sat down with us… listened to us and these things reminded us of our tribal ways'.[46] In 1968, as Wyndham became residents' preferred location, the mission closed and all salvageable equipment was removed to the town. It was much later that some of the community decided to return to the former mission, now named Oombulgurri.[47]

Sunday Island (1898-1964)

After the first Forrest River expedition, ex-pearler Sydney Hadley established his own non-denominational 'mission' on Sunday Island with the aim of creating an independent, self-supporting place where Bardi and Jawi people could be protected from pearling crews.[48] Hadley maintained the mission at his own expense for five years until he received a government grant in 1903. Its main industry was beachcombing for trochus shell and *bêche-de-mer* or trepang. Attempts to farm tropical crops like coffee, cotton, rubber and bananas, failed. Hadley's focus was on protection rather than religious conversion; his inclusive and eclectic mission approach attracted the disapproval of other Christian missionaries.[49]

Sunday Island was taken over by the Australian Aborigines Mission (AAM) in 1924, years after Hadley had approached them for assistance. The fundamentalist methods of the AAM entailed zealous evangelisation. Following an organisational split in 1929 the parent body, renamed United Aborigines Mission (UAM), retained control of Sunday Island. A move to Wotjulum on the mainland in the mid-1930s proved unpopular with many of the Bardi and Jawi people who either remained on the island or went to the Catholic mission at Lombadina. The Aborigines Department stopped subsidising the mission in 1939 and commenced negotiations for its transfer to the Catholics but negotiations ceased with the outbreak of war. During the war older Bardi who had returned to Sunday Island regained control over their own people, eroding the control of the UAM whose personnel were removed from the mission and whose boats were destroyed by the Army. The Army employed Bardi men in different capacities, opening up new contacts and experiences for them and their people.[50]

After the war the UAM regained control and, despite severe criticism from residents and officers of the Department of Native Affairs, it did not withdraw from Sunday Island until 1962. The Department could not get the Bardi people to abandon the island. Older community members remained, but school aged children were sent to lodge at Amy Bethel Hostel in Derby for their education, and their families followed, most of whom were housed on the town reserve. Nevertheless there were ongoing attempts by some Sunday Islanders to return and eventually some settled at One Arm Point within sight of Sunday Island.

Port George IV (Kunmunya) (1910–c. 1950), Wotjulum (1951–1956), Mowanjum (1956–)

When the Presbyterian Assembly was established in Western Australia in 1901 its Foreign and Aboriginals' Committee immediately started planning for a mission in the north-west. It was not until 1910 that W. J. S. Rankin and Dr John S. Yule were appointed to go north to investigate that possibility. The following year, Robert and Frances Wilson went to Walcott Inlet to start a mission. This was the country of the Worora people; the Wunambal people from the north of the Prince Regent River and the Ngarinyin people also passed that way. The Wilsons found it impossible to settle at Walcott Inlet. Port George IV Mission commenced in October 1912 on their second attempt.

Right Port George IV Mission (Kunmunya), 1936. Rev. J. R. B. Love and family.
Courtesy of State Library of Western Australia (53002P).

In December 1914, 25-year-old James Robert Beattie Love went to Port George as a relief missionary and supervised the transfer of the mission to a nearby site that became Kunmunya. Between 1915 and 1925 a succession of missionary couples at Kunmunya each stayed for one or two years. In 1926 the Presbyterian Board of Missions seriously considered closing the mission due to high staff turnover.[51]

The Board's appointment of Reverend Love and his wife Margaret to the mission in August 1927 was a critical decision. Love, who had been impressed with Kunmunya on his first visit, brought a new lease of life based on mutual respect. He deplored paternalism and racism. Unlike other Kimberley missionaries, Love instituted regular camp meetings where people were encouraged to discuss their problems and make their own decisions; this later formed the basis of a Council of Elders with decision-making responsibilities. He embarked on a study of the Worora language and culture and by 1929, when the new church was built, Love, with a team, had translated nine chapters of the Gospel of Mark into Worora. He subsequently translated other biblical works. Love's work engendered a deep love for the Old and New Testaments in the local people, enculturating Christianity into their own belief systems. They reciprocated Love's trust by sharing information about their culture and traditions.[52] When Bob and Margaret Love left in 1940, they were sorely missed and 'it was as though Kunmunya had died' when he died in February 1947.[53]

As Kunmunya residents were aging, Commissioner Middleton offered the government station Munja to the Presbyterians free of charge. In 1951 the mission transferred to Munja on the coast near Cockatoo and Koolan Islands in Umida country. The Worora, Ngarinyin and Wunumbul could not agree to live together at Munja but accepted the former UAM site at Wotjulum instead.

In 1956 the community moved again, to a location they named 'Mowanjum' near Derby, well outside their traditional lands. Later they transferred to a final location, 'New Mowanjum', ten kilometres outside Derby at the start of the Gibb River Road. This site is on country belonging to the Nyigina, from whom they had to seek permission to settle. Although the artificial gathering in one settlement of at least three different language groups created tensions, this is where the community has remained since the Presbyterians withdrew.[54]

UAM and Australian Inland Mission - Halls Creek (1943-)

The UAM and the Australian Inland Mission (AIM) were evangelising churches that had their roots in La Perouse in New South Wales. Originally supported by Baptist, Methodist and Congregational churches, in the 1940s UAM became more fundamentalist after the Baptists, Church of Christ and Brethren churches took charge. The UAM was based in Derby from the 1940s when it began itinerant work visiting Halls Creek, Moola Bulla and surrounding cattle stations in Gija, Gooniyandi and West Jaru country. When Moola Bulla closed in 1955, most of the 250 evicted inmates were taken to Halls Creek before the UAM at Fitzroy Crossing agreed to take them, caring for them on Bunuba country. Gija and West Jaru people soon left, finding jobs on stations closer to their own country. The UAM was considered a safe haven by these people and the first conversions of the Moola Bulla–Halls Creek people were recorded at the Fitzroy Crossing Mission.

Above Napier Range near Lillimilura north-west of Fitzroy Crossing. Photo – Mike Donaldson

Christian missions and government stations

Christian missions in the Kimberley worked in parallel with government depots and feeding stations established as the government's preferred alternative to missions. Relationships between them fluctuated with departmental leadership and government policy. People were transferred between missions and government settlements like Moola Bulla (1910),[55] Violet Valley (1912), Munja (1927) and Udialla (1946). As a result of this flow, many Kimberley people had family connections in all the institutions. In 1939 a Presbyterian mission was established on Moola Bulla with Reverend Hovenden as schoolteacher. When Moola Bulla closed in 1955 some of its residents transferred to other missions.

Conclusion

Missions in the Kimberley left a mixed legacy. Their primary aim was to 'civilise' Aboriginal people through conversion to Christianity by providing a safe haven and a regular food source. Nevertheless, missions contributed to the breakdown of family and community. Missions relied on the hard work of the Aboriginal people to sustain enterprises like cattle and horse breeding, production of fruit and vegetables and building projects, established for the benefit of the communities.

The experiences reported by mission residents range from harsh ill-treatment from some missionaries to very positive relationships with others who were loved and respected. Individuals who were raised by missionaries value the refuge the missions provided from hunger and itinerancy and the introduction to education and skills which prepared them for life in the wider community. Under the leadership of particularly enlightened missionaries the languages and traditions of the residents were maintained and fostered.

World War II was a watershed in the history of the Kimberley: Aboriginal people gained a new sense of autonomy when most *gadia* evacuated from the north-west. Availability of income and re-location of former pastoral workers to reserves close to town brought a different way of life. With the introduction of the policy of self-determination in the early 1970s, Aboriginal people of the Kimberley gained even greater autonomy over their own affairs. Those who lived on missions on their own lands, for example, in Kalumburu, Beagle Bay, La Grange, Balgo and Forrest River, re-claimed the mission lands, marking the end of the era of mission management of Aboriginal communities. Christianised Aboriginal people, and those who gained an education through the missions, have come to dominate the Aboriginal political landscape in the Kimberley and Australia.

Notes

1 I use the word 'White' to refer to the hegemony of the colonising groups. The word '*gadia*' is the vernacular equivalent in the Kimberley.

2 For an overview of Aboriginal-settler relations, refer to N. Green, 'Aborigines and White Settlers in the Nineteenth Century' and G. C. Bolton, 'Black and White after 1897' in C. T. Stannage (ed.), *A New History of Western Australia*, UWA Press, Nedlands, 1981; J. Milroy, J. Host and T. Stannage (eds), *Wordal, Studies in Western Australian History*, vol. 22, Centre for Western Australian History, University of Western Australia, 2001; P. Hetherington, *Settlers, Servants and Slaves: Aboriginal and European Children in nineteenth century Western Australia*, UWA Press, Nedlands, 2002; J. T. Reilly, *Reminiscences of Fifty Years' Residence in Western Australia*, Sands & McDougall Ltd, Perth, 1903.

3 For an overview of the history of the Catholic Church in the Kimberley refer to Margaret Zucker, *From Patrons to Partners: A History of the Catholic Church in the Kimberley, 1884–1984*, University of Notre Dame Australia Press, Fremantle, 1994.

4 *Western Australian Catholic Record*, 21 February 1884.

5 11 Feb 1884, Bishop M. Griver, Perth, to Father D. McNab, Perth, Archives of the Catholic Archdiocese of Perth (ACAP).

6 D. F. Bourke, *The History of the Catholic Church in Western Australia 1829–1979*, Catholic Archdiocese of Perth, Perth, 1979, pp. 144, 156; 5 Jul 1886, Bishop M. Griver, Perth, to Cardinal Simeoni, Rome, ACAP.

7 Sr B. Nailon and Fr F. Huegel (eds), *This is your place: Beagle Bay Mission 1890–1990,* Beagle Bay Community/Magabala Books, Beagle Bay, 1990; B. Nailon, *Emo and San Salvador*, vols 1 & 2, Brigidine Sisters, Echuca (Vic.), 2004–2005.

8 Bishop M. Gibney, Diary 27 May – 13 September 1890 (edited by Daisy Bates), *Sunday Times*, Perth, 27 Nov, 4 Dec, 11 Dec, 18 Dec 1927.

9 12 Jul 1888, Bishop M. Gibney, Perth, to the Colonial Secretary, Perth, ACAP. See also Gibney, 'Report on the Trappist Mission, Beagle Bay', reproduced in full in Reilly.

10 Gibney, Diary, *Sunday Times*, 4 Dec 1927.

11 B. Nailon, *Nothing is Wasted in the Household of God: Vincent Pallotti's Vision in Australia 1901–2000*, Spectrum Publications, Richmond (Vic.), 2001, p. 20; Nailon, *Emo and San Salvador*, vol. 1; M. Durack, *The Rock and the Sand*, Constable, London, 1969, p. 134.

12 Minute Paper for the Executive Council 2336/99 in State Records Office of Western Australia (SROWA), AN 1/2, Acc 144/1898, Trappist Mission Beagle Bay Half Yearly Report ending 31 December 1898.

13 Nailon, *Nothing is Wasted*; G. Walter, PSM, *Australia: Land, People, Mission*, Pallottine Society, Limburg (Germany), 1928, Bishop of Broome, [Broome], 1982.

14 C. Choo, *Mission Girls: Aboriginal Women on Catholic Missions in the Kimberley, Western Australia, 1900–1950*, UWA Press, Crawley, 2001, Chapter 5.

15 Walter, Evidence, in *Report of the Royal Commission on the Condition of the Natives* (Roth Report), Government Printer, Perth, 1905.

16 Walter, Evidence, 1905.

17 12 October 1906, Father G. Walter, Superior, Beagle Bay Mission to Chief Protector of Aborigines, Perth, SROWA, AN 1/2, Acc 255, 24/1906, Beagle Bay Mission; Choo, *Mission Girls*.

18 T. Cooper, *Unless the grain falls: A History of the Early Salesian Years in Australia*, Provincial Office [Salesian Order], Oakleigh (Vic.), 1996.

19 Choo, *Mission Girls*, Chapter 8.

20 Annual Report of the Aborigines Department, 1907; Sister Mechtilde, *The Missionary Adventures of the Sisters of St John of God*, dissertation (institution unknown), 1961; Durack, *The Rock and the Sand.*

21 Choo, *Mission Girls*, Chapters 4 & 5.

22 ibid., Chapter 6.

23 E. Perez OSB, *Kalumburu: The Benedictine Mission and the Aborigines 1908–1975*, Benedictine Mission, Kalumburu, 1977.

24 E. Perez OSB (translator), *The Diary of Bishop Torres*, The Kalumburu Book Trust, 1986.

25 C. Choo, 'The Impact of War on the Aborigines of the Kimberley' in *On the Homefront: Western Australia in World War II* edited by Jenny Gregory, UWA Press, Nedlands, 1996, pp. 134–44.

26 C. Choo, 'Dormitories at Kalumburu Mission 1908 – 1962', *New Norcia Studies*, No. 16, September 2008, pp. 23–33.

27 I. Crawford, *we won the victory: Aborigines and Outsiders on the North-West Coast of the Kimberley*, Fremantle Arts Centre Press, Fremantle, 2001, Chapter 10.

28 A. Mungala Chalarimeri, *The Man from the Sunrise Side*, Magabala Books, Broome, [2001], p. 149.

29 B. F. McCoy, *Holding Men: Kanyirninpa and the Health of Aboriginal Men*, Aboriginal Studies Press, Canberra, 2008, Chapter 2; F. Byrne OSB, *A Hard Road: Brother Frank Nissl, 1888-1980, a life of service to the Aborigines of the Kimberley*, Tara House Publishing, Nedlands, 1989, Chapter 13; Zucker, *From Patrons to Partners*, Chapter 12; Nailon, *Nothing is Wasted*, pp. 112–17.

30 28 May 1955, Patrol Report of J. Beharell, SROWA, Acc 3412, Box 4, 23.24, Missions. Balgo Pallottine – Reports – Annual & Patrol.

31 26 Sep 1960, Patrol Report of W. J. Courtney, Welfare Inspector, Halls Creek, SROWA, Acc 3412, Box 4, 23.24; R. M. and C. H. Berndt, *Survey of the Balgo Hills Area (Southern Kimberley, Western Australia)*, University of Western Australia, March 1960.

32 Byrne, *A Hard Road*; Zucker, *From Patrons to Partners*.

33 Referred to as 'Lagrange' in some early texts.

34 Community Pay Tribute to Priest, *7.30 Report*, 25 Mar 2010, http://www.abc.net.au/7.30/content/2010/s2856437.htm, accessed 26 Mar 2010.

35 N. McMaster C.Ss.R., *Locating an Indigenous Church: Critical Mission in Remote Australia*, private publication, Halls Creek, 2001; N. McMaster, *The Catholic Church in Jaru and Gija Country: Reworking a Context of Evangelisation in the Kimberley*, David Lovell Publishing, Melbourne, 2008.

36 C. Halse, *A Terribly Wild Man*, Allen & Unwin, Crows Nest (NSW), 2002, Chapters 5 & 6.

37 Green, *The Forrest River Massacres*, Fremantle Arts Centre Press, Fremantle,1995, Chapter 6.

38 Halse, *A Terribly Wild Man*, pp. 99-100.

39 J. B. Gribble, *Dark Deeds in a Sunny Land: Blacks and Whites in North West Australia*, Daily News, Perth, 1905 (Preface dated 1886), reprinted, UWA Press with Institute of Applied Aboriginal Studies, Western Australian College of Advanced Education, Nedlands, 1987.

40 Halse, *A Terribly Wild Man*, p. 101.

41 C. Nungulla McDonald (with Jill Finnane), *when you grow up*, Magabala Press, Broome, 1996.

42 G. T. Wood, 'Royal Commission of Inquiry into Alleged Killing and Burning of bodies of Aborigines in East Kimberley and into Police methods when effecting arrests', *Western Australian Votes & Proceedings*, 1927, Paper No. 3.

43 Green, *The Forrest River Massacres*, p. 222; Halse, *A Terribly Wild Man*, Chapter 6.

44 E. R. Gribble, *Forty Years with the Aborigines*, Angus & Robertson, Sydney, 1930.

45 27 Aug 1924, letter, Allen Bachelor, Secretary, Australian Board of Missions, to Western Australian Government, refers to the Mission's success in the production of cattle and cotton, and its attempts to be self supporting.

46 McDonald (with Finnane), *when you grow up*, p. 57.

47 N. Green (ed.), *The Oombulgurri Story: A pictorial history of the people of Oombulgurri, 1884-1988*, Focus Education Services, Cottesloe (WA), 1988, pp. 110–19.

48 Durack, *The Rock and the Sand*, p. 130.

49 M. V. Robinson, *Change and Adjustment among the Bardi of Sunday Island, North-Western Australia*, unpublished Master of Arts Thesis (Anthropology), University of Western Australia, 1973, pp. 161–5.

50 ibid.

51 J. W. Paton, *Kunmunya Mission: the move from Port George IV sites and some notes on Aboriginal words and customs in period 1915–18*, undated, Battye Library, PR 14529/KUN/1-0/41.

52 J. R. B. Love, *Stone-Age Bushmen of To-day: Life and Adventure among a Tribe of Savages in North-Western Australia*, Blackie & Son, London, 1936; *The Leader*, 2 June 1934, 'Visitors from the Far North-West, Life at Kunmunya Mission Station, One neighbour – and sixty miles away', Battye Library, PR 14529/KUN/3-0/41.

53 M. McKenzie, *The Road to Mowanjum*, Angus & Robertson, Sydney, 1969.

54 Refer to Crawford, *we won the victory*, pp. 34-6, for description of tribal groups relevant to this account and their affinity to country; pp. 191-4, for the establishment of Mowanjum; M. A. Jebb, *Blood, Sweat and Welfare: A History of White Bosses and Aboriginal Pastoral Workers*, UWA Press, Crawley, 2002, pp. 7, 271; D. Mowaljarlai and D. Utamorrah, *Visions of Mowanjum: Aboriginal Writings from the Kimberley*, Rigby, Adelaide, 1980.

55 Kimberley Language Resource Centre, *Moola Bulla: In the Shadow of the Mountain*, Magabala Books, Broome, 1996; S. Toussaint and H. Rumley, 'For their Own Benefit?: A Critical Overview of Aboriginal Policy and Practice at Moola Bulla, East Kimberley, 1910–1955', *Aboriginal History*, Vol. 14, 1–2, 1990.

Impacts of settlement and development in the Kimberley, 1965–2010

Bill Bunbury

In this presentation I want to concentrate on the impact of changes in the pastoral industry since the 1960s, the changing relationships between pastoralists and Aboriginal people and the subsequent history of pastoralism for both parties.

Much of the following is based on a three-part Radio National 'Hindsight' documentary series I made in 2000: 'It's Not The Money It's the Land'.

The subject was the impact of the Equal Wages Case of 1965 for Northern Australian Aboriginal pastoral workers. As a sequel I wrote a book, using the same title, published by Fremantle Arts Press in 2002.

For me first awareness of a key event in this story came in 1997.

I had been asked to make a presentation at the National Reconciliation Convention in Melbourne. 'Chances lost chances taken' was about 19th century opportunities for Reconciliation with the original Australians which had either been foregone or firmly grasped.

But also at that conference I became aware of a mid-twentieth century opportunity which, while well intended, would affect the lives of many Indigenous workers and their families throughout the Northern Territory and the Kimberley. It would also affect pastoralists and the way they had run stations for at least half a century.

At that conference Sir James Gobbo, then Governor of Victoria, recalled the 1965 Conciliation and Arbitration Commission's decision to grant Equal Wages to Aboriginal stockmen. The consequences, he felt had not been what the Commission might have hoped for.

It set me thinking. In the 1970s and early 1980s I had occasionally driven through small Northern Territory and Kimberley towns, Katherine, Halls Creek and Fitzroy Crossing, recording interviews and moving on to the next town.

Opposite
Aboriginal Stockmen mustering on Rosewood Station, ca.1900.
Courtesy of State Library of Western Australia (004376D, 3364B/75)

But what I'd failed to apprehend was why so many Aboriginal families clung to the edge of those communities. They were certainly living rough – often literally camped on the edge of town.

How did this come about? What had happened to bring so many people to the fringes of a town and town life that was doing very little for them?

It's a story that begins in the last part of the 19th and early 20th century when pastoralists entered the Kimberley and the Northern Territory. First contact with the original inhabitants was frequently followed by conflict over the use of land. Both groups wanted water and access to good pasture. The introduction of cattle and sheep offered easier hunting and Indigenous tribes took to killing the white man's livestock, with inevitable reprisals by the Europeans.

Eventually this conflict was resolved by mutual need. The pastoralist might have had superior weapons but he did not want a major war on his hands. Aboriginal people saw benefit in entering the pastoral economy. This also suited pastoralists in country where white labour was scarce and costly.

A native population offered the pastoralist many advantages; knowledge of country and soon-developed skills from the new labour force. Aboriginal people too were curious about station work and often took readily to station life.

For Aboriginal people, living on what had now become stations also meant still living in their own country, even if it meant dependence on the pastoralist for food, clothing and welfare, in exchange for labour.

The compensation? Some retention of traditional culture alongside the new pastoral economy.

It was an arrangement, which, while feudal in terms of employment conditions, did provide both parties with benefits and in many cases trust and friendship existed between pastoralist and stock worker.

Some stations treated their Indigenous populations better than others and it is impossible to generalise on a good–bad basis.

Much of the interaction depended on individual relationships.

To some extent Aboriginal culture could survive in this situation. Obligations to country through ceremony could be sustained and traditional law passed on to younger people. On the other hand in

the early years, workers were tied to the stations, often with little freedom of movement or opportunity to seek work elsewhere.

Essentially pastoralists had an Indigenous community living alongside them, if not always in the way they had done once.

This way of life persisted until the Commonwealth Conciliation and Arbitration Case for Equal Wages for northern pastoral workers in 1965.

Wages as cash in hand, let alone Equal Wages, were unfamiliar in the workaday world of station life. Physical isolation from towns also meant there was little opportunity for Aboriginal people to become familiar with money and how the money economy worked because they rarely saw cash. Interestingly, white workers on stations didn't see much cash either day to day.

Apart from hand-outs of clothing and tucker and occasional pocket money, say at race-time meetings when the community might go to town, there was little familiarity with money which would have prepared Indigenous workers for the receipt of regular wages.

Above Stockmen in the bush, Karunjie Station, ca. 1940–1960. Courtesy of State Library of Western Australia (007879D, BA1327/37).

However World War Two caused the first crack in this laissez-faire regime. The Australian Army, when it recruited Aboriginal labour for defence projects, paid wages, causing many station workers to question why this never happened inside the cattle grid. At war's end fewer were prepared to resume station life.

The unions' role is interesting here, notably the NAWU – the Northern Australian Workers Union. Prior to World War Two this union had not supported Aboriginal workers on pastoral stations, partly because they saw Indigenous labour as competitive with a white workforce, particularly during the depressed 1930s. Moreover there were almost no Aboriginal members. The concept of unions, like cash, was not in the forefront of Indigenous thinking.

However by the time the Equal Wage Case came up in 1965, union attitudes had shifted, partly due to the leadership of men like union organiser Dexter Daniels at Wave Hill and President of the NAWU, Joe McGinness, both notable and respected Indigenous leaders. These men were at the forefront of the campaign for Equal Wages.

When the Commission hearings took place in 1965 only two parties were present to provide evidence for and against the case. John Kerr, later Governor General, represented the pastoralists and the NAWU represented the workers. The NAWU stated its case minimally. The union saw Equal Wages as a long overdue restitution of almost a century of semi-slavery and assumed that the verdict would inevitably reflect natural justice.

QC, Hal Wootten, was then Junior Counsel assisting John Kerr, and despite his brief, personally sympathetic to the Aboriginal workers' arguments. However he was keenly aware that those most affected by the decision were not present. He noticed that:

> There was no contact with Aborigines by anybody in the case, the union advocate, the judges or anybody. The Aborigines were completely outside. It was all white fellows arguing about them and what ought to happen to them.

One of the ironies most apparent to Hal Wootten was the fact that it was the pastoralists who raised the question of how this decision would benefit Aboriginal workers.

> They said, 'We can see this is going to be very painful for aborigines and we wouldn't like that to happen but it's going to be one of the consequences if this decision is made.'

Pastoralists, in effect, argued that once Equal Wages came in they could no longer sustain the traditional station economy, where the pastoralist or his manager fed and clothed everybody, including dependants. However in the light of a changed situation they argued that they could only retain a few selected workers. The rest, wives, children, older people and those termed 'Slow workers' would have to take their chance elsewhere.

Internationally the Commission's hands were also tied. Inevitably Australia could not, in the eyes of the world, continue to tolerate a feudal economy within a democracy.

It was also influenced by views about assimilation in the 1960s. While the Commission was well aware that, as the pastoralists warned, payment of Equal Wages would result in massive unemployment and dislocation, it awarded in favour of Aboriginal workers on the grounds of 'equal treatment for All Australians', hinting as it did so, that the Commonwealth Government would pick up the tab if disaster ensued. It did and proved costly and long-lasting.

Some pastoralists were well aware of the likely social dislocation – and anticipated the breakdown in European–Aboriginal relationships.

Annette Henwood from Fossil Downs station recalls that several pastoralists in the Kimberley met to try to work out how to implement the scheme more gradually to ease the major upheaval they anticipated. However when the Award was pushed through its application on most stations meant loss of country and loss of work.

Hoping to allay the worst effects the Commission had in fact proposed a three-year delay in implementing the Award – to give the pastoral economy time to adjust. Unfortunately, while the application came late to the Kimberley, it came with large lay-offs and great disruption.

Anticipating this possibility the West Australian government had encouraged the retention of Aboriginal communities on station properties, partly because when the inevitable dislocation occurred after the payment of the Award, it was well aware that the small towns of the Kimberley would not be able to cope with a large influx of displaced people.

The government's worst fears were realised in the 1970s when hundreds left the stations and crowded on to the reserves of Halls Creek, Fitzroy Crossing and Wyndham. They had lost their work, their skills and most importantly their country, which was the essence of their identity and which gave spiritual and physical meaning to their lives. Now, in town, they faced the worst risks, unemployment, exposure to alcohol, boredom, and loss of morale. Adults were no longer role models for their offspring, unable now to teach them skills they had absorbed and used every day.

One of the last stations to be affected was Gordon Downs, 120 kilometres south of Halls Creek. Here the people had been scarcely aware of what the Equal Wage decision would mean to them.

When I spoke with them in 2000, well after they returned to Gordon Downs, few stockmen could recall seeing money and certainly not the 'big money' after 1965. What the decision of 1965 ultimately meant was exile in Halls Creek – temporarily 'losing' their country.

But that very word 'losing' can be 'lost in translation'. I remember when recording interviews at Gordon Downs – how easy it was to misuse this participle.

I'd asked the people what they felt about losing their land. The conversations were in Djaru, with local interpreter, Patsy Mudgabel translating as we went for the benefit of the later audience, the radio listeners.

During a break in recording Patsy tactfully told me that the stockmen could not understand my question about 'losing the land'. In their view they had never lost it. Rather, the land had lost them for a while. Country and obligations to country were always in their consciousness in exile at Halls Creek. Land was in people's heads and in their hearts. It only awaited their physical return.

And it's here that the story begins to turn round.

While the 1970s and early 1980s were a period of massive dislocation they also created a strong reaction which found expression in political growth and revival of spirit among Aboriginal communities in the North-West and elsewhere. Organisations like the Kimberley Land Council emerged to help people cope with dispossession and help them get back to country, with considerable help from the Commonwealth Government under Prime Minister Malcolm Fraser.

Some Aboriginal communities have now regained their own country and run pastoral properties on their own terms, sometimes simply as communities free from the pressures and problems of urban life.

It is often hard for other Australians to appreciate how much this meant to people who had been taken out of their own country.

Ribnga Green, who was Development Officer for the Kimberley Land Council at Halls Creek, went with the Gordon Downs people when they eventually returned to their own country. I'll quote from his interview.

> People were back in their country so they could sing songs again and dance dances and do things that they'd been doing for aeons of time. To see those sorts of changes was the highlight of my working career. I don't think anything will quite equal that.

But the story doesn't end there and it is easy to over-simplify a very complex situation. While important, the Equal Wage Decision wasn't the only factor in a changing pastoral scene.

I remember driving back from Gordon Downs to Broome early one morning in September 2000. Just as I turned south along the Broome-Derby road three helicopters rose up in front of me. I couldn't see the cattle they were mustering. They were invisible in the scrub. It was a vivid reminder of how much had changed in the pastoral industry since 1965.

Above Stockmen with cattle at the Drysdale River, Kalumburu, 1966. Courtesy of State Library of Western Australia (341653PD).

Mechanisation, the use of motorbikes and more intensive cattle raising have replaced open-range pastoralism where the stockman and the horse were once essential.

It is inevitable too that Indigenous families would have left the stations at some stage. Many, with increased mobility, wanted more from life and often sought educational opportunities for their children. But the question remains. Could we have done it better? Could we have avoided the uprooting, the loss of morale and heartbreak which accompanied that sudden dispersal from country?

Former Reconciliation Council member, the late Ric Farley, thought so. I put it to him that one could argue that the payment of Equal Wages was inevitable, one of those leaps across a ravine that simply had to happen. But as he responded:

> The ravine certainly was there and it had to be crossed but I'm not sure if it had to be crossed in a single leap. I think if the commission had approached the issue in a way that they're tending to do now, recognising that there is a surviving Aboriginal culture and a surviving Aboriginal system of law. If things had been approached in a more pragmatic way then perhaps the impact would not have been as great.

So is this episode just a slice of history, one where we can shrug our shoulders and say, "Well it was a mistake and we wouldn't do things that way now." Or is this story still important?

Ric Farley's response is also helpful again.

> Yes, because it's one of the reasons that Indigenous people now find themselves facing the sorts of problems that they do. One of the questions often asked is, "Why can't Aboriginal people get a job like anyone else? Why are so many people hooked on alcohol or drugs, living on the edge of river banks or around large towns and cities?"
>
> People have to understand that a lot of Aboriginal people were really forced into that position. They were not doing it by choice. That's not how people would choose to live if they had a choice but it's what's been imposed on them by the forces of history. People need to understand that and out of that understanding hopefully will come a much more informed debate about what needs to happen in the future.

By the 1980s the major impact of the wage decision of 1965 had been felt. The Noonkanbah Dispute of 1980 was perhaps its last manifestation; a direct expression of the anxiety Indigenous people felt about being exposed yet again to the negative aspects of white society, as they saw it.

Aboriginal people have become pastoralists themselves – sometimes with mixed success.

Some lands taken up were too small for viable pastoral enterprise, sometimes on stations abandoned as unviable by former pastoralists.

However economic success has not always been the sole driving force of Indigenous moves 'back to country'. Noonkanbah, in Aboriginal eyes, is still the benchmark for much of the attempt to go back, with its dual emphasis on getting clear of town life and its attendant ills, and the re-establishing of traditional culture and spiritual relation to land.

In part the leaders of the move 'back to country', as Steve Hawke has observed, the elders who could remember station life from the mid-20th century, were conservative and, in a paradoxical way, also romantic. An attempt to re-establish the image of the stockman, a saddled and booted horseman, in a distinctive uniform, has not, in an age of rapidly changing technology, always attracted younger players.

Many of the younger men, if they have work at all, now work in the mining industry – at Argyle Diamond Mine for example, where Aboriginal employment has been sought and culture respected, or in other jobs, sometimes in the towns their fathers or uncles left to go back to country.

Some younger workers, however, like those recruited to the stock rider's life at Roebuck Downs Station near Broome have felt the appeal of the life their parents and grandparents led, preferring life in the saddle to a long shift in a mine or an office. This project was initiated and supported by the Indigenous Land Corporation.

The Roebuck Plains' story however has not been replicated across the Kimberley. Its proximity to Broome with its relatively large population has helped develop a labour pool, an advantage not enjoyed by more remote parts of the Kimberley.

Technology has not increased employment on stations. Improved watering systems, where cameras can monitor bores, lessen the need for the horse-borne station hand, who once rode out to check windmills and pumps. Mechanical mustering, as I've mentioned earlier, has replaced many longer spells on horseback. Fencing too, imposed as a result of the veterinary campaign to rid Northern Australia of cattle diseases, and the use of feedlots now further limit the role of the traditional horseman.

Alan Lawford, Station Manager at Bohemia Downs, told me recently that, currently, of the 28 Aboriginal pastoral properties in the Kimberley, only 10 now show a profitable return.

This is comparable, incidentally, with pastoralism in general in the Kimberley, in an era of low cattle prices and high station running expenses. An additional burden, unless management is very hard-headed, is that the cultural notion of sharing means that profit can be quickly dispersed throughout the station community. The gains for these communities are often social rather than financial.

However that gain is not lightly dismissed if we consider the alternative. Families live on country with less exposure to alcohol and the malaise of unemployment. If we take happiness as a measure of success then an outstation can offer positives.

The Indigenous station can, and frequently does, perform another useful social role. Magistrates, in conjunction with Aboriginal elders, sometimes send young offenders to these stations in order to let them learn a more disciplined life. They see this as a more positive alternative to juvenile detention, and time on stations relieves the taxpayer of the more expensive cost of imprisonment.

Alternative rural activities have also extended the Indigenous relationship to country. The formation of the Kimberley Fire project has provided employment and income for Aboriginal fire preventers. The Yirriman project in particular, working from Derby, has assisted stations like Jarlmadanga (Mt Anderson) with fire prevention activity.

European pastoralism in the Kimberley has also changed, not only technically as we've seen, but also in terms of the market situation, the physical environment and employment.

In terms of work, while once a pastoral station had a large labour force on its doorstep in the shape of a traditional community, stations now run with smaller numbers and often with an itinerant white (*and sometimes black*) workforce. Pastoral work has always had a seasonal emphasis and better roads and transport mean that employees can be called in as needed.

Markets too have changed. Cattle exports expanded with the Air Beef Scheme from Mount House in the 1950s and early 1960s. But now improved roads carry cattle to Wyndham and Broome for the live export market. Indonesia is a major customer for Kimberley cattle and in recent years has sustained the industry.

The landscape has also had some respite, the decline of sheep and de-stocking of many stations has led to an improvement in many parts of the Kimberley.

Native Title Agreements, while initially greeted with suspicion by some pastoralists, have in many cases proved workable.

Rob Gillam, the current President of the Pastoralists and Graziers Association WA, has pointed out that in some areas, the local Indigenous community often proved the best guardian against misuse of access. It was important to them that they and not people from other places enjoyed the benefit of hunting and visiting important sites. Their presence could help monitor the situation, ensuring that gates were shut and water not left running.

Above Stockman at Kalumburu 1966. Courtesy of State Library of Western Australia (333826PD).

And much water has flowed under many bridges in the Kimberley since the 1965 Equal Wage Decision and pastoralism has changed accordingly. Much of that change was inevitable but the efforts of Aboriginal leaders to overcome the negative effects of that decision deserve our respect.

For European pastoralists too there have been major adjustments and changes; greater environmental concern and adaptation, but perhaps also the recognition that in this vast region both European and Indigenous Australians have found ways to live with the land and recently in closer understanding of each other.

The complex relationship of European pastoralist and Aboriginal countryman has not always been understood by people beyond the sphere of station life and work. At one time there was a measure of mutual interdependence. Station work alone saw to that.

Mary Durack once spoke of the Aboriginal community at Ivanhoe as our 'workers by day and saviours by night, people who knew the country, were aware of coming floods and the approach of hostile groups'.

The pastoralist provided sanctuary and the Aboriginal stood sentry.

Now, even if both no longer always share the same station, much has been learnt about Kimberley country and how to care for it. Land can own people in the long run – not the other way round.

In closing I'd particularly like to thank Rob Gillam, President of the PGA, Peter McEntee and Alan Lawford of Bohemia Downs Station for their considerable contribution to my more recent knowledge of the Kimberley scene.

Further reading

Bunbury, B. *It's Not The Money It's The Land: Aboriginal Stockmen and the Equal Wages Case*. Fremantle Arts Centre Press, Fremantle, 2002.

Hawke, S. and Gallagher, M. *Noonkanbah: Whose Land, Whose Law*. Fremantle Arts Centre Press, Fremantle, 1989.

Opposite
The Kimberley's fertile and well watered basaltic plains make ideal cattle country. Drysdale River. Photo – Mike Donaldson